The Business of Sports

The Business of Sports

Volume 3
Bridging Research and Practice

EDITED BY BRAD R. HUMPHREYS
AND DENNIS R. HOWARD

Praeger Perspectives

Westport, Connecticut
London

Library of Congress Cataloging-in-Publication Data

The business of sports / edited by Brad R. Humphreys and Dennis R. Howard.
p. cm.
Includes bibliographical references and index.
ISBN 978-0-275-99340-5 ((set) : alk. paper) — ISBN 978-0-275-99341-2 ((vol. 1) : alk. paper) — ISBN 978-0-275-99342-9 ((vol. 2) : alk. paper) — ISBN 978-0-275-99343-6 ((vol. 3) : alk. paper)
1. Professional sports—Economic aspects. 2. Sports—Economic aspects. 3. Sports administration. I. Humphreys, Brad R. II. Howard, Dennis Ramsay, 1945–
GV716.B89 2008
796.06′91—dc22 2008008547

British Library Cataloguing in Publication Data is available.

Library of Congress Catalog Card Number: 2008008547
ISBN: 978-0-275-99340-5 (set)
978-0-275-99341-2 (vol. 1)
978-0-275-99342-9 (vol. 2)
978-0-275-99343-6 (vol. 3)

First published in 2008

Praeger Publishers, 88 Post Road West, Westport, CT 06881
An imprint of Greenwood Publishing Group, Inc.
www.praeger.com

Printed in the United States of America

The paper used in this book complies with the Permanent Paper Standard issued by the National Information Standards Organization (Z39.48–1984).

10 9 8 7 6 5 4 3 2 1

Contents

Preface

Interaction between researchers and practitioners frequently leads to significant improvements in both research and practice, although it may take some time for the process to bear fruit. While such interaction is relatively common in disciplines like engineering and computer science, it is not as common in sports, and even less common in the sports business. However, consider the effects of the path-breaking statistical research on the performance of baseball players by Bill James. Although his work was initially disregarded by industry professionals, James's research is now widely used by Major League Baseball teams and he consults for the Boston Red Sox. Based on anecdotes in Michael Lewis's *Moneyball*, Bill James's research has had a significant impact on Major League Baseball.

Movement scientists have also been influential in changing athletic performance in a number of individual sports. By studying the mechanics of athletes in sports like athletics, gymnastics, and swimming, researchers in kinesiology and movement science have improved the performance of athletes.

In volume 3 of *The Business of Sports*, we attempt to bridge the gap between business-related research on sports and the sports industry. The goal is to promote two-way interaction between researchers and sports industry practitioners. Scholarly research on the sports business has much to offer the sports industry, and careful attention to the important insights and experience of practitioners can lead research in new and exciting directions. Volume 3 contains chapters on topics that we feel holds great promise for productive future interaction between sport researchers and sport practitioners.

Perhaps the most exciting area for interaction between researchers and practitioners is the evaluation of player performance. For decades, player evaluation and scouting was exclusively the domain of "bird dog" scouts employed by professional sports teams. These scouts were primarily former players, and their evaluations of player performance were primarily qualitative and subjective. However, the past decade has seen a quantitative revolution in the evaluation of player performance. Teams in every major sport in the world—from soccer to ice hockey—have begun to explore the quantification of player evaluation. The first two chapters in volume 3 examine the frontiers of quantitative analysis of athletic performance.

In the first chapter of volume 3, economist David Berri describes a method of statistically analyzing the performance of professional basketball players. Berri believes that, much like the baseball players' market before Billy Beane's success as the general manager of the Oakland Athletics, the market for NBA players contains significant inefficiencies. Berri posits that NBA executives make persistent, systematic mistakes when evaluating players and has developed a method based on currently available statistics that can be used to exploit these inefficiencies.

John Charles Bradbury has spent considerable time analyzing the on-field performance of Major League Baseball players. Bradbury's chapter is an overview of the quantitative techniques used to evaluate the performance of professional athletes. Bradbury shows how these tools can provide powerful new insights into player behavior. Anyone who wanted more details on how the A's evaluate talent after reading *Moneyball* will find this chapter informative.

Many large cities in the United States have struggled to revitalize their urban cores over the past few decades. Invariably, these attempts involve the renovation of existing sports venues or the construction of new ones. Can professional sports play a role in revitalizing American cities? Mark Rosentraub has a foot in both academia and practice. Rosentraub is an academic who has consulted on a number of high-profile urban redevelopment projects that had professional sports venues as their centerpiece. In his chapter, Rosentraub discusses some of the successes and failures of sports facilities as engines of urban redevelopment.

Professional sports teams face a number of difficult problems. Some have been discussed in detail in previous chapters. Daniel Mason addresses revenue-sharing in professional sports leagues, an especially thorny issue. Every major sports league in North America engages in some form of revenue-sharing. But, as Mason points out, revenue-sharing generates a number of important incentives in sports leagues, and not all of them lead to an enhanced experience for fans. At the core of the revenue-sharing problem is an interesting economic concept, the "principal-agent problem." Since this problem can be found in many settings in sport, and in other industries, this chapter has important insights in a number of business settings.

A large number of professional sports teams in North America now play in newly built facilities. Despite the large amount of construction that has recently taken place, the near future promises to hold even more sport facility construction projects. How should sports facility construction projects be financed? The U.S. Congress addressed this issue in the 1980s when they explicitly prohibited professional sports facilities from being financed with tax-exempt bonds. However, a number of recent new stadium construction projects have been financed in ways that challenge the ban on tax-exempt financing of sport-facility construction. These challenges raise important questions about the role of sports in the economy. Dennis Zimmerman, a long-time analyst for the Congressional Budget Office and the Congressional Research Service, reviews the controversy surrounding the use of tax-exempt bonds to finance sports facility construction.

Sports fans enjoy watching athletes give maximum effort in pursuit of victory, and the organizers of sports events earn the largest profits when they induce athletes to put forth maximum effort. But maximum effort is difficult to sustain, and athletes seeking long and profitable careers have an incentive to put forth the minimum effort required to win a given contest. This can lead to interesting economic problems in sports, especially individual sports. Peter von Allmen examines this tension between the organizers of individual sporting events like foot races and golf tournaments and explains how tournament organizers have devised compensation schemes to overcome this problem. This chapter provides insight into the skewed compensation schemes used in marathon races and other individual sports.

The performance of athletes is easily observable. Even if it is difficult to quantify and analyze, every sports fan and Monday morning quarterback can observe and evaluate the performance of a player. But what about managers and coaches? Managers play an important role in the performance of sports teams. As fans, we can occasionally catch a glimpse of the powerful effect that managers have on athletic outcomes—go for one or two, punt or try to pick up a first down, pull the goalie—this is the tip of the proverbial iceberg as most of the decisions made by managers and coaches are either impossible to observe or take place out of sight. This does not mean that coaches and managers cannot be evaluated. Economists have devised several methods to evaluate outcomes when specific events or decisions cannot be easily observed. Carlos Barros and Mário Teixeira provide an introduction to the analysis of efficiency frontiers, a powerful tool for evaluating both the performance of sports coaches and managers and, as this chapter shows, the overall effectiveness of sports organizations.

As we write this preface, the Seattle SuperSonics, an NBA team playing in the fourteenth-largest media market in the United States, may be moved to Oklahoma City, Oklahoma, currently the nation's forty-sixth-largest media market. What makes a viable market for a major-league sports franchise? How many viable markets exist in North America? Since the western exodus of the Dodgers and Giants from New York City in the 1950s, franchise moves have been of intense interest to sports fans. This has continued for decades, as sports teams continue to move across North America. Michael Davis examines franchise moves and the determinants of a viable host market for a professional sports team. Davis sheds light on where teams may move and which teams may move, interesting topics for both sports fans and sports business executives.

Only one top tier sport in all of North America does not crown a post-season championship based on a knock-out elimination process: NCAA Football in the "Bowl Subdivision." Sports fans and media commentators constantly bemoan the lack of a college football playoff. As a number of previous chapters in *The Business of Sports* have pointed out, the design of tournaments is fundamentally an economic decision made by the organizers of sports leagues. Michael Mondello traces the history of the college bowl system and examines this system through the lens of economics. The chapter identifies a number of institutional factors that keep the bowl system in place and explores the incentives created by this system. Mondello also offers an alternative to the existing system that avoids many of the existing flaws.

Reverse-finish talent dispersal drafts have been a feature of professional sports leagues since the early part of the twentieth century. Drafts are so ingrained in the fabric of professional sports that many fans never stop to think about how drafts came to be a part of North American professional sports, what they are intended to accomplish, and how effective drafts are at accomplishing their stated goals. But drafts do not have to be an integral part of a professional sports league. The major professional football leagues in Europe do not have talent dispersal drafts. Kevin Quinn takes a careful look at these questions. This chapter contains two conclusions that will probably surprise even the most informed sports fan: despite the claims by sports leagues, drafts do little to promote competitive balance in sports leagues; and despite the seemingly large salaries paid to rookie professional athletes, drafts almost certainly reduce the earnings of athletes.

Agents play an increasingly important role in professional sports. As recently as twenty years ago, it was not uncommon for players to negotiate their own contracts, eschewing advice from professional agents. However, the modern sports market contains significant opportunities for athletes to earn money from sources outside athletic performance, contracts have become more complex, and higher salaries provide players with incentives to engage in sophisticated financial management practices. The relationship between players and agents is not as straightforward as might appear at first glance. Daniel Mason and Gregory Duquette discuss the interesting features of the relationship between professional athletes and their agents. Because the agent-athlete relationship has many factors in common with the extensively researched principal-agent contracting relationship an extensive body of scholarly research exists in which to understand how athletes and agents interact.

Many sports fans of a certain age have fond memories of collecting and trading sports cards. Taking a longer perspective, baseball cards, in one form or another, have been around since the late nineteenth century. Despite this long history, a number of interesting events have taken place in the baseball card industry over the past twenty years that fundamentally changes this industry. Arthur Zillante documents the interesting economic history of the baseball card industry—the story of the firms that produce baseball cards and their rocky relationship with athletes and teams. Zillante's story contains interesting elements of intellectual property rights, antitrust law violations, product differentiation, and the surprising revelation of a long-lived industry in decline.

ACKNOWLEDGMENTS

A project on the scale of *The Business of Sport* is a huge undertaking. From inception to publication, it has taken a long time and a lot of work—more than either of us realized when we first took on this project. We could not have completed it without the help of many people, all of whom deserve our deepest thanks and appreciation. First and foremost, we thank each and every one of our contributing authors. We have been blessed to work with such a talented group, and we gratefully acknowledge the contributions of all of these hard-working individuals.

We also got a tremendous amount of editorial support from the staff at Praeger Publishers/Greenwood Press. Praeger is an excellent, professional, well-run publishing house, and the efforts of the editors there have made significant contributions to the project. We thank all of the Praeger/Greenwood editorial staff members who assisted us in the completion of *The Business of Sport* for their help. We also thank Jane Ruseski, Brian Soebbing, Dan "Professor Puck" Mason, Tiffany Richardson, Angela Ronk, Jill Gurke, Amie Cowie, Craig Depken, Andy Zimbalist, Rick Zuber, and Paul Swangard for their help, support, and valuable input. We couldn't have done this without you.

One

A Simple Model of Worker Productivity in the National Basketball Association

David J. Berri

The study of sports by economists has grown rapidly in the past three decades. Although the output of this industry is monetarily insignificant in the aggregate economy, the industry does offer data on worker productivity, which has proven quite useful to applied economists. As Lawrence Kahn notes, the sports industry is the only place where researchers can "know the name, face, and life history of every production worker and supervisor."[1] Such data can be employed in the study of a number of issues including the prevalence of racial discrimination, the relationship between pay and worker productivity, and the evaluation of managerial ability.[2]

Given the wealth of data available, it is curious how such abundance has been employed. Consider the data generated by the sport of baseball. Extensive worker productivity data exists for this sport from the mid-1870s to the present. How have researchers employed such data? In Gerald Scully's seminal investigation of baseball's reserve clause, the productivity of a hitter was measured with slugging percentage, or total bases divided by at-bats.[3] To calculate slugging percentage, one only needs to know how many at-bats a player took, as well as his production of singles, doubles, triples, and home runs. These five measures are then utilized to create a simple measure of a hitter's productivity. In addition to imposing the relative value of each factor, slugging percentage ignores the impact of variables such as walks and stolen bases.

Given the limits of this measure, one might expect that as computing power increased, researchers would move to more sophisticated measures of worker productivity. Surprisingly, though, in thirteen studies published from

1982 to 2002, slugging percentage was still employed as the primary measure of a hitter's output.[4] Why do researchers utilize a measure that fails to fully employ the richness of the data generated by Major League Baseball (MLB)?

The virtue of slugging percentage is that it is both simple and relatively accurate. *The Wages of Wins* reported that slugging percentage explained 81 percent of the variation in runs scored.[5] In contrast, 94 percent of the variation in runs scored was explained by a more complex measure developed by John Thorn and Pete Palmer.[6] Although Thorn and Palmer's work, and others in the sabermetrics tradition, can offer greater accuracy, their work fails to match the simplicity of slugging percentage.[7]

One could argue that the availability of a simple and accurate measure of productivity has been a significant contributing factor to the abundance of research employing baseball data. In contrast, the lack of a simple productivity measure may have stunted research employing worker-productivity data from professional basketball.[8]

A metric for basketball that offers the simplicity of slugging percentage was offered in *The Wages of Wins.* This metric—titled Win Score—incorporates much of what a player does on the basketball court in a simple formula. *The Wages of Wins* was intended for a general audience, hence the math and econometrics utilized to create Win Score were not fully presented. The purpose of this chapter is to provide the details behind this work.

These details will begin with a review of the efforts offered by the industry, members of the media, and academic researchers to measure player performance in the National Basketball Association (NBA). With this review in hand, a model will be constructed that will initially move from the simple to the complex, yet eventually return to a simple equation that accurately measures the output of a NBA player.

A BRIEF REVIEW OF EXISTING MEASURES OF WORKER PRODUCTIVITY IN THE NBA

Table 1.1 lists the various aspects of player and team productivity the NBA tracks each season.[9] The table begins with team wins and winning percentage, followed by the two primary determinants of wins, points scored and points surrendered per game. As will be noted, the remaining statistics impact how many points a team tabulates and allows per contest played.[10] Variables tabulated for the team are listed in alphabetical order, followed by the data employed in this chapter that is tracked for a team's opponent. The sample statistics reported are drawn from fifteen NBA regular seasons, beginning with the 1991/92 campaign and concluding with the 2005/06 season.

TABLE 1.1
Team and Player Statistics for the National Basketball Association

Variable	Calculation	Notation	Mean	Maximum	Minimum	Standard Deviation
Wins		WINS	39.918	72.000	8.000	13.283
Games played		GM	79.837	82.000	50.000	8.043
Winning percentage	WINS/GM	PCT	0.500	0.878	0.134	0.158
Points scored		PTS	97.727	118.683	81.900	5.606
Opponent's PTS		DPTS	97.727	114.780	83.400	5.791
Assists		AST	22.303	29.244	15.640	2.298
Blocked shots		BLK	5.090	8.366	3.037	0.967
Defensive rebounds		RBD	29.479	33.549	24.927	1.588
Field goals attempted		FGA	81.295	92.439	71.220	3.816
Field goals made		FGM	36.852	45.939	30.780	2.548
Free throws attempted		FTA	25.771	33.451	17.988	2.480
Free throws made		FTM	19.220	24.927	14.500	1.912
Free throw percentage	[FTM/FTA]	FT	0.746	0.829	0.662	0.028
Offensive rebounds		RBO	12.638	18.463	9.427	1.551
Personal fouls		PF	22.414	28.073	18.000	1.707
Points per shot	[PTSFGA]/FGA	PPS	0.966	1.079	0.848	0.041
Points from field goal attempts	[PTS-FTM]	PTSFGA	78.507	94.976	65.100	4.946
Steals		STL	8.078	12.841	5.610	1.035
Turnovers		TO	15.243	18.988	11.354	1.277
Total rebounds	RBO+RBD	TREB	42.117	48.134	35.634	2.022
Opponent's RBD		DRBD	29.479	34.232	24.537	1.673
Opponent's FGA		DFGA	81.295	93.878	68.756	3.882
Opponent's FGM		DFGM	36.852	45.329	30.341	2.796

(continued)

TABLE 1.1 *(continued)*

Variable	Calculation	Notation	Mean	Maximum	Minimum	Standard Deviation
Opponent's FT	[DFTM/DFTA]	DFT	0.746	0.780	0.694	0.015
Opponent's FTA		DFTA	25.771	37.451	19.720	2.766
Opponent's FTM		DFTM	19.220	28.671	13.940	2.101
Opponent's RBO		DRBO	12.638	16.463	9.598	1.224
Opponent's PPS	[DPTSFGA]/DFGA	DPPS	0.965	1.079	0.845	0.038
Opponent's PTSFGA	[DPTS-DFTM]	DPTSFGA	78.507	93.159	65.800	5.271
Opponent's TO		DTO	15.193	20.622	11.634	1.360

Sources: Sporting New Official NBA Guide, 2006/07 edition, NBA.com, ESPN.com, and Sportsillustrated.cnn.com.
Notes: D—Represents the opponent's accumulation of the factor; that is, the opponent's total scoring = DPTS. Sample: 1991/92 to 2005/06.

The difficulty with the data generated by the NBA is that the marginal value of each factor is not intuitively clear. For example, a rudimentary understanding of baseball is all one needs to understand that a home run has a greater impact on wins than a single. The relative value of player performance measures in basketball, though, is not quite as intuitive. Which has a greater impact on wins, points or assists? Is a rebound worth more than a blocked shot?

The answer to these questions is crucial to measuring the output of an NBA player. Few basketball players excel at every aspect of the game. Consequently, comparing players who offer such diverse output sets is quite difficult. To overcome this hurdle, a variety of indices have been offered by members of the media, NBA insiders, and academic researchers to summarize each player's contribution to team success. What follows is a brief review of these efforts.

The Measures of the Media and the NBA

The general approach offered by members of the media follows in the democratic tradition of Western civilization. In ascertaining the Most Valuable Player, members of the All-NBA teams, and the Rookie of the Year, sportswriters simply vote. A problem with this method lies in its subjective nature. In addition to disagreements over which players should be granted these awards, members of the media also disagree about how a term such as "Most Valuable" should even be defined. Certainly the subjective method has its flaws. To overcome problems inherent to the democratic approach, a number of objective models have been developed.

The most common objective measure resembles the model offered on the NBA's official Web site. According to NBA.com, when an NBA coach evaluates a player's performance he refers to the player's efficiency. What does the NBA mean by efficiency? The answer lies in equation (1).[11]

$$\text{NBA Efficiency} = (PTS + TREB + STL + BLK + AST) - (FGA - FGM) - (FTA - FTM) - TO, \quad (1)$$

where PTS is points, TREB is total rebounds, STL is steals, BLK is blocked shots, AST is assists, FGA is field goals attempted, FGM is field goals made, FTA is free throws attempted, FTM is free throws made, and TO is turnovers. The NBA's index is quite similar to Dave Heeran's TENDEX system, Robert Bellotti's Points Created model, and the method IBM employed in ascertaining its player of the year.[12] An apparent problem with these models is that no attempt is made to ascertain the relative value of each statistic. Consequently, although these indices are easy to construct, the ability of these measures to truly assess worker productivity is not clear.

Academic Models

Economists, well trained in the art of econometrics, have generally sought to measure worker productivity via regression analysis. The estimated model begins with a measure of team performance, either wins or the ratio of points scored and points surrendered, as the dependent variable. The independent variables are comprised of a variety of player-performance measures.

The choice of player-performance measures typically includes every measure available to the researcher. For example, Frank Scott, James Long, and Ken Sompii, include measures of shooting efficiency (field-goal percentage and free-throw percentage), total rebounds, assists, and personal fouls.[13] Factors such as turnovers, blocked shots, and offensive and defensive rebounds were excluded. The reason for this choice lay in the variables the NBA collected. The excluded variables were not collected for individual players until the mid-1970s. Scott, Long, and Sompii, though, sought to examine the entire decade of the 1970s, forcing these authors to employ fewer variables.

In contrast, Thomas Zak, Cliff Huang, and John Siegfried, as well as Robert McCormick and Robert Clement, Richard Hofler and James Payne, and David Berri examined later years.[14] Hence each study employed most, if not all, of the variables ignored by Scott, Long, and Sompii. A difficulty with these works, though, is that little effort was made to ascertain theoretically how each variable impacted team wins.

Consider the impact of blocked shots and defensive rebounds. Two events can follow a blocked shot. The team that blocks the shot can rebound the basketball. In such an instance, the team has both prevented its opponent from scoring and given itself a chance to score. If the team that blocks the shot, though, fails to gather in the rebound, then the impact of the blocked shot is insignificant. The other team retains possession of the ball and hence still has an opportunity to add to its point total. In other words, independent of defensive rebounds, blocked shots do not impact the outcome of games.

A similar story can be told with respect to assists and personal fouls. The former improves a team's shooting efficiency. Once we note a team's level of efficiency, though, the number of assists a team accumulates offers no additional explanatory power. Personal fouls lead to free-throw attempts by the opponent. Again, once we know the number of free throws an opponent takes, personal fouls do not aid our ability to explain wins. In essence, the value of blocked shots, assists, and personal fouls cannot be determined via a simple regression of wins on these statistics. With a bit of work, though, a value for these factors can be determined.[15]

Before we get to the value of blocked shots, assists, and personal fouls, we first need to construct a model of team wins. This process will begin with a very simple model. Step by step the simple model will be made more complex. Eventually, though, these steps will lead to a simple equation—Win Score—that will accurately measure the productivity of an individual basketball player.

MODELING WINS IN THE NBA: MOVING FROM THE SIMPLE TO THE COMPLEX TO THE SIMPLE

As noted, the NBA tabulates a variety of statistics to evaluate the productivity of an individual player. To evaluate the productivity of an NBA player, we need to connect all the statistics tracked for individuals to team wins. The first impulse is to simply regress wins on the host of statistics the NBA tracks. This approach, as detailed above, is flawed. With a bit of work, though, one can build a model that connects wins to much of what a player does. And then, as will be shown, with a bit more work one can ascertain the value of everything else the initial model does not incorporate.

We begin the process of building this model with the work of John Hollinger and Dean Oliver.[16] Both of these authors argued separately, as equation (2) illustrates, that wins in the NBA are primarily determined by a team's offensive and defensive efficiency.

$$\text{Wins} = a_0 + a_1\text{Offensive Efficiency} + a_2\text{Defensive Efficiency} + e_{2i}, \quad (2)$$

where efficiency is measured by dividing points scored (or allowed) by the number of possessions in a game.

To measure possessions—which we will refer to specifically as possessions employed—each author employed a similar calculation.[17]

$$\text{Possessions Employed (PE)} = \text{FGA} + b_1\text{FTA} + \text{TO} - \text{REBO} \quad (3)$$

Two difficulties exist with the Hollinger-Oliver model. First, it is not entirely clear that wins can be defined in terms of a team's relative ability to elicit points from possessions. Second, the Hollinger-Oliver definition of possessions only considers points scored, offensive rebounds, turnovers, and shot attempts. Defensive rebounds are not included. This factor, though, likely impacts team wins and therefore should be included in any measure of player productivity. Hence, a better model needs to be developed.[18]

Step 1: Connecting Team Wins to Points Scored and Surrendered

The building of a better model begins with equation (4), where wins in professional basketball are connected to points scored and points surrendered.

TABLE 1.2
Estimated Coefficients for Equation (4)

Variables	Coefficients
Constant	0.517[a]
	(13.605)
PTS	0.033[a]
	(70.700)
DPTS	−0.033[a]
	(−66.588)
Adjusted R^2	0.941
Observations	429

[a]Denotes significance at the 1 percent level.
Notes: Dependent variable is regular season winning percentage. Sample: 1991/92 to 2005/06. t-statistics in parentheseis below each coefficient.

$$PCT = c_0 + c_1 PTS + c_2 DPTS + e_{4i} \quad (4)$$

Equation (4) was estimated with fifteen seasons of aggregate regular season team data, beginning in 1991/92 and concluding with the 2005/06 campaign.[19] As reported in Table 1.2, the total points a team scores and surrenders per game explains 94.1 percent of the variation in team winning percentage. Such a result is not surprising since by definition wins are defined by these two factors.[20]

The number of points a team scores is entirely determined by the number of shots a team takes and the efficiency at which these shots are successfully converted. Shot attempts include field-goal attempts (FGA) and free-throw attempts (FTA), while shooting efficiency is defined in terms of points per shot (PPS) and free-throw percentage (FT).[21] This basic identity is illustrated by equations (5) and (6).[22]

$$PTS = PPS^*FGA + FT^*FTA \quad (5)$$

$$DPTS = DPPS^*DFGA + FT^*DFTA \quad (6)$$

Given these two identities, we now can relate team wins to eight measures of player and team performance. The next step is to explain how many field goals a team will attempt per game.

Step 2: Explaining Field-Goal Attempts

To attempt a field goal, a team must first acquire the ball. A team gains possession of the ball each time it forces a turnover (DTO) or rebounds an errant shot by the opponent. One should note the difference between a defensive rebound (REBD) and a team rebound (REBTM). A defensive rebound is a rebound of an opponent's missed shot that can be credited to a specific individual player. If a rebound cannot be credited to an individual player, a team rebound is recorded.[23]

If a team fails to force a turnover or rebound a missed shot, the opponent will eventually make a shot. By rule a team will acquire possession of the ball each time an opponent makes a field-goal attempt (DFGM). The team also acquires possession after an opponent makes a free throw (DFTM), but since players are often awarded more than one free throw at a time, only a fraction of made free throws result in a change in possession.[24]

The number of possessions a team acquires (PA) is determined by the factors listed in equation (7). Given our discussion of DFTM, the value of d_1 is less than 1.

$$\text{Possessions Acquired (PA)} = \text{DTO} + \text{REBD} + \text{REBTM} + \text{DFGM} + d_1{*}\text{DFTM} \tag{7}$$

Once a team has acquired possession of the ball, it has the right to take one field-goal attempt. This is not the only option available. A team could also commit a turnover (TO), which results in a loss of one field-goal attempt. If the team takes a shot from the field and misses, it can acquire an additional shot attempt by rebounding the errant shot (REBO). Finally, the team can draw a personal foul. The free-throw attempts that result serve as a substitute for field-goal attempts. Free-throw attempts are equal to a fraction of field-goal attempts, since more than one free throw can be taken on a given possession. If we know the number of possessions acquired, turnovers, offensive rebounds, and free-throw attempts, we can determine how many field-goal attempts a team will take. This is illustrated for the team by equation (8). As our discussion of free throws indicates, f_1 will be less than 1.

$$\text{FGA} = \text{DTO} + \text{REBD} + \text{REBTM} + \text{DFGM} + d_1{*}\text{DFTM} - \text{TO} + \text{REBO} - f_1{*}\text{FTA}, \tag{8}$$

where

$$\text{DTO} + \text{REBD} + \text{REBTM} + \text{DFGM} + d_1{*}\text{DFTM} = \text{PA}$$

and

$$d_1 < 1 \text{ and } f_1 < 1.$$

Step 3: Calculating Team Rebounds

Of the factors that lead a team to take a field-goal attempt, data is readily available for both the team and individual. The exception is team rebounds that result in a change of possession. This factor is not reported by the NBA. Given the data we have, though, we can construct an estimate for team rebounds that change possession. The first step in this process is ascertaining the value of d_1 and f_1.

To ascertain the value of these unknowns we first must acknowledge that each time a team gains possession of the ball (DFGM, RBD, DTO), or retains possession of the ball (RBO), it acquires the right to one field-goal attempt. Each time a team loses possession of the ball (TO), it has lost one field-goal attempt. The value of the opponent's free throws (DFTM) and free-throw attempts (FTA)—in terms of field-goal attempts—is not equal to 1. To estimate the value of these latter factors we construct a variable that we will call—for want of a better name—FGADIF. This calculation of this variable is noted in equation (9).[25]

$$\text{FGADIF} = \text{FGA} - (\text{DFGM} + \text{REBD} + \text{DTO} + \text{REBO} - \text{TO}) \qquad (9)$$

FGADIF is calculated by subtracting from FGA all the factors that are worth one field-goal attempts. In other words, equation (8) is rewritten so that everything that is worth one field-goal attempt is on the right hand side while the factors worth less than one field-goal attempt are on the left hand side of the equation. As illustrated in equation (10), we can then regress FGADIF on DFTM and FTA to ascertain the values of d_1, f_1, and REBTM.

$$\text{FGADIF} = g_0 + d_1\text{DFTM} + f_1\text{FTA} + e_{10} \qquad (10)$$

The estimation of this equation, reported in Table 1.3, allow us to estimate both the value of free throws in terms of field-goal attempts, and the

TABLE 1.3
Estimated Coefficients for Equation (10)

Variables	Coefficients
Constant	5.074[a]
	(14.566)
DFTM	0.461[a]
	(30.212)
FTA	−0.449[a]
	(36.217)
Adjusted R^2	0.819
Observations	429

[a]Denotes significance at the 1 percent level.

Notes: Dependent variable is the difference in field goals attempted. Sample: 1991/92 to 2005/06. t-statistics in parentheses below each coefficient.

TABLE 1.4
Re-Estimated Coefficients for Equation (10)

Variables	Coefficients
Constant	5.346[a]
	(69.328)
DFTM, FTA	0.453[a]
	(40.694)
Adjusted R^2	0.820
Observations	429

[a]Denotes significance at the 1 percent level.
Notes: $d_1 = -f_1$. Dependent variables is FGADIF. Sample: 1991/92 to 2005/06. t-statistics in parentheses below each coefficient.

number of possession-changing team rebounds a team garners per game. With respect to the former, the estimation of equation (10) reveals that the suggested values of DFTM and FTA are in absolute terms quite similar. A Wald test suggests that that the coefficients for variables are indeed statistically equal in absolute value. Consequently one could re-estimate equation (10) and impose the following restriction:

$$d_1 = -f_1$$

The results of this re-estimation, reported in Table 1.4, reveal that the value of a free throw made or attempted, in terms of field-goal attempts, is 0.45. With this information in hand, we can now estimate team rebounds. Given that team rebounds are the only factor missing in our estimation of field-goal attempts, one can ascertain each team's accumulation of this variable via the calculation of equation (11).

$$\text{REBTM} = g_0 + e_{10i} \tag{11}$$

For example, e_{10} was equal to -0.088 for the Detroit Pistons during the 2005/06 season. With the estimated value of g_0 equivalent to 5.346, the Pistons averaged an estimated 5.258 team rebounds that changed possession per game.

Step 4: Revisiting Points Scored

With team rebounds estimated, we can now connect field-goal attempts to each action a team takes to acquire and maintain possession of the ball. Given that field-goal attempts are a key determinant of points scored, we are also now able to expand our understanding of how teams accumulate points.

From equation (8) we see that field-goal attempts are determined by free-throw attempts, offensive rebounds, turnovers, and possessions acquired. Given this list, coupled with what we know of points scored from equation (5), we now can see that the number of points a team scores is determined by the following list of factors: PPS, FT, FTA, REBO, TO, DFGM, DFTM, REBD, REBTM, DTO.

So now we have expanded our list of factors that determine points scored from the four factors listed in equation (5) to the ten factors reported above. After all this effort, we can now create a model of wins that incorporates much of what is tabulated for individual players.

Step 5: Explaining Wins in Terms of Points per Possession

The ten factors that explain points scored can be divided into two groupings. From equation (7) we can see that DFGM, DFTM, REBD, REBTM, and DTO are simply possessions acquired.

The first five factors on our list include exactly the same factors employed in the calculation of offensive efficiency. To see this, consider that the calculation of PPS and FT requires four statistics: PTS, FTM, FGA, and FTA. And since FTM is simply a part of PTS, one can see that this list of factors, PPS, FT, FTA, REBO, TO, contains the same elements as this list: PTS, FGA, FTA, REBO, TO. And this latter list is simply the elements comprising offensive efficiency, or PTS/PE. Consequently, as equation (12) illustrates, points scored is determined by offensive efficiency and possessions acquired.

$$PTS = PTS/PE * PA \tag{12}$$

Like equations (5) and (6), equation (12) is also an identity. The number of points a team scores must be a function of how many possessions the team acquires multiplied by how many points a team scores per possession. A similar argument can be made concerning the number of points a team surrenders. In other words, we expect DPTS to be defined as illustrated in equation (13).

$$DPTS = DPTS/DPE * DPA \tag{13}$$

With our new definitions of points scored and points surrendered, we now know that wins are determined by the following list of factors: PTS/PE, PA, DPTS/DPE, and DPA, where DPE is the opponent's possessions employed and DPA is the opponent's possessions acquired.

This list can be further simplified. The number of possessions a team employs and acquires is virtually identical to the number of possessions employed and acquired by the opponent.[26] As a consequence, we can make two changes to our list. First, PA, a factor that positively impacts wins, must cancel DPA, a factor that negatively impacts wins. So one can estimate wins with equation (14).

$$\text{Wins} = h_0 + h_1{}^*\text{PTS/PE} - h_2{}^*\text{DPTS/DPE} + e_{14i} \quad (14)$$

Looking back at the work of both Hollinger and Oliver, we see that equation (14) is equivalent to what these authors proposed. Certainly we have shown that the focus on offensive and defensive efficiency adopted by Hollinger and Oliver does allow one to theoretically explain team wins. Hence the first issue with respect to the Hollinger-Oliver model has been resolved.

Nevertheless, we wish to connect wins to statistics tabulated for the team—and its players—that we are analyzing. And the inclusion of DPE does not help us with that objective. Fortunately we find that the number of possessions the opponent employs (DPE) is virtually equivalent to the possessions acquired (PA) by the team.[27] Hence we can rewrite equation (14) as follows:

$$\text{Wins} = j_0 + j_1{}^*\text{PTS/PE} - j_2{}^*\text{DPTS/PA} + e_{15i} \quad (15)$$

Table 1.5 reports the estimation of equation (15). The results reveal a model that explains 94.3 percent of team wins. In other words, the explanatory power of a model based on points scored and surrendered per possession is equivalent to equation (2), where wins were related to only points scored and surrendered.

TABLE 1.5
Estimated Coefficients for Equation (13)

Variables	Coefficients
Constant	0.496[a]
	(6.798)
PTS/PE	3.134[a]
	(62.746)
DPTS/PA	−3.133[a]
	(55.016)
Adjusted R^2	0.942
Observations	429

[a]Denotes significance at the 1 percent level.
Notes: Dependent variable is regular season winning percentage. Sample: 1991/92 to 2005/06. t-statistics in parentheses below each coefficient.

THE MARGINAL VALUE OF THE INDIVIDUAL STATISTICS

The Impact of Points and Possessions

With equation (15) estimated, we can now ascertain the marginal value of much of what each team and player does upon the court. By taking the derivative of wins with respect to PTS and PE, one can ascertain the impact of an additional point and possession on team wins. The results of these calculations are reported in Table 1.6.[28] From this table we can see each additional point adds 0.033 wins while each possession employed subtracts 0.034 victories. A similar calculation produces the marginal impact of DPTS and PA.

As one can see in equations (16) and (17), the similarity in these values is not a coincidence.

$$\text{Marginal Value of PTS} = [\,j_1 * \text{PE}^{-1}] \tag{16}$$

$$\text{Marginal Value of PE} = j_1 * \text{PTS} * \text{PE}^{-2} * -1 = [\,j_1 * \text{PE}^{-1}] * [\text{PTS} * \text{PE}^{-1}] * -1 \tag{17}$$

The difference between these equations is [PTS/PE]*−1. The average value of this ratio from 1991/92 to 2005/06 is 1.02.[29] Consequently the average marginal value of PTS and each of the elements of PE are virtually equal.[30] This finding will be important in the construction of Win Score.

Given these values, we can now, as noted in Table 1.7, ascertain the value of the statistics tabulated for the players and the team. The team factors—which are associated with team defense—include variables that cannot be assigned to individual players. Consequently team variables cannot be easily incorporated in our measure of worker productivity.[31] The list of player factors, though, which includes points, field-goal and free-throw attempts, offensive rebounds, turnovers, steals,[32] and defensive rebounds, can be employed in our evaluation of individual players.

TABLE 1.6
Marginal Value of Player and Team Factors, Derived from Equation (13)

Variable	Marginal Value
Points	0.033
Possessions employed	(0.034)
Points surrendered	(0.033)
Possessions acquired	0.034

TABLE 1.7
Marginal Value of Player and Team Defensive Factors, Derived from Table 1.6

Player Factors	Marginal Value
PTS	0.033
FGA	(0.034)
FTA	(0.015)
RBO	0.034
TO	(0.034)
RBD	0.034
STL	0.034
Team Defensive Factors	**Marginal Value**
DPTS	(0.033)
DFGM	0.034
DFTM	0.015
DTO-STL	0.034
RBTM	0.034

The Impact of Personal Fouls, Blocked Shots, and Assists

We now have ascertained the impact of much of what a player does on wins. There are still three factors, though, that are tabulated for the player which are not on our list. These include personal fouls, blocked shots, and assists. With a bit of work, though, a value for each of these variables can be determined.

Personal Fouls

From Table 1.7 we learned the impact of an opponent making a free throw (DFTM) on team wins. Free throws are taken by the opponent when a player commits a personal foul. It is important to remember that not all personal fouls lead to free throws. Still, we can allocate the percentage of free throws an opponent takes to each player according to the percentage of personal fouls each player commits. For example, Al Harrington of the Atlanta Hawks committed 14.7 percent of the team's personal fouls in 2005/06. Consequently, of the 1,768 free throws made by Atlanta's opponents, we can assign 14.7 percent—or 259.1—to Harrington. And since we know the impact the opponent's free throws have on wins, we have now estimated the impact of Harrington's propensity to commit crimes on the basketball court.[33]

Blocked Shots

Blocked shots are also not part of any element of equation (15). Like personal fouls, though, blocked shots relate directly to a factor connected to team wins. To ascertain the value of a blocked shot, one can regress the opponent's two-point field goals made on a team's blocked shots and the opponent's field-goal attempts. These results are reported in Table 1.8.

From this table we see that each blocked shot reduces the made two-point shots by the opponent by −0.58. Given the value of a made two-point shot by the opponent, we can surmise that each blocked shot is worth 0.019 wins, or 58 percent of 0.032 wins.[34]

Assists

The last variable tracked for the individual to be incorporated is assists. Of all the variables tracked, this one is the only judgment call. An assist is credited when the official scorer believes a pass led to another player scoring. Hence, unlike points, rebounds, turnovers, and so on, a player's assists are somewhat subjective.

Not only are assists subjective, they also do not directly impact team wins. In other words, we have shown that wins are determined by offensive and defensive efficiency. Once we know a team's efficiency levels, knowing assists does not change our assessment of a team. This can be seen empirically by simply adding assists to equation (15), a step that demonstrates that assists do not statistically impact wins once one has noted the efficiency metrics. Theoretically this result should not surprise, since if two teams have the

TABLE 1.8
Determining the Value of a Blocked Shot

Variables	Coefficients
BLK	−0.578[a]
	(8.853)
DFGA	0.556[a]
	(27.846)
Adjusted R^2	0.876
Observations	429

[a]Denotes significance at the 1 percent level.

Notes: Dependent variable is opponent's two-point field goals made. Sample: 1991/92 to 2005/06. Dummy variables for each team and year were included in the model. t-statistics in parentheses below each coefficient.

same levels of efficiency, the wins produced will be the same regardless of how many assists the teams accumulate.

Although assists do not impact wins directly, assists do have value. And this value can be uncovered by looking at the determinants of an individual player's productivity. Specifically, as noted in *The Wages of Wins*, we expect that a player will be more productive on a team where teammates get more assists than he will be on a team with fewer assists. To capture this impact, player per-minute performance was regressed on a collection of factors, including past performance, games played, experience level, position played, roster stability, per-minute productivity of teammates, quality of coaching, and the per-minute assists of a player's teammates.[35] The results indicate that each additional assist by a teammate does positively impact a player's per-minute productivity. With a bit of work, it was shown that each assist is worth about 0.67 points.[36]

Before moving on, it is important to note one implication of the model used to derive the value of an assist. It has been argued that a player's performance in the NBA is dependent upon the performance of his teammates. Although it is the case that increases in the productivity of teammates diminishes the production of a player, the impact is relatively small. The analysis used to derive the value of an assist also indicates that a 50 percent increase in the productivity of teammates would only reduce per-minute performance of a player by 13 percent.[37] In sum, much of what a player does is independent of his teammates.

The Value of a Player's Actions on the Court

With personal fouls incorporated in the model, and the impact of blocked shots and assists ascertained, we now have values for every statistic tabulated for an individual player. These are reported in Table 1.9.

One should note that rather than focus on points and field-goal attempts, Table 1.9 reports the impact of converting a three-point field-goal attempt. These are calculated from the values reported in Table 1.7, where we saw that each point was worth 0.033 wins while each field-goal attempt cost −0.034. A made three-pointer gives a team three points (0.099), while costing −0.034. So the net value is 0.065. A similar process reveals that a made two-point field goal is worth 0.032 wins. Made free throws—which are calculated by noting the value of a point and a free-throw attempt—are worth 0.018 points. Missed field-goal and free-throw attempts simply reflect the value of the corresponding shot attempt.

The remaining factors in Table 1.9 for the players are taken from Table 1.7 or the discussion of blocked shots and assists. As for the team's statistics listed, these are determined according to the same process reported above.

TABLE 1.9
Marginal Value of All Player and Team Factors

Player Variables	Marginal Value
Three-point field goal made (3FGM)	0.065
Two-point field goal made (2FGM)	0.032
Free throw made	0.018
Missed field goal (FGMs)	−0.034
Missed free throw (FTMs)	−0.015
Offensive rebounds	0.034
Defensive rebounds	0.034
Turnovers	−0.034
Steal	0.034
Opponent's free throws made	−0.018
Blocked shot	0.019
Assist	0.022

Team Variables	Marginal Value
Opponent's three-point field goals made (D3FGM)	−0.065
Opponent's two-point field goals made (D2FGM)	−0.032
Opponent's turnovers	0.034
Team rebounds	0.034

CALCULATING WINS PRODUCED

With values for each statistic ascertained, we can now employ the following steps to calculate how many wins each player produces.

Step 1: Calculating Production per 48 minutes (P48)

The first step, illustrated with equation (18), simply involves multiplying each player's accumulation of each statistic by the corresponding value in Table 1.9.

$$\begin{aligned} \text{PROD} = {} & \text{3FGM}^*0.065 + \text{2FGM}^*0.032 + \text{FTM}^*0.018 \\ & + \text{FGMS}^*{-0.034} + \text{FTMS}^*{-0.015} + \text{REBO}^*0.034 \\ & + \text{REBD}^*0.034 + \text{TO}^*{-0.034} + \text{STL}^*0.034 \\ & + \text{DFTM}^*{-0.018} + \text{BLK}^*0.019 + \text{AST}^*0.022 \end{aligned} \tag{18}$$

Two of the factors used to measure PROD—blocked shots and assists—are not part of offensive or defensive efficiency. As noted, each of these elements of a player's performance does not impact wins directly, but does alter the productivity of teammates. In essence, both blocked shots and assists represent a transfer of production from one player to another. Given the nature of these two stats, not only does one have to note the value of the blocked shots and assists a player accumulates, but also one needs to consider the accumulation of these factors by a player's teammates.[38]

To do this, we calculate how many blocked shots and assists a team accumulates per 48 minutes played. We then note for each team how their accumulation of blocked shots and assists differs from the league average. For example, the Utah Jazz in 2005/06 averaged 0.117 blocked shots and assists per 48 minutes played. The league average was 0.108. Consequently, for each player on the Jazz, 0.009—or the difference between Utah's accumulation and the league average—was subtracted from each player's per-48-minute PROD. As noted in equation (19), with the adjustment for blocked shots and assists by teammates (MATE48) incorporated, a player's production per 48 minutes (P48) can be calculated.[39]

$$P48 = [PROD / \text{Minutes Played}]*48 - MATE48 \qquad (19)$$

It is important to note that the adjustment for the teammates' assists and blocked shots is quite small. The average difference in 2005/06 of MATE48—in absolute terms—was only 0.007. As noted in Table 1.10, this is quite small relative to 0.294, or the average value of production per 48 minutes (P48) for the 2005/06 season.

Step 2: Adjust for Position Played

Table 1.10 illustrates not only the overall average, but also the average by position played for the 2005/06 campaign.[40] Players in the NBA are assigned one of five positions. In the backcourt we find point guards and shooting guards. These players tend to accumulate larger numbers of

TABLE 1.10
Average Productivity at Each Position, 2005/06

Position	Average P48
Centers	0.368
Power forwards	0.366
Small forwards	0.264
Shooting guards	0.230
Point guards	0.244
League average	0.294

turnovers, primarily because ball handling is a primary responsibility of backcourt performers. Furthermore, guards tend to gather few rebounds. In the frontcourt we find small forwards, power forwards, and centers. These players tend to accumulate a larger number of rebounds and a smaller number of turnovers. Hence, relative to guards, frontcourt performers will tend to have higher levels of productivity.

To illustrate, an average center from 1993/94 to 2004/05 captured 12.4 rebounds per 48 minutes. An average point guard only captured 4.7 boards in this time. So a center who accumulated eight rebounds per 48 minutes is well below average, while a point guard with the same quantity of boards is well above average. Given that these positions are complements rather than substitutes, to accurately measure the productivity of a player in the NBA one must compare the productivity of a player relative to the position the player plays.

This is accomplished simply by subtracting from each player's P48 the average performance by a player at his position. As noted in *The Wages of Wins*, virtually all of a player's value is determined by his statistical performance relative to the position he played.

Step 3: Adjusting for Team Statistics

Although one could stop after these first steps—a point to be made again below—one can consider the various factors only tracked for the team. Table 1.9 lists several statistics—again associated with team defense—the NBA does not connect to individual players. These include three-point and two-point field goals made by the opponent, opponent's turnovers that are not steals, and team rebounds.[41]

To account for these factors, the methodology put forward by Scott, Long, and Sompii, as well as Berri, will be adopted.[42] Specifically, the team defensive factors will be allocated across the members of a team according to the minutes each player played. Given the nature of team defense, it makes sense that if you play 15 percent of a team's minutes that you are responsible for 15 percent of a team's defensive factors. This approach allows defensive ability to vary when we look at players on different teams, but we will charge the same per-minute defensive factor to each player on a specific team.[43]

The first step in allocating these team statistics is simply noting the value of the team factors accumulated. This step is illustrated in equation (20).[44]

$$\text{Value of Team Factors} = \text{D3FGM}^{*}{-0.065} + \text{D2FGM}^{*}{-0.032} + \text{DTO}^{*}0.034 + \text{REBTM}^{*}0.034 \qquad (20)$$

All of these factors are weighted according to the values previously noted. Our next step is comparing the value of team factors, per 48 minutes played, to the average per 48 minute value we see in the league. In other words, TM48 is calculated by subtracting the league average team adjustment from each team's adjustment. For example, the Detroit Pistons in 2005/06 had a team adjustment that was 0.011 below the league average, which means this team was an above-average defensive team. Hence, to incorporate the team adjustment, each player's P48 performance on the Pistons was increased by 0.011.

$$\text{TM48} = [(\text{Value of Team Factors / Minutes Played by Team}) * 48] - \text{League Average Value of Team Factors per 48 minutes played} \quad (21)$$

As one can see in Table 1.11, TM48 is relatively small. We noted earlier that average productivity per 48 minutes is 0.294. The average TM48—in absolute terms—is only 0.010. It is important to also note that the correlation coefficient between unadjusted and adjusted production per 48 minutes is 0.99. In sum, adjusting for the team defensive factors does not alter our assessment of individual players.

Step 4: Moving from Relative Wins Toward Wins Produced

A player's impact on wins is almost entirely a function of the statistics the player accumulates relative to what one would expect from a player at that position. But if we stop with steps 1 and 2, all we would know is a player's production of relative wins. For the league, the summation of relative wins would be 0.

To get at total wins we add to each player's per-48-minute production the number of wins an average player would produce in the league in this time frame. The average team will win 0.500 games per 48 minutes played. So an average player will produce approximately 0.1 wins per 48 minutes.[45] When we add this quantity to each player's adjusted production per 48 minutes we can see each player's Win Produced per 48 minutes (WP48).

Given all these steps, we can see in equation (22) how the WP48 of each player is calculated.

$$\text{WP48} = \text{P48} - \text{POS P48} + \text{TM48} + 0.1 \quad (22)$$

Once we have calculated WP48 it is fairly simple to measure Wins Produced. All one needs to do is divide WP48 by 48, and then multiply by the number of minutes played.

The Accuracy of Wins Produced

To assess the accuracy of this approach we turn to Table 1.12, where the summation of the Wins Produced by each team's players is compared to

TABLE 1.11
Value of TM48, 2005/06

Eastern Conference Teams	TM48	Western Conference Teams	TM48
Atlanta Hawks	−0.009	Dallas Mavericks	0.010
Boston Celtics	0.007	Denver Nuggets	−0.008
Charlotte Bobcats	−0.003	Golden State Warriors	−0.003
Chicago Bulls	0.027	Houston Rockets	0.003
Cleveland Cavaliers	−0.005	Los Angeles Clippers	−0.005
Detroit Pistons	0.011	Los Angeles Lakers	−0.003
Indiana Pacers	0.008	Memphis Grizzlies	0.023
Miami Heat	−0.005	Minnesota Timberwolves	0.010
Milwaukee Bucks	−0.004	New Orleans Hornets	−0.003
New Jersey Nets	0.016	Phoenix Suns	−0.022
New York Knicks	−0.006	Portland Trail Blazers	−0.013
Orlando Magic	0.003	Sacramento Kings	−0.006
Philadelphia 76ers	−0.017	San Antonio Spurs	0.021
Toronto Raptors	−0.018	Seattle Supersonics	−0.027
Washington Wizards	0.001	Utah Jazz	0.017
Average League TM48 in Absolute Terms			0.010

actual wins. The absolute difference between these two values for the 2005/06 season is only 3.2 wins. As noted in *The Wages of Wins*, from 1993/94 to 2004/05, this average difference was 2.4. In sum, a team's Wins Produced is tied quite closely to actual wins. And this is not surprising. The calculation of Wins Produced simply involves allocating to the players the outcome of a model connecting wins to offensive and defensive efficiency. Since offensive and defensive efficiency explains 94 percent of wins, Wins Produced will also have the same explanatory power.

THE WIN SCORE MODEL

The Wins Produced algorithm produces an accurate evaluation of player productivity, but it lacks the simplicity of slugging percentage or OPS. Fortunately, one can create a simple model from the results already reported. From Table 1.7 it was seen that points, rebounds, steal, turnovers, and field-goal attempts have virtually the same impact—in absolute terms—on wins. We have also seen that free-throw attempts, personal fouls, blocked shots, and assists—again in absolute terms—have a smaller impact than points, rebounds, and so on. For simplicity we can argue that the impact of these latter four factors in absolute terms is 0.5. Put all this together and we get the Win Score model, which is calculated as follows for player i in year t:

TABLE 1.12
Evaluating the Accuracy of Wins Produced, 2005/06

Teams	Summation of Wins Produced	Actual Wins	Difference in Absolute Terms
San Antonio Spurs	59.2	63	3.8
Detroit Pistons	58.9	64	5.1
Dallas Mavericks	57.4	60	2.6
Phoenix Suns	56.1	54	2.1
Miami Heat	51.2	52	0.8
Memphis Grizzlies	50.9	49	1.9
Los Angeles Lakers	47.7	45	2.7
Cleveland Cavaliers	47.0	50	3.0
Washington Wizards	45.9	42	3.9
Indiana Pacers	45.8	41	4.8
Los Angeles Clippers	45.1	47	1.9
Sacramento Kings	45.1	44	1.1
New Jersey Nets	44.5	49	4.5
Chicago Bulls	42.8	41	1.8
Denver Nuggets	41.8	44	2.2
Orlando Magic	38.2	36	2.2
Milwaukee Bucks	38.2	40	1.8
Golden State Warriors	37.3	34	3.3
Boston Celtics	37.0	33	4.0
Houston Rockets	36.7	34	2.7
Minnesota Timberwolves	36.0	33	3.0
Philadelphia 76ers	35.9	38	2.1
Utah Jazz	34.0	41	7.0
New Orleans Hornets	33.3	38	4.7
Toronto Raptors	33.2	27	6.2
Seattle Supersonics	32.8	35	2.2
Charlotte Bobcats	30.4	26	4.4
Atlanta Hawks	28.2	26	2.2
New York Knicks	23.9	23	0.9
Portland Trail Blazers	15.3	21	5.7
Average Difference			**3.2**

$$\text{WIN SCORE}_{it} = \text{PTS}_{it} + \text{TREB}_{it} + \text{STL}_{it} + 1/2{*}\text{BLK}_{it} + 1/2{*}\text{AST}_{it} - \text{TO}_{it} - \text{FGA}_{it} - 1/2{*}\text{FTA}_{it} - 1/2{*}\text{PF}_{it} \quad (23)$$

Comparing Win Score per-minute to P48 we find a 0.99 correlation coefficient. In other words, whether we use the actual values reported in Tables 1.7 and 1.8, or the simplified Win Score model, the assessment of players is essentially the same.

It is important to note that Win Score is appropriate if you are comparing a player relative to himself or to other players playing the same position. In other words, if you are doing a study of how player performance changes

TABLE 1.13
Average Win Score Per Minute at Each Position, 1994/95 to 2004/05

Position	Average Win Score per Minute
Centers	0.225
Power forwards	0.215
Small forwards	0.152
Shooting guards	0.128
Point guards	0.132
League average	0.170

over time, or what factors impact player productivity, Win Score is appropriate. If you wish to know if a player at one position is offering more than another at a different position, then one has to adjust for position played. As illustrated in Table 1.13, Win Score per-minute for centers and power forwards tends to be higher than what we observe for guards.

One can calculate Position Adjusted Win Score (PAWS).[46] One can then compare PAWSmin—or PAWS adjusted for minutes played—to WP48. This comparison reveals that our evaluation of players is virtually identical by each approach. For example, for the 2005/06 season we find that PAWSmin has a 0.994 correlation with WP48. This result is consistent with the contention that player performance is primarily about the statistics the player generates relative to the position the player plays. The adjustment for team factors, which Win Score and PAWS ignores, has virtually no impact on the final assessment of individual players.

WIN SCORE VERSUS NBA EFFICIENCY

At first glance it appears that Win Score and NBA Efficiency are essentially the same model. Differences exist with respect to how assists and blocked shots are valued. Win Score also incorporates personal fouls, while the NBA's metric does not. The truly important difference, though, lies with respect to the valuation of shot attempts.

The NBA model values equally missed field goals and missed free throws. More important, though, is the impact of made shot attempts. As noted, a made shot results in a change of possession. Therefore, making a shot moves a team closer to winning the game, but also imposes a cost. According to the NBA model, though, a player does not bear the cost of a shot attempt if the attempt is successful. Consequently, according to the NBA's calculations,

a player only needs to successfully make 33 percent of his two-point field-goal attempts and 25 percent of his three-pointers for the benefits of the player's shooting to equal the costs.[47] If a player exceeds these percentages, and is able to take a large number of his team's shot attempts, the player's value according to the NBA's method can be quite high. In contrast, the method proposed here imposes the cost of each shot attempt, regardless of whether the shot is made or not. As a result, a player must connect on at least 50 percent of two-point shots and 33 percent of three-pointers.

To illustrate this point, consider the case of Allen Iverson. Iverson was chosen first overall in the draft in 1996 and was named Rookie of the Year for the 1996/97 campaign. For the 2001/02 season, Iverson was named MVP of the NBA. Three times he has been named both first team All-NBA and second team All-NBA. Clearly Iverson is regarded as one of the better players in the NBA by the national media. And his career per game average in NBA Efficiency, 21.4, is well above the NBA average of 15.4.[48]

The 2005/06 campaign was Iverson's tenth season in the league. Across these ten years he has averaged twenty-eight points per game. From three-point range he has averaged 4.1 attempts per game, which he has converted at a rate of 31.0 percent. From inside the arc he has converted at a rate of 44.5 percent. His PPS for his career has been 0.897, well below the average mark of 0.956 we see across Iverson's ten years. In sum, Iverson scores, but he scores inefficiently. The NBA Efficiency model, despite the name of this measure, fails to penalize inefficiency. Consequently, because Iverson surpasses the meager thresholds imposed by the NBA's model, his inefficient scoring actually increases his value according to NBA Efficiency. The results reported here, though, suggest that Iverson's shooting—which wastes his team's scarce supply of shot attempts—reduces the likelihood his team will win.

And we can see this when we look at Iverson's Wins Produced and Win Score. Across his ten-year career he has produced 51.1 wins and posted a WP48 of 0.086. His Win Score per-minute is 0.115, below average for a guard. It is true that in four years—1997/98, 1998/99, 2004/05, and 2005/06—his WP48 was above average. In six years, though, he was below average. If we put the good and bad together, the picture that emerges is of a slightly below-average performer.

The difference between industry or popular perception, and the view offered by Wins Produced and Win Score, is not unique to Iverson. For the 2005/06 regular season, 118 players accumulated at least 2,000 minutes played. These players were ranked both in terms of PAWSmin and NBA Efficiency per-minute.[49] The difference between the rankings was then calculated and utilized to construct a list of the ten most overrated and underrated players in the NBA. These lists are reported in Tables 1.14 and 1.15.

TABLE 1.14
The Most Overrated Players for 2005/06

Overrated Players	Team	Difference in Rankings	Rank PAWSmin	PAWSmin	Rank NBA Efficiency per Minute	NBA Efficiency per Minute	PPS	Points per Game	Points per Minute
Al Harrington	Atlanta	−61	114	−0.072	53	0.467	0.957	18.6	0.507
Zach Randolph	Portland	−51	108	−0.059	57	0.465	0.885	18.0	0.524
Nenad Krstic	New Jersey	−49	110	−0.060	61	0.458	1.016	13.5	0.438
Carmelo Anthony	Denver	−48	66	0.000	18	0.576	0.985	26.5	0.722
Allen Iverson	Philadelphia	−38	51	0.022	13	0.607	0.934	33.0	0.767
Chris Webber	Philadelphia	−38	63	0.002	25	0.556	0.883	20.2	0.525
Primoz Brezec	Charlotte	−37	101	−0.050	64	0.457	1.034	12.4	0.453
Richard Hamilton	Detroit	−29	84	−0.017	55	0.466	1.023	20.1	0.570
Mark Blount	Boston-Minnesota	−28	118	−0.117	90	0.395	1.016	11.3	0.408
Zaza Pachulia	Atlanta	−28	91	−0.024	63	0.457	0.902	11.7	0.372
	AVERAGES	**−40.7**	**90.6**	**−0.038**	**49.9**	**0.490**	**0.964**	**18.5**	**0.528**

TABLE 1.15
The Most Underrated Players for 2005/06

Underrated Players	Team	Difference in Rankings	Rank PAWSmin	PAWSmin	Rank NBA Efficiency per Minute	NBA Efficiency per Minute	PPS	Points per Game	Points per Minute
Andre Iguodala	Philadelphia	56	17	0.082	73	0.426	1.081	12.3	0.326
Josh Childress	Atlanta	51	16	0.083	67	0.449	1.167	10.0	0.330
Eddie Jones	Memphis	49	46	0.026	95	0.381	0.993	11.8	0.363
Chris Duhon	Chicago	40	52	0.017	92	0.393	0.985	8.7	0.300
Delonte West	Boston	38	30	0.046	68	0.449	1.096	11.8	0.346
Smush Parker	LA Lakers	37	61	0.008	98	0.374	1.047	11.5	0.339
Shane Battier	Memphis	33	58	0.014	91	0.394	1.081	10.1	0.288
Antonio Daniels	Washington	32	72	−0.004	104	0.360	0.878	9.6	0.336
Luther Head	Houston	32	77	−0.009	109	0.327	0.986	8.8	0.306
Raja Bell	Phoenix	31	69	−0.003	100	0.370	1.126	14.7	0.393
	AVERAGES	**39.9**	**49.8**	**0.026**	**89.7**	**0.392**	**1.044**	**10.9**	**0.333**

Iverson in 2005/06 was ranked thirteenth in NBA Efficiency per minute, but only fifty-first in PAWSmin. The difference of 38 between these rankings was the fifth largest difference found among the overrated players. Topping the list was Al Harrington, who was ranked fifty-third in NBA Efficiency but only one-hundred-fourteenth (out of 118) in Win Score. Although Win Score is a more accurate reflection of Harrington's impact on wins, it appears Indiana Pacers heeded the NBA Efficiency metric. In the summer of 2006 Harrington signed a four-year, $35.3-million contract with the Pacers.[50] In other words, the Indiana Pacers signed a player ranked in the bottom ten in the league in overall productivity to a contract that was going to pay him close to $9 million per season. Given that the average NBA player is paid less than half what Harrington will receive, it appears that he might be overpaid.[51]

If we look at these two lists, an interesting pattern emerges. The average NBA player in 2005/06 scored 0.400 points per minute. All of the underrated players scored at a slower per-minute rate. Consequently, the NBA Efficiency metric—which is dominated by scoring—rates these players relatively low. In the overrated list we see that nine of the ten players listed score at an above average rate. The overrated players, though, have an average PPS of 0.964, which is below the league average mark of 0.98. In sum, the overrated players are above average in scoring output but below average in shooting efficiency. The construction of the NBA Efficiency metric, though, fails to penalize these scorers for inefficiency. Consequently these players are rated higher than their contribution to wins would suggest. The underrated players fail to score, so the NBA's metric discounts their contribution. In terms of wins, though, many of the underrated are actually quite valuable.[52]

Although the list of underrated does include some very valuable players, none of these players are in the top ten in PAWSmin. This list is revealed in Table 1.16. As one can see, the player with highest PAWSmin is Kevin Garnett, a ranking also granted by the NBA's metric. Once we move off the top spot, though, differences emerge. The most striking is seen with respect to Ben Wallace. Wallace ranked in the top ten in blocked shots, steals, and rebounds. But his inability to score dragged down his ranking in the NBA's metric. His PAWS, and also his Wins Produced, indicated that Wallace was indeed one of the top ten players in the league. Although scorers tend to attract the attention of the media and fans, Wallace shows that a player can dramatically impact outcomes in the NBA without tallying many points.

TABLE 1.16
The Most Productive Players at Each Position in 2005/06

Top Players	Team	Position	Difference in Rankings	Rank PAWSmin	PAWSmin	Rank NBA Efficiency per Minute	NBA Efficiency per Minute
Jason Kidd	New Jersey	Point guard	16	3	0.153	19	0.576
Dwayne Wade	Miami	Shooting guard	−1	6	0.116	5	0.698
LeBron James	Cleveland	Small forward	−3	9	0.106	6	0.691
Kevin Garnett	Minnesota	Power forward	0	1	0.196	1	0.778
Ben Wallace	Detroit	Center	28	5	0.140	33	0.525
Steve Nash	Phoenix	Point guard	3	4	0.143	7	0.681
Paul Pierce	Boston	Shooting guard	−2	13	0.099	11	0.626
Andrei Kirilenko	Utah	Small forward	11	11	0.104	22	0.568
Shawn Marion	Phoenix	Power forward	2	2	0.182	4	0.715
Dwight Howard	Orlando	Center	3	14	0.096	17	0.578

CONCLUDING OBSERVATIONS

To conclude, let's list a few of the basic lessons learned.

- The box score statistics the NBA tracks for individual players can be linked directly to team wins. Hence, the wins a player produces can be estimated.
- Although player performance is impacted by the production of teammates, the impact is relatively small.
- The model the NBA lists on its website—NBA Efficiency—over-values scoring and does not offer sufficient penalties for inefficient shooting.

Although each of these lessons is important, the primary purpose of this essay was to detail the Win Score model. As noted, research on baseball has been made easier by metrics like slugging percentage, which simply and accurately capture a baseball player's productivity. The Win Score measure described here offers the same simplicity and accuracy for analysis of professional basketball.

Thus far this metric—or something quite similar—has been employed in published studies examining shirking by workers, determinants of attendance on the road, player performance in the playoffs, and competitive balance in the NBA.[53] Additionally, Win Score is also being employed in working papers examining coaching, two studies of the NBA draft, a study of racial bias in the sports media, and a study of racial bias among NBA referees.[54] Although the creator of Win Score—that would be me—is more than happy having a near monopoly on publishing studies with this measure, one would hope that other researchers will follow the lead of Price and Wolfers and take advantage of the Win Score metric. As noted, many of the stories people have told with player statistics in baseball can also be told using basketball data. Hopefully the Win Score metric will make the telling of these stories that much easier.

ACKNOWLEDGMENT

The model presented here benefited from numerous discussions with Dean Oliver, author of *Basketball on Paper: Rule and Tools for Performance Analysis*. Any errors are still the responsibility of the author.

NOTES

1. Lawrence M. Kahn, "The Sports Business as a Labor Market Laboratory," *Journal of Economic Perspectives* 14, no. 3 (Summer 2000): 75.

2. For a review of the literature examining the prevalence of racial discrimination prior to the 1990s, see Lawrence M. Kahn, "Discrimination in Professional Sports: A

Survey of the Literature," *Industrial Labor Relations Review* 44 (April 1991): 395–418. More recent studies of racial discrimination in professional baseball were conducted by Torben Andersen and Sumner J. La Croix, "Customer Racial Discrimination in Major League Baseball," *Economic Inquiry* 29 (October 1991): 665–677; Andrew Hanssen, "The Cost of Discrimination: A Study of Major League Baseball," *Southern Economic Journal* 64, no. 3 (January 1998): 603–627; and F. Andrew Hanssen and Torben Anderson, "Has Discrimination Lessened Over Time? A Test Using Baseball's All–Star Vote," *Economic Inquiry* 37, no. 2 (1999): 326–352. Racial discrimination in professional basketball was recently examined by Jeffery A. Jenkins, "A Reexamination of Salary Discrimination in Professional Basketball," *Social Science Quarterly* 77 (September 1996): 594–608; Matthew S. Dey, "Racial Differences in National Basketball Association Players' Salaries," *American Economist* 41 (Fall 1997): 84–90; Barton Hughes Hamilton, "Racial Discrimination and Professional Basketball Salaries in the 1990s," *Applied Economics* 29 (1997): 287–296; Mark Gius and Donn Johnson, "An Empirical Investigation of Wage Discrimination in Professional Basketball," *Applied Economics Letters* 5 (1998): 703–705; Orn B. Bodvarsson and Raymond T. Brastow, "A Test of Employer Discrimination in the NBA," *Contemporary Economic Policy* 17 (1999): 243–255; Orn B. Bodvarsson and Raymond T. Brastow, "Do Employers Pay for Consistent Performance? Evidence from the NBA," *Economic Inquiry* 36, no. 1 (April, 1998): 145–160; Ha Hoang and Dan Rascher, "The NBA, Exit Discrimination, and Career Earnings," *Industrial Relations* 38, no. 1 (January 1999): 69–91; Robert E. McCormick and Robert D. Tollison, "Why Do Black Basketball Players Work More for Less Money?" *Journal of Economic Behavior and Organization* 44 (2001): 201–219; Orn B. Bodvarsson and Mark D. Partridge, "A Supply and Demand Model of Co-Worker, Employer, and Customer Discrimination," *Labour Economics* 8 (2001): 389–416; James Richard Hill, "Pay Discrimination in the NBA Revisited," *Quarterly Journal of Business and Economics* 43, nos. 1 and 2 (Winter 2004): 81–92; Lawrence M. Kahn and Malav Shah, "Race, Compensation and Contract Length in the NBA, 2001–2002," *Industrial Relations* 24, no. 3 (July 2005): 444–462; Richard C. K. Burdekin, Richard T. Hossfeld, and Janet Kiholm Smith, "Are NBA Fans Becoming Indifferent to Race: Evidence from the 1990s," *Journal of Sports Economics* 6, no. 2 (May 2005): 144–59. For a recent review of the literature see David J. Berri, "Economics and the National Basketball Association: Surveying the Literature at the Tip-off," in *The Handbook of Sports Economics Research,* ed. John Fizel (Armonk, N.Y.: M. E. Sharpe, 2005), 21–48. The issue of pay and productivity has been examined in both directions. Gerald W. Scully, "Pay and Performance in Major League Baseball," *American Economic Review* 64 (1974): 917–930; Marshall H. Medoff, "On Monopsonistic Exploitation in Professional Baseball," *Quarterly Review of Economics and Business* 16 (1976): 113–121; Paul M. Sommers and Noel Quinton, "Pay and Performance in Major League Baseball: The Case of the First Family of Free Agents," *Journal of Human Resources* 17, no. 3 (Summer 1982): 426–436; Henry J. Raimondo, "Free Agents' Impact on the Labor Market for Baseball Players," *Journal of Labor Research* 4, no. 2 (Spring 1983): 183–193; James Richard Hill and William Spellman, "Professional Baseball: The Reserve Clause and Salary Structure," *Industrial Relations* 22, no. 1 (Winter 1983): 1–19; James Richard Hill, "The Threat of Free Agency and Exploitation in Professional Baseball, 1976–1979," *Quarterly Review of*

Economics and Business 25, no. 4 (Winter 1985): 68–82; Frank Scott Jr., James Long, and Ken Sompii, "Salary vs. Marginal Revenue Product Under Monopsony and Competition: The Case of Professional Basketball," *Atlantic Economic Journal* 13 (1985): 50–59; Thomas H. Bruggink and David R. Rose Jr., "Financial Restraint in the Free Agent Labor Market for Major League Baseball: Players Look at Strike Three," *Southern Economic Journal* 56, no. 4 (April 1990): 1029–1043; Paul M. Sommers, "An Empirical Note on Salaries in Major League Baseball," *Social Science Quarterly* 71, no. 4 (December 1990): 861–867; Durland, Dan, Jr., and Paul M. Sommers, "Collusion in Major League Baseball: An Empirical Test," *Journal of Sport Behavior* 14, no. 1 (March 1991): 19–29; Andrew Zimbalist, "Salaries and Performance: Beyond the Scully Model," in *Diamonds Are Forever: The Business of Baseball*, ed. Paul Sommers (Washington, D.C.: Brookings Institution Press, 1992), 109–133; Andrew Zimbalist, *Baseball and Billions* (New York: Basic Books, 1992); Asher A. Blass, "Does the Baseball Labor Market Contradict the Human Capital Model of Investment?" *Review of Economics and Statistics* 74 (1992): 261–268; Don N. MacDonald and Morgan O. Reynolds, "Are Baseball Players Paid Their Marginal Product?" *Managerial and Decision Economics* 15, no. 5 (Sept.–Oct. 2994): 443–457; Anthony Krautmann, "What's Wrong with Scully: Estimates of a Player's Marginal Revenue Product," *Economic Inquiry* 37, no. 2 (April 1999): 369–381; Anthony Krautmann, Elizabeth Gustafson, and Lawrence Hadley, "Who Pays for Minor League Training Costs?" *Contemporary Economic Policy* 18, no. 1 (January 2000): 37–47; Anthony Krautmann and Margaret Oppenheimer, "Contract Length and the Return to Performance in Major League Baseball," *Journal of Sports Economics* 3, no. 1 (February 2002): 6–17: 1each examined the impact productivity has upon a worker's wage in professional sports. Anthony Krautmann ("Shirking or Stochastic Productivity in Major League Baseball?" *Southern Economic Review* [April 1990]: 961–968), Paul M. Sommers ("The Influence of Salary Arbitration on Player Performance," *Social Science Quarterly* 74, no. 2 [June 1993]: 439–43), and Joel Maxcy, Rodney Fort, and Anthony Krautmann ("The Effectiveness of Incentive Mechanisms in Major League Baseball," *Journal of Sports Economics* 3, no. 3 [August 2002]: 246–255) examined how compensation impacts player productivity.

Notable papers examining the role of baseball managers include John Ruggiero, Lawrence Hadley, Gerry Ruggiero, and Scott Knowles, "A Note on the Pythagorean Theorem of Baseball Production," *Managerial and Decision Economics* 18 (1997): 335–342; Ira Horowitz, "Pythagoras's Petulant Persecutors," *Managerial and Decision Economics* 18 (1997): 343–344; Ira Horowitz, "Pythagoras, Tommy Lasorda, and Me: On Evaluating Baseball Managers," *Social Science Quarterly* 75 (1994): 413–419; Ira Horowitz, "On the Manager as Principal Clerk," *Managerial and Decision Economics* 15 (1994): 187–194; Lawrence M. Kahn, "Managerial Quality, Team Success, and Individual Player Performance in Major League Baseball," *Industrial and Labor Relations Review* 46, no. 3 (April 1993): 531–547; Gerald W. Scully, "Managerial Efficiency and Survivability in Professional Team Sports," *Managerial and Decision Economics* 15 (1994): 403–411; Philip K. Porter and Gerald W. Scully, "Measuring Managerial Efficiency: The Case of Baseball," *Southern Economic Journal* 48 (1982): 642–650. Coaching in the National Football League was examined by L. Hadley, M. Poitras, J. Ruggiero, and S. Knowles, "Performance Evaluation of National Football League Teams," *Managerial and Decision Economics* 21 (2000): 63–70. College basketball coaching has been examined by both

John L. Fizel and Michael P. D'Itri in "Managerial Efficiency, Managerial Succession and Organizational Performance," *Managerial and Decision Economics* 18 (1997): 295–308, and Robert C. Clement and Robert E. McCormick, "Coaching Team Production," *Economic Inquiry* 27 (April 1989): 287–304. Finally, coaching in the NBA has been previously analyzed by Jeffrey Pfeffer and Alison Davis-Blake, "Administrative Succession and Organizational Performance: How Administrator Experience Mediate the Succession Effect," *Academy of Management Journal* 29, no. 1 (March 1986): 72–83 and Robert E. McCormick and Robert C. Clement, "Intrafirm Profit Opportunities and Managerial Slack: Evidence from Professional Basketball," In *Advances in the Economics of Sports*, ed. Gerald W. Scully (Greenwich, Conn.: JAI Press, 1992).

3. Gerald W. Scully, "Pay and Performance in Major League Baseball," *American Economic Review* 64 (1974): 917–930.

4. Studies utilizing slugging percentage include Sommers and Quinton, "Pay and Performance in Major League Baseball"; Raimondo, "Free Agents' Impact on the Labor Market; Bruggink and Rose, "Financial Restraint in the Free Agent Labor Market; Hill, "Threat of Free Agency and Exploitation"; Durland and Sommers, "Collusion in Major League Baseball"; Sommers, "Influence of Salary Arbitration on Player Performance"; Anthony Krautmann and Margaret Oppenheimer, "Free Agency and the Allocation of Labor in Major League Baseball," *Managerial and Decision Economics* 15, no. 5 (Sept.–Oct. 1994): 459–469; Krautmann, "What's Wrong with Scully: Estimates"; Krautmann, Gustafson, and Hadley, "Why Pays for Minor League Training Costs?"; Maxcy, Fort, and Krautmann, "Effectiveness of Incentive Mechanisms"; Krautmann and Oppenheimer, "Contract Length and the Return to Performance"; and Brian L. Goff, Robert E. McCormick, and Robert D. Tollison, "Racial Integration as an Innovation: Empirical Evidence from Sports Leagues," *American Economic Review* 92, no. 1 (March 2002): 16–26. Sommers ("Influence of Salary Arbitration on Player Performance") also employed a player's batting average while Krautmann, Gustafson, and Hadley ("Why Pays for Minor League Training Costs?") added a hitter's runs-batted-in. Slugging percentage has not been the only measure of productivity chosen. Medoff ("On Monopsonistic Exploitation in Professional Baseball"), Hill and Spellman ("Professional Baseball"), and MacDonald and Reynolds ("Are Baseball Players Paid Their Marginal Product?") measured a hitter's productivity with runs scored. Such a choice ignores the impact a player's hitting has upon the scoring of teammates. Paul M. Sommers ("An Empirical Note on Salaries in Major League Baseball." *Social Science Quarterly* 71, no. 4 [December 1990]: 861–867) utilized a player's batting average, or simply hits divided by at-bats. Batting average ignores the quality of a player's hits and is generally considered inferior to slugging average. Finally, Zimbalist ("Salaries and Performance"; *Baseball and Billions*) utilized slugging percentage with a player's on-base percentage in the construction of a summary statistic he labeled PROD.

5. David J. Berri, Martin B. Schmidt, and Stacey L. Brook. *The Wages of Wins: Taking Measure of the Many Myths in Modern Sports* (Stanford, Calif.: Stanford University Press, 2006).

6. J. Thorn and P. Palmer, *The Hidden Game of Baseball: A Revolutionary Approach to Baseball and Its Statistics* (New York: Doubleday, 1984). The Thorn and Palmer work is called linear weights. This was utilized by Asher Blass ("Does the Baseball Labor Market Contradict the Human Capital Model") in a study of monopsonistic exploitation in MLB.

7. The Sabermetric movement is led by the Society for American Baseball Research (SABR). As Bill James notes, the Sabermetric movement can best be described as "the search for objective knowledge about baseball" (David Grabiner, "The Sabermetric Manifesto," www.baseball1.com/bb-data/grabiner/manifesto.html).

8. A simple search in ECONLIT conducted in January 2007 indicates how much research has been completed utilizing data from baseball and basketball. Searching ECONLIT for all journal articles that contain the key word "baseball" yields 404 papers. A similar search with the key word "basketball" yielded a list of only 137 articles.

9. The player and team data utilized in this study can be found in the 2006/07 *Sporting News NBA Guide*.

10. With the exception of the 1998/99 campaign, the NBA played eighty-two games in each regular season. The 1998/99 season was delayed by the first lockout in NBA history and hence the season was only fifty games. Given the difference in games played, the data employed in this study is not season aggregates, but rather per-game averages.

11. Equation (1) can be found at the following Web site: http://www.nba.com/statistics/efficiency.html

12. Dave Heeran, *Basketball Abstract, 1991–1992 Edition* (Englewood Cliffs, N.J.: Prentice-Hall, 1992). TENDEX was first formulated by Heeran in 1959. Heeran begins with a model identical to the one currently employed by the NBA, but then weights each player's production by both minutes played and the average game pace his team played throughout the season being examined.

Robert Bellotti, *The Points Created Basketball Book, 1992–1993* (New Brunswick, N.J.: Night Work Publishing, 1996). Bellotti's Points Created model, published in 1988, is also quite similar. Bellotti begins with the basic TENDEX model and then simply subtracts 50 percent of each player's personal fouls. Jeffrey Jenkins ("Reexamination of Salary Discrimination") employed the Points Created model in a study of racial discrimination.

It does not appear that IBM still offers the player of the year award. From 1983–1984 to 2001–2002, though, IBM did utilize a simple formula to identify its choice for player of the year. The formula used by IBM differed from the above models by subtracting field-goal attempts rather than missed field goals. The IBM award also ignored the impact of missed free throws, and weighted player productivity by both team wins and team statistical productivity.

13. Scott, Long, and Sompii, "Salary vs. Marginal Revenue Product," 50–59.

14. Thomas A. Zak, Cliff J. Huang, and John J. Siegfried, "Production Efficiency: The Case of Professional Basketball," *Journal of Business* 52 (1979): 379–393; McCormick and Clement, "Intrafirm Profit Opportunities and Managerial Slack"; Richard A. Hofler and James E. Payne, "Measuring Efficiency in the National Basketball Association," *Economic Letters* 55 (1997): 293–299; David J. Berri, "Who Is Most Valuable? Measuring the Player's Production of Wins in the National Basketball Association," *Managerial and Decision Economics* 20, no. 8 (Fall 1999): 411–427.

15. Zak, Huang, and Siegfried ("Production Efficiency") found that both blocked shots and assists were statistically insignificant in a model designed to explain wins in the NBA. With respect to the latter, these authors noted the relationship between passing and shooting efficiency in explaining the statistical insignificance of assists.

16. John Hollinger, *Pro Basketball Prospectus 2002* (Washington, D.C.: Brassey's Sports, 2002); Dean Oliver, *Basketball on Paper* (Washington, D.C.: Brassey's, 2004).

17. The difference between Hollinger and Oliver is the value of b_1. Hollinger argues that it is 0.44. As will be shown, the results reported here are quite consistent with Hollinger's value. In Oliver's measure of possessions, the weight placed on free-throw attempts is 0.4. Oliver does not derive his measure by regression analysis but rather by examining in detail a collection of NBA games. Oliver found that on average, 40 percent of all free throws end possessions.

18. In evaluating players Hollinger and Oliver do consider defensive rebounds, as well as other factors not included in the definition of offensive and defensive efficiency. Neither author, though, employed regression analysis to ascertain the value of the statistics tracked for individual players.

19. The equation was estimated via ordinary least squares. As with all models estimated in this study, White Heteroskedasticity–Consistent standard errors are reported.

20. Points scored and points surrendered are the sole determinants of wins in a single game. Over the course of a season, though, teams score more points than they need to win, and surrender more points than necessary to lose. These excess points tend to even out over the course of a season. But this tendency is not perfect, hence equation (4) does not explain 6 percent of team wins.

21. Points-per-shot (Rob Neyer, "Who Are the "True" Shooters?" in *STATS Pro Basketball Handbook, 1995–1996* [New York: STATS Publishing, 1995], 322–323) is the number of points a player or team accumulates from its field-goal attempts. Its calculation involves subtracting free throws made from total points, and then dividing by field goals attempted. Employing points per shot, rather than field-goal percentage, allowed for the impact of three-point shooting to be captured more efficiently.

22. One could rewrite equation (4) in light of (5) and (6). Such a step produces a model with the same explanatory power as equation (4), but now wins are defined in terms of eight factors (PPS, FT, FGA, FTA, DPPS, DFT, DFGA, DFTA), not just two (PTS, DPTS).

23. Team rebounds are basically an accounting device. The number of missed shots and rebounds should equal at the end of a game. If a missed shot goes out of bounds, though, a rebound cannot be credited to an individual. Likewise, if a player misses the first of two free throws, no rebound can be recorded for an individual player. Hence, these events are also listed as team rebounds. One should note that only team rebounds that result in a change of possession are included in the estimation of team rebounds that follows. Team rebounds associated with misses on the first of two free throws are not included. In other words, the calculation of team rebounds employed here is not equivalent to what is reported in the box score at the end of a game. One should also note that all team rebounds are treated as defensive rebounds. It is possible to have a team rebound on the offensive end. It is not clear, given the methodology employed, how the number of offensive team rebounds would be measured. It is clear, though, that measuring team offensive rebounds would not change the story being told.

24. Free-throw attempts are awarded if a player is fouled while shooting. The number of free throws is related to the number of points a shot was worth. For example, two shots are awarded when a player is fouled attempting a two-point shot. If the shot is successful, only one free throw is awarded. Finally, after a team has committed four

team fouls per regulation period, each additional foul leads to two free throws by the opponent.

25. The construction of FGADIF forces the value of DFGM, RBD, DTO, RBO, and TO to equal, in absolute terms, one field goal attempt.

26. Given the calculation of team rebounds, this must be the case. One must also note that the number of possessions the team employs and acquires virtually equals the number of possessions the opponent employs and acquires.

27. Following the same process we can estimate the number of possessions employed by the opponent (DPE) and acquired by the opponent (DPA). There is a 0.99 correlation between DPE and PE, as well as between DPA and PA.

28. As noted in *The Wages of Wins*, there are basically two methods one can employ to derive the values reported in Table 1.6. The first method begins by regressing wins on points scored per possession employed and points allowed per possession acquired. Then one takes the derivative of wins with respect to points scored, possessions employed, points allowed, and possessions acquired. From this, one refers to the calculation of possessions employed and possessions acquired to determine the value of each of the statistics comprising these measures. If you do not like this approach, one could just regress wins on points scored and points surrendered, which is equation (4). Then, because teams average about one point per possession—the exact number is 1.02 for the seasons stretching from 1991/92 to 2005/06—you could simply argue that one point is worth one possession. Either approach will basically result in the same values for the various statistics listed in Table 1.6.

29. The calculation of equations (14) and (15) utilized the average number of points and possessions per game. One could also estimate the marginal value of points and possessions for each individual team.

30. It is very important to note that this result can be uncovered with a bit of adjustment to the model of productivity reported in Berri ("Who Is Most Valuable?"). In this paper, which explicitly examined player productivity in the NBA, wins were regressed on PPS, FT, FTA, REBO, REBD, AST/TO, DTO, and DPTS. Assists do not belong in this model since once one knows shooting efficiency, knowing the passing that led to that level of efficiency is irrelevant. In other words, as discussed earlier, assists do not directly lead to more wins by themselves, but indirectly cause teammates to produce more wins. So this is one deficiency in Berri (ibid.). Additionally this model from 1999 ignores team rebounds. If we correct for the problem with respect to assists and team rebounds, and simply regress wins on PPS, FT, FTA, REBO, REBD, REBTM, TO, DTO, and DPTS, one learns the following: the impact of rebounding and turnovers is statistically the same. At least, the Wald Test is unable to reject the hypothesis that all the coefficients for these variables, in a statistical sense, are the same. Consequently Berri's 1999 work, when modified somewhat, confirms the argument we make here. Rebounds and turnovers have the same impact on wins. Furthermore, the estimated impact of rebounds and turnovers is 0.03, which is what we report here. We would also add that when we take the modified Berri 1999 model and derived the value of points and field-goal attempts, we also see that these are worth 0.03 in absolute terms. Again, that is what we report here. So whether one regresses wins on possessions and efficiency, or one regresses wins directly on the individual statistics, the answer is essentially the same.

31. Following Scott, Long, and Sompii ("Salary vs. Marginal Revenue Product") and Berri ("Who Is Most Valuable?"), team factors can be utilized in the evaluation of individual players. Each of these authors allocated variables tracked for the team to individual players according to the number of minutes the player played.

32. If the opponent commits a turnover and one can identify the player on the team who is responsible, the identified player is given credit for a steal. So the opponent's turnovers include all of the steals each individual player on the team garners. In Table 1.7 the value of a steals are listed among statistics tabulated for players while the opponent's turnovers that are not steals (DTO – STL) are listed among team variables. One should also note that a small number of turnovers are not recorded for individual players. One could therefore add team turnovers to the list of team factors in Table 1.6.

33. In *The Wages of Wins* an alternative approach was suggested. If you regress the opponent's free throws made on personal fouls you learn that each personal foul is worth about 1.14 free throws made by the opponent. Consequently, the value of a personal foul can be considered to be approximately the same as the value of a made free throw by the opponent, which we have already said costs a team 0.018 wins. The 1.14 figure was taken from a model estimated with data from 1993/94 through the 2004/05 season. Dummy variables were included for the years and teams examined. The model explains about 88 percent of the variation in the opponent's free throws made.

34. A blocked shot does not lead to a one-to-one reduction in the opponent's two-point field goals. This is likely due to the fact that all shots a player blocks were not going to actually go in. We would also add that we could look at the impact blocked shots have on made three-point baskets by the opponent. Unfortunately, we do not have data on whether a player blocked a two-point or three-point attempt. We assume that most blocked shots are for two-point attempts, hence we simply restricted our examination of blocks to these shots.

35. Here is how the value of an assist was ascertained for *The Wages of Wins*. A player's per-minute unassisted Win Score (i.e., Win Score without assists) was calculated. This was then regressed on the various factors listed in the text. The results indicated the per-minute unassisted Win Score was statistically linked (at least statistically significant at the 10% level or better) to a player's per-minute unassisted Win Score the previous season, the winning percentage of the head coach, the stability of a team's roster, games played, wins produced per minute by a player's teammates, whether the player was a center, power forward, or small forward, whether the player had played more than twelve years, and the number of assists per minute accumulated by teammates. Except for the wins production of teammates and a player being old, each factor had a positive impact on player performance. This model suggests that assists do have a positive and significant impact on teammate performance. For the definition of these factors one is referred to *The Wages of Wins* and David J. Berri and Anthony Krautmann, "Shirking on the Court: Testing for the Dis-Incentive Effects of Guaranteed Pay," *Economic Inquiry* 44, no. 3 (July 2006): 536–546. One should note that the causality probably goes both ways because assists, since one only is credited with an assist if a basket is scored after a pass. Hence, this result may overstate the value of an assist.

36. As noted in *The Wages of Wins*, here are the specific steps followed to determine the value of an assist.

- From our per-minute productivity model we learned that a one-unit increase in team assists increased per-minute productivity by 0.64.
- We adjusted per-minute unassisted productivity for each player in 2004/05 for the quantity of assists accumulated by the player's teammates.
- Next we determined for each team in 2004/05 the quantity of a team's simple unassisted productivity that was determined and not determined by assists. We then allocated the quantity of production that was due to assists across the members of the team according to the number of assists each player accumulated.
- Once this allocation was complete, we had a simple measure of unassisted productivity that was adjusted for assists. We wondered then how much assists matters. So we regressed our adjusted per-minute productivity on both our simple unassisted per-minute measure and the number of assists the player had accumulated per minute. The coefficient on assists from this regression was 0.67. From this we concluded that each assist was worth 0.67 the value of a point, rebound, and so on, or everything of equal value in our simple unassisted productivity model.

Again, as noted in the previous note, this probably overstates the value of an assist. Certainly one could envision additional work in this area to further refine the valuation of this one factor of production.

37. The average value for wins produced by teammates per minute was 0.00212. The average value of per-minute productivity employed was 0.0939. Given an estimated coefficient for per-minute teammate wins of −11.456, the elasticity of per-minute teammate wins was −0.259.

38. The calculation of the player's production of wins simply involved assigning credit for each element of offensive and defensive efficiency to the players. Assists and blocked shots are not part of either efficiency measure. Therefore, to incorporate these factors in our evaluation of the players, we must subtract the value of assists and blocked shots as the team level. This step does not change our evaluation of the team, but does alter our evaluation of individual players. If a player is relatively better at blocking shots and/or assists, his value will increase. If a player is relatively worse, his value will decline.

39. As noted in *The Wages of Wins*, per-minute performance is a very small number. For the average NBA player this value would be 0.006.

40. Position played is noted at websites such as Sportillustrated.cnn.com. The allocation of minutes on each team was used to estimate the precise position each player played. This estimation presumed that teams always employ a point guard, shooting guard, small forward, power forward, and center.

41. One should add team turnovers to this list. An example would be a twenty-four-second clock violation. The value of a team turnover is equal to the value of a turnover.

42. Scott, Long, and Sompii, "Salary vs. Marginal Revenue Product"; Berri, "Who Is Most Valuable?"

43. 82games.com does provide estimates for how well a team performs defensively with different players on the court. These estimates of a player's contribution to defense could also be used to allocate the team defensive factors across a team's players. At The Wages of Wins Journal (dberri.wordpress.com) the data from 82games.com was used to

evaluate the defensive contribution of the Washington Wizards in 2006/07. The results revealed that whether team defense was allocated according to minutes played or according to the 82games.com measure of player defense, the evaluation of players was essentially the same.

44. By accounting for these statistics, not only do we account for the level of defense played on the team but also the pace the team generally plays. Team pace is a factor many have noted to be important in evaluating a player. If a team plays at a faster pace, its players will have more statistics, and hence any statistical measure will inflate the value of these players. Adjusting for the team defensive factors also corrects for this bias.

45. This is not exactly accurate. Teams do play overtime games. So per forty-eight minutes the average team actually wins 0.099 games. The actual value of 0.099 is used in the calculation of Win Produced per forty-eight minutes.

46. The PAWS acronym was originated by Brian Platnick. At The Wages of Wins Journal (dberri.wordpress.com) readers were asked to create a name for Win Score adjusted for position played. Platnick's suggestion of Player Adjusted Win Score, or PAWS, was chosen as the best name.

47. The same critique offered for NBA Efficiency also applies to John Hollinger's (2002) Player Efficiency Rating (PER), except the problem is even worse. Hollinger argues that each two-point field goal made is worth about 1.65 points. A three-point field goal made is worth 2.65 points. A missed field goal, though, costs a team 0.72 points. Given these values, with a bit of math we can show that a player will break even on his two-point field-goal attempts if he hits on 30.4 percent of these shots. On three-pointers the break-even point is 21.4 percent. If a player exceeds these thresholds, and virtually every NBA played does so with respect to two-point shots, the more he shoots the higher his value in PERs. So a player can be an inefficient scorer and simply inflate his value by taking a large number of shots.

48. This calculation is based on a sample of all players from 1993/94 through the 2005/06 campaign who played at least forty-one games and twenty-four minutes per game in a season. In all 2,023 player observations met this criteria.

49. Metrics like NBA Efficiency, Points Created, TENDEX, and John Hollinger's Player Efficiency Rating are not adjusted for position played. This is because a player's scoring dominates each player's evaluation by these models. Given that scoring rates are similar across all positions, the evaluation of players by these metrics tends not to vary tremendously by players at different positions. When utilizing a metric that is not dominated by scoring, it is clear that position played does impact the evaluation of performance and hence must be noted in measuring productivity.

50. This number was taken from an article posted at ESPN.com: "Pacers Get Harrington from Hawks for First-Round Pick," http://sports.espn.go.com/nba/news/story?id=2557921.

51. The Pacers expected to contend with the addition of Harrington, but after forty games in 2006/07 the team had only won twenty games. Consequently Harrington, a player who was supposed to lead the team into contention, was traded to the Golden State Warriors.

52. As noted in *The Wages of Wins*, NBA Efficiency—relative to Wins Produced—is a better predictor of both salaries in the NBA and the coaches voting for the All-Rookie team. In other words, a metric that overvalues scoring is also found to be fairly consistent with player evaluation in the NBA.

53. Berri and Krautmann, "Shirking on the Court," 536–546; David J. Berri and Martin B. Schmidt, "On the Road with the National Basketball Association's Superstar Externality," *Journal of Sports Economics* 7, no. 4 (November 2006): 347–358; David J. Berri and Erick Eschker, "Performance When It Counts? The Myth of the Prime-Time Performer in the NBA," *Journal of Economics Issues* 39, no. 3 (September 2005): 798–807; David J. Berri, Stacey L. Brook, Aju Fenn, Bernd Frick, and Roberto Vicente-Mayoral, "The Short Supply of Tall People: Explaining Competitive Imbalance in the National Basketball Association," *Journal of Economics Issues* 39, no. 4 (December 2005): 1029–1041.

54. David J. Berri, Michael Leeds, and Michael Mondello, "Is It the Teacher or the Students? Understanding the Role of the Coach in the National Basketball Association," presented by Berri and Mondello at the Western Economic Association, San Francisco, July, 2005; David J. Berri, Stacey L. Brook, and Aju Fenn, "From College to the Pros: Predicting the NBA Amateur Player Draft," presented at the Southern Economic Association, Washington D.C., November, 2005; Berri et al., "Short Supply of Tall People"; David J. Berri and Aju Fenn, "Is the Sports Media Color-blind?" presented at the Southern Economic Association, New Orleans, November 2004; Joseph Price and Justin Wolfers, "Racial Discrimination among NBA Referees," mimeo, University of Pennsylvania, Philadelphia.

Two

Statistical Performance Analysis in Sport

John Charles Bradbury

When it comes to valuing performance in sports, academics have relied heavily on the conventional wisdom, using the statistics traditionally valued by fans.[1] This is understandable because those who follow sports have developed a sense of what succeeds and what fails in games. But what happens if the traditional benchmarks used for evaluating player performance are not the best options to use for valuing athletic accomplishments? Some common statistics used to evaluate players include the batting average in baseball, points in basketball, and the quarterback rating in football. At the end of the season it is common to hear sportswriters to proclaim the leader in these categories as the best hitter, scorer, or quarterback. The problem is that, though all of these metrics are positively correlated with winning in their respective sports, there are other statistics that are better suited for evaluating player performance. Failure to recognize superior metrics is harmful, not just to sports managers and fantasy team owners, but to social scientists who use sports data as a laboratory for testing theories of human behavior. The goal of this chapter is to demonstrate why this is the case.

Social scientists are increasingly using sports events to test hypotheses that are difficult to examine in the real world. Because sports have well-defined costs and benefits, the games provide an opportunity to observe how players respond to incentives in a controlled setting. For example, criminal activity is a difficult area to study, because criminals attempt to conceal their illegal actions. A social scientist who studies crime is limited to what is visible, which may not contain some important factors because a portion of the illegal activity studied remains unobserved. The correlative to crime in sports is breaking rules. Unlike real world crime, rule violations in sports are visible to an arena of spectators, and the punishments are well known to all participants. A researcher wishing to study models of crime now has a natural laboratory.

One important question that interests researchers studying criminal behavior is how the size of law enforcement affects crime. Looking at the relationship between police force size and criminal activity paints a confusing picture. Where criminal activity is high, police activity is typically high; and where few crimes are committed, the police presence is usually low. The causal relationship between criminal activity and law enforcement is difficult to determine. Do police cause crime, do police flock to areas with high crime to lessen it below what it would otherwise be, or does police presence have no impact at all? In sports, rule changes that impact the law enforcement officers on the field (referees) have provided insight into how players limit their criminal activity according to the level of enforcement. McCormick and Tollison used the introduction of a third referee to college basketball games to gauge the impact of an extra "policeman" on committing fouls during the course of a game.[2] The authors conclude that the additional referee lowered fouling by a substantial margin—a 50 percent increase in the policing force was associated with a 34 percent reduction in fouls. Furthermore, they found that the additional referee improved the general quality of the game as scoring increased. A similar study, Heckelman and Yates, analyzes the same enforcement change in hockey.[3] The addition of a referee in the NHL led to more penalties being called; however, the authors conclude that increased enforcement did not deter players from committing fouls.

These examples demonstrate the results of sports studies are useful beyond understanding the sport under examination.[4] Although the studies are about sports, the results have implications for researchers in other fields. Researchers have used sports as a laboratory to study issues such as racial discrimination, market inefficiency, contract incentives, and income inequality. Because social scientists continue to utilize the expansive data sets and controlled settings of sports games, they must be sure to understand what the statistics in the games reveal about performance. For example, if a researcher intends to use baseball data to explore fan racial discrimination, the researcher must know how to identify the productivity of the players studied in order to quantify the impact of race. Interpreting metrics incorrectly can lead to false rejections of correct hypothesis and acceptances of incorrect hypotheses.

This chapter examines the consequences of improper evaluation of athletic performance in the economic study of sports and the properties of useful measures of performance in sports. It concludes with a discussion of the importance of understanding the meaning of statistics in sports.

WHY METRICS OF PERFORMANCE ARE IMPORTANT

Empirical Methods

A typical study that uses sports games to test hypotheses is normally based on a linear regression model in which variation in the dependent variable Y is the factor to be explained about player i, such as his salary. Variation in the dependent variable is explained by X, a single independent variable, or a vector of several variables, that are factors of prime interest to the researcher, such as the race of a player. The model typically contains a vector of control variables, C, that are important to determining the dependent variable independent of factors in X. The model is estimated using multiple regression analysis, which holds constant the many relevant factors to measure marginal impacts (i.e., parameters in the model) of individual factors included in the regression model. One parameter measures the impact of X on Y, controlling for the effects of relevant factors in vector C. Another vector of parameters capture individual impacts of the control variable factors on Y. These models typically contain a constant term, and all contain an unobservable equation error term, or random error term. If, after controlling for the other factors, estimates of the parameter on the control variable X are statistically significant, then we can feel comfortable attributing changes in player performance, captured by Y, to changes in X with some confidence.

There is nothing incorrect about the general functional form of such multiple regression models as long as they are properly specified. The problem with relying on the conventional wisdom to choose control variables to proxy ability is that we have little reason to suspect these metrics are correct, other than the fact that sports fans continue to use them. If the conventional wisdom is wrong, and the researcher is relying on the conventional wisdom to properly control for an important influence on the dependent variable, then the model will be misspecified. Due to the exclusion of relevant omitted factors that are correlated with variable(s) of interest, X, the estimate of the parameter on X will be biased—a phenomenon called omitted variable bias. On the margin, this bias may be large enough to cause the researchers to err in evaluation of a hypothesis, as well as cause misestimation of regression coefficients.

The continued use of a method is evidence of its efficiency; however, inefficiencies in the traditional methods have been a recent subject of debate in sports. In his recent bestselling book, *Moneyball*, Michael Lewis reveals the Oakland A's methods of using of new metrics of performance to gain an edge on its rivals in Major League Baseball.[5] While the "insights" that Lewis describes in his narrative may be a bit overstated, it certainly merits further investigation of inefficiency.

Hakes and Sauer examined one of the supposed inefficiencies in the baseball market highlighted in *Moneyball*: the underpricing of on-base percentage relative to slugging percentage.[6] The authors find that Lewis's claim is correct: teams were undervaluing the on-base percentage. How did twenty-nine other general managers miss the importance of the on-base percentage in generating runs so that one team could purchase this skill so cheaply? If the market for baseball talent is efficient, then players ought to be properly valued by the baseball labor market. It turns out that this was a short-term mistake, as Hakes and Sauer noted that the mispricing existed only for a short time and disappeared almost as soon as the book was published.

The lesson of *Moneyball* for sports researchers is that the statistics that fans often use to evaluate players are not the best measures of performance. While television broadcasts and scoreboards list the batting average of every player before he steps to the plate in order to inform the viewer about the quality of the hitter, better metrics for evaluating players exist.

Is it typical for popular sports statistics to be inferior metrics of player quality? The answer is difficult to know because researchers have not evaluated the information contained in sports statistics in more than a few areas. Some statistical-savvy sports fans have been evaluating old metrics and developing new ones for decades. However, the vast majority of these studies have not undergone the formal peer-review process that academics expect. While many of these studies may yield correct findings, they ought to be examined more rigorously before anyone uses their results to choose control variables in academic studies.

From the few academic studies done, it is clear that researchers studying sports ought to place greater emphasis on the usefulness of different metrics before pursuing more ambitious social science experiments in sports games. Later in this chapter, I discuss a few economic studies of sports productivity metrics that find many common statistics to be flawed. Also, it is likely that yet-undiscovered metrics outperform the current popular metrics in many sports. If researchers wish to employ sports as a social science laboratory, it is important to properly evaluate old metrics and search for new ones.

An Example of Omitted Variable Bias

Economists frequently use sports to examine racial discrimination, because the games allow researchers to control for ability—the main determinant of worker compensation—which is difficult to isolate in most labor markets. In a world without racial prejudice, workers ought to be compensated according to their ability, not race. In sports, players who are equally productive ought to be paid the same, regardless of their race. If players of a racial group receive compensation different from their contributions to team revenue—which economists refer to as the marginal revenue product of labor—then this is evidence of discrimination. The findings of the studies on player salaries are mixed, with older studies finding more evidence of discrimination against minorities than newer studies.[7]

One strand of empirical studies on racial discrimination in sports focuses on consumer discrimination against players using the baseball-card market. The baseball-card market contains a fixed stock of cards that are traded on a secondary market of collectors. The market prices generated by these transactions reveal fans' willingness to pay for different player cards, where traders value players according to their on-field productivity. Typically, fans are willing to pay more (less) for superior (inferior) players' cards. If, after accounting for other relevant factors, fans value players differently by race, this is evidence of racial discrimination by consumers. The empirical findings of these studies are mixed.

Nardinelli and Simon employ the 1989 prices of 1970 Topps baseball cards and find evidence of racial discrimination against nonwhite players, with discrimination against Hispanic players being more pronounced than for blacks. Andersen and La Croix use the 1985 prices of Topps baseball cards from several yearly series. The results show consumer discrimination against black players, but no discrimination against Hispanic players. McGarrity, Palmer, and Poitras, using 1994 prices of 1974 Topps baseball cards, finds little evidence of discrimination against black or Hispanic players.[8] The authors of the latter study argue that although their findings contradict the former studies, their results are superior because the study relies on a set of cards more appropriate for analysis and they employ a better econometric technique.[9] Fort and Gill use an alternative measure of race—it is continuous and based on a survey of market participants—and find evidence of racism against black and Hispanic players.[10]

All of the studies employ a functional form similar to the statistical model described above; where the focus of the study is the impact of the race variables on the dependent variable (card price), while controlling for the ability of the player represented on the card using a vector of performance statistics. Because of the censored nature of card prices—all cards circulate at a minimum positive price, sometimes called the common player price—the authors use the tobit multiple-regression method, or similar estimation methods, to estimate the impacts that account for the biases in the censored data.

These studies are excellent examples of how useful sports data can be to study an important social issue. The authors have examined the subject more thoroughly that I can discuss in this chapter. It is not my intent to accept or reject the findings of these previous studies; instead, I wish to show how the choice of the performance metric can influence the regression results, using a similar example.

Using 2006 price data for 1980 Topps cards for 334 hitters, I estimate a model explaining the variation in the logarithm of the difference between a baseball-card price and the common player-card price of all players. Card prices are from the 2006 Beckett's Baseball Card Online Price Guide.[11]

To investigate the role of performance variables in producing omitted variable bias, I estimate several different models with different statistics as explanatory variables. The first model uses a popular hitting metric: the career batting average (AVG) of the player. Though it is a common statistic, there are many other superior measures of hitter quality. The other specifications include metrics that convey more information about the hitter. These metrics are on-base percentage (OBP) and slugging percentage (SLG), on-base percentage plus slugging percentage (OPS), and linear weights (LWTS).

Table 2.1 lists the results of the different regression specifications. In all models, the coefficient for black players is never statistically significant. The estimate of the impact for being Hispanic, though, is sensitive to the chosen specification.[12] Model 1 lists the results using the batting average as the ability control variable. The results indicate that, after controlling for the factors included in the model, cards of Hispanic players sell for less than white players at a statistically significant level. However, in models 2 to 4, the Hispanic coefficient is not statistically significant. Not only does this demonstrate the sensitivity of regression coefficients to performance metrics, but also that the traditional metric with inferior information yields misleading results. A researcher wishing to study consumer racial demonstration using baseball cards, but who only has a minor interest in baseball, might unintentionally use an inferior metric and feel justified in finding racial prejudice against Hispanics by baseball fans.

It is important to note that previous studies of racial discrimination in the baseball-card market do not rely on the batting average to proxy talent. I want to emphasize that the purpose of this exercise to is to demonstrate the sensitivity of regression coefficients to different performance specifications, not to critique past studies. I use the batting average in this example because it is a popular measure of player skill that does not include important information about ability. The results demonstrate that researchers using the sports laboratory need to be careful in choosing performance proxies.

In the following section, I highlight some of the useful metrics that are available for evaluating players in baseball, basketball, and football. However, sports researchers should emphasize further evaluation of these metrics, and the development of new statistics to proxy player quality, in order to

TABLE 2.1
Tobit Estimates of Impact of Race on Baseball Card Price

Variable	AVG 1	OBP, SLG 2	OPS 3	LWTS 4
Race				
Black	0.01871	0.01659	0.00347	0.00873
	[0.17]	[0.14]	[0.03]	[0.08]
Hispanic	0.23803	0.15587	0.16677	0.15411
	[1.98][b]	[1.32]	[1.41]	[1.35]
Performance Control Variables				
AVG	6.28655			
	[2.33][b]			
OBP		3.37389		
		[1.89][a]		
SLG		0.70312		
		[0.49]		
OPS			1.57456	
			[1.87][a]	
LWTS				0.00061
				[1.57]
Other Control Variables				
Plate Appearances	0.00019	0.00019	0.00018	0.00018
	[5.29][c]	[4.62][c]	[4.58][c]	[3.94][c]
Rookie Card	0.0047	0.00238	0.003	0.00256
	[0.50]	[0.25]	[0.32]	[0.27]
First Base	0.42403	0.45141	0.47468	0.42616
	[1.89][a]	[2.21][b]	[2.19][b]	[2.27][b]
Second Base	0.41416	0.43471	0.41903	0.40764
	[1.74][a]	[1.76][a]	[1.78][a]	[1.81][a]
Third Base	0.30957	0.34954	0.3739	0.32732
	[1.50]	[1.90][a]	[1.92][a]	[1.89][a]
Catcher	0.08816	0.14821	0.17102	0.14571
	[0.51]	[0.89]	[0.98]	[1.00]
Designated Hitter	0.35783	0.45925	0.46302	0.43333
	[1.36]	[1.77][a]	[1.76][a]	[1.86][a]
Outfield	0.31482	0.35648	0.3757	0.3273
	[1.58]	[1.85][a]	[1.86][a]	[1.95][a]
Constant	6.71819	2.45494	3.9583	4.17617
	[0.37]	[0.13]	[0.21]	[0.22]
Pseudo R^2 [d]	0.33	0.33	0.33	0.36
χ^2	62.02	75.13	66.15	62.18
Observations	334	334	334	334

[a]Significant at 10 percent.
[b]Significant at 5 percent.
[c]Significant at 1 percent.
[d]The squared correlation of the regression-predicted price and actual price.
Notes: Robust z-statistics in brackets.

minimize the problems of omitted variable bias when researchers use sports data to test economic hypotheses.

GOOD PERFORMANCE METRICS

What makes a performance metric good? Two factors are important: the accuracy of measuring value and degree to which the metric reflects skill. The first quality is important for knowing what a player contributes to team success on the field. The many things players do on the field have different impacts on how the team performs. A batter who hits forty doubles in baseball is going to produce more value than the player who hits forty singles. However, just because a player performs in a way that contributes some value does not mean it is the result of player skill. Most athletic outcomes are a product of skill and luck, and disentangling the two can be difficult, especially in team sports. What if the difference between a hit being a single and a double is solely a product of random chance? Though the doubles hits are more valuable than singles, we would not want to say the player with forty doubles is more valuable than the player with forty singles, because he did not perform any better than the other player; luck intervened. Also, in team games, players depend quite a bit on their teammates. If a quarterback leads the league in passing yards, how much of his success is due to individual skill and the skill of his receivers? Disentangling teammate spillovers is also an important consideration.

One method researchers can use for separating skill from luck is to look at repeat performances of players. If performance is a product of skill, then the athlete in question ought to be able to replicate that skill. If other factors, such as random chance or teammate spillovers, are responsible for the performance, then we ought not observe players performing consistently in these areas over time. A common way to gauge the degree of skill contained in a performance metric is to observe its correlation year to year. If metrics for individual players do not vary much from year to year, then it is likely that players have a skill in that area. If there is no correlation, then it is likely that other factors are heavily influencing the metric. In the latter case, even if a particular metric appears to have a powerful influence on the overall performance of the team, its utility as a measure of quality is limited.[13]

In the following subsections, I evaluate several popular metrics used to evaluate athletes in baseball, basketball, and football. I focus on baseball more than other sports for several reasons. First, because players take turns batting, the impact of teammate spillovers is small compared to other team sports.[14] Therefore, the metrics are easier to evaluate in baseball than in other team sports. Second, the analysis of baseball statistics is further advanced than in other fields, thanks to an active community of fan-scholars who have been studying the game for several years. This field is commonly known as sabermetrics.[15] The most prominent member of the sabermetrics community is Bill James, who has written several books on baseball and has worked in the front office of the Boston Red Sox for several seasons. Finally, my contributions to the sports economics community have been in baseball; therefore, it is the field about which I am most knowledgeable.

Baseball

Baseball has three main components: hitting, pitching, and fielding. Because fielding is so difficult to measure, I will exclude it from the analysis. However, the growing public availability of fielding data should soon yield many new fielding metrics for scholars to study.[16]

Hitting

The object of hitting is to score runs for the team. Because players take turns hitting and depend on each other to contribute to scoring, I must use team-level data to estimate the association between batting metrics and scoring. Using a sample of data from 2000–2005, I estimate the impact of five metrics on runs scored by league: AVG, OBP, SLG, OPS, and LWTS. I also test the impact of both OBP and SLG on runs in a single equation.

AVG is the number of hits divided by total at-bats. OBP is the sum of hits, walks, and hit-by-pitch divided by plate appearances. SLG is a batting average that weights each hit in the numerator by the total number of bases the hitter advanced (i.e., singles are counted once, doubles are counted twice, and so on). OPS is the sum of OBP and SLG, and was developed by Thorn and Palmer. While OPS is intuitively unappealing, it happens to correlate well with LWTS, but is much simpler to calculate. LWTS is the estimated number of runs generated above or below the league average, based on the linear weights system of Thorn and Palmer.[17] The system weights several offensive events according to their run-generating tendencies.

Table 2.2 lists the R^2 of each of the models on run scoring by league. The R^2 indicates how much of the variance of runs scored is explained by the variance of the metric(s) in a linear regression. AVG, the statistic for which the leagues' batting titles are awarded, explains less of the variance (63% and 67%) than any of the other metrics. While OBP and SLG explain more than AVG on their own, combined they are even more powerful. Included separately in the same regression model, the statistics explain 92 percent of the difference in runs scored across teams. When added together as OPS, the model is nearly as informative, explaining 90 percent.

TABLE 2.2
Explained Variance (R^2) of Offensive Metrics on Runs Per Game, 2000–2005

Metric	NL	AL
AVG	0.67	0.63
OBP	0.82	0.84
SLG	0.82	0.79
OBP, SLG	0.92	0.92
OPS	0.90	0.90
LWTS	0.91	0.93

Depending on the time period and league, these values may change slightly; however, combined OBP-SLG and LWTS are superior measures of run production, compared to the other options.

In terms of reflecting skill, all of the metrics correlate well from year to year across players, though AVG varies more than the other metrics. Table 2.3 lists the year-to-year correlation coefficients and R^2 for hitters with a minimum of 400 plate appearances in consecutive seasons from 1980–2005. Figure 2.1 shows the relationships graphically, where a tighter relationship around the regression line indicates more year-to-year stability of the metric. Given that the other performance variables gauge run-scoring more accurately and proxy a skill set better than AVG, they are better choices as performance control variables for explaining observed variation in card prices.

Pitching

Pitching statistics contain less information about pitcher run prevention than hitting statistics do for run production. While batters face pitchers on their own, pitchers jointly prevent runs with their fielders. Baseball fans traditionally evaluate pitchers according to how many "earned runs" they allow

TABLE 2.3
Year-to-Year Correlations of Offensive Metrics in Baseball, 1980–2005

Metric	R	R^2
AVG	0.47	0.22
OBP	0.64	0.41
SLG	0.67	0.45
OPS	0.65	0.43
LWTS	0.70	0.49

FIGURE 2.1
Year-to-Year Correlations of Offensive Metrics in Baseball, 1980–2005

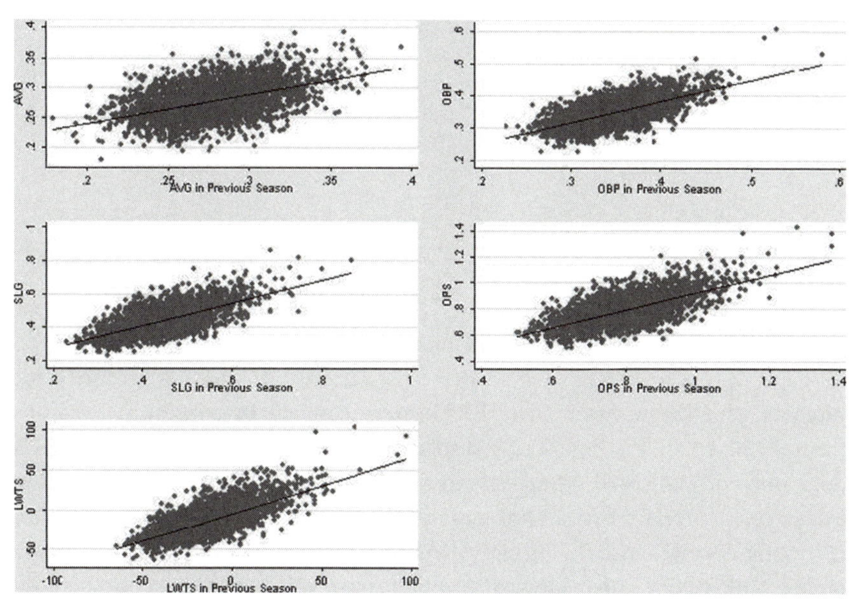

(ERA)—total earned runs divided by innings pitched and multiplied by 9. As Table 2.4 shows, ERA explains 97 percent of the difference in runs allowed across teams from 2000 to 2005. Other skills that pitchers possess, such as striking out batters (K9), preventing walks (BB9), and limiting home runs (HR9), have much less impact on run prevention.[18] Including strikeouts, walks, and home runs in a single regression explains a bit more than each factor individually. Fielding Independent Pitching (FIP)—a metric that combines walks, strikeouts, and homers into a single metric, like OPS is for OBP and SLG—explains runs allowed about the same as the regression

TABLE 2.4
Explained Variance (R^2) of Pitching Metrics on Runs Allowed per Game, 2000–2005

Variable(s)	NL	AL
ERA	0.97	0.97
K	0.15	0.21
BB	0.25	0.48
HR	0.55	0.45
K, BB, HR	0.77	0.65
FIP	0.75	0.63

TABLE 2.5
Year-to-Year Correlations of Pitching Metrics in Baseball, 1980–2005

Variable	R	R^2
BABIP	0.24	0.06
ERA	0.37	0.14
K9	0.79	0.62
BB9	0.64	0.42
HR9	0.47	0.19

including its components separately.[19] However, this is not sufficient to say that ERA is superior to these other metrics.

Table 2.5 reports the year-to-year correlations of pitching statistics for pitchers who threw more than 100 innings pitched in consecutive seasons from 1980 to 2005. Figure 2.2 displays the relationship graphically. ERA does not correlate well from year to year. All of the components of ERA, except one, correlate better from year to year than ERA. The lone exception is batting average on balls in play (BABIP). With a few minor exceptions a pitcher influences runs allowed through four channels: strikeouts, walks, home runs, and balls in play. The first three events do not require the

FIGURE 2.2
Year-to-Year Correlations of Pitching Metrics in Baseball, 1980–2005

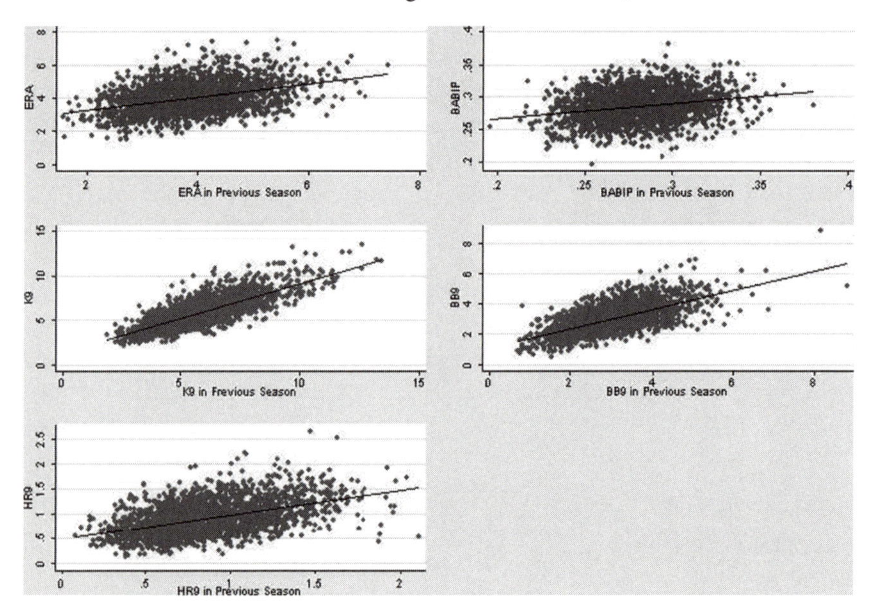

TABLE 2.6
Variance of ERA Explained by its Components, 1980–2005

Variable	Explained Variance of ERA (R^2)
BABIP	0.31
K9	0.04
BB9	0.10
HR9	0.41

pitcher to rely on his fielders to help put the batter out. It is this last area, where pitchers do not seem to have much skill. BABIP is the number of non–home run hits that a pitcher gives up, divided by the number chances a pitcher gives his fielders to make outs. Since 86 percent of all plate appearances result in a ball being put in play, the earned runs allowed by a pitcher are heavily influenced by his BABIP—an area in which pitchers have little ability. Table 2.6 shows that BABIP explains much more of the variance of a pitcher's ERA than strikeouts or walks, though not home runs. This explains why ERA does not correlate well from season to season: pitchers appear to have little skill at preventing hits at balls in play, yet their performance in this area is a major determinant of ERA. ERA is a metric that is contaminated with luck; therefore, its usefulness as a measure of pitchers' ability to prevent runs is muted.

The non-BABIP components of ERA, also known as Defense Independent Pitching Statistics (DIPS), provide more reliable information about the skill of a pitcher than ERA. This is an interesting finding that was first discovered by McCracken.[20] Bradbury verifies McCracken's results and finds that the labor market for pitchers reveals that major-league front offices must have also been aware of this, as they paid pitchers according to their DIPS performance rather than the traditional statistics such as ERA and winning percentage.[21]

Using baseball as an example, it is apparent that just because a traditional sports metric has survived the test of time among fans, it does not mean that it is an adequate ability control variable for econometric studies of sports. The above analysis demonstrates that two of the most popular metrics for evaluating players are not optimal choices for measuring player ability.

Basketball and Football

Team games like basketball and football, where players interact during the play of the game, are much more difficult to analyze than a sequential game like baseball. While this makes some studies using data from these sports difficult, the teammate spillovers are interesting in and of themselves. Many nonsports activities more accurately mirror the interaction in basketball and football than baseball, which is why researchers have used these sports in their studies. I discuss one performance metric from each sport; both of which come from a recent book on sports economics.

In basketball, players are generally valued according to their scoring abilities. This is not surprising given the object of the game is to score more points than the other team. However, it would be wrong to focus solely on a metric because of its direct impact on scoring. Other skills that players contribute to maximizing wins are steals, blocks, assists, and shooting attempts. Berri, Schmidt, and Brook developed a method for weighting these many characteristics, according to their contributions to winning, to generate a single metric, Win Score.[22] While the authors are not the first persons to investigate methods for evaluating performance in basketball, their model predicts team performances well.[23] They also find that Win Score is positively correlated from season to season, indicating that the metric captures player skill. Furthermore, they demonstrate that NBA teams overvalue scoring in the labor market.

Berri, Schmidt, and Brook also developed a metric for evaluating quarterbacks in football, QB Score (QB Score = Yards − (3 × Plays) − (50 × Turnovers)). The statistic has the advantage of being simple to calculate and it predicts a quarterback's impact on winning more than the popular NFL QB Rating. Unfortunately, like ERA for pitchers, though it captures a player's contribution to a team, it does not correlate well from year to year. Therefore, its use to proxy ability is limited. However, because so few academic studies on football exist, there are few other options for evaluating players.

CONCLUSION

This chapter highlights the importance of understanding the information contained in sports statistics. Because researchers continue to use sports games as a social science laboratory, further investigation of the sports themselves is necessary. An empirical study of consumer racial discrimination in the baseball-card market demonstrates the sensitivity of results to the choice of productivity statistics used as control variables. Common statistical methods are subject to bias when the researcher relies on inferior metrics; therefore, researchers ought to be cautious when choosing statistical measures of player ability.

Furthermore, our understanding of how to measure performance in sports is young. Thus, there is a need for further development of more accurate methods of player productivity if social scientists wish to use sports as an empirical testing ground. Even in baseball, where measures of productivity are far ahead of most other sports, there is room for further understanding. The new metrics in basketball and football require scrutiny from scholars, and there is much room for the development of new statistics in these and other sports.

NOTES

1. In Chapter 1 of this volume, David J. Berri notes that eleven sports economics studies from 1982–2002 employ the slugging percentage to proxy hitting ability in baseball, despite the fact that it is not the best available metric.

2. R. E. McCormick and R. D. Tollison, "Crime on the Court," *Journal of Political Economy* 92, no. 2 (1984): 223–235.

3. J. C. Heckelman and A. J. Yates, "And a Hockey Game Broke Out: Crime and Punishment in the NHL," *Economic Inquiry* 41, no. 4 (2003): 705–712.

4. See B. L. Goff and R. D. Tollison, *Sportometrics* (College Station: Texas A&M University Press, 1990), for further examples of empirical tests of economic hypotheses using sports.

5. M. L. Lewis, *Moneyball: The Art of Winning an Unfair Game* (New York: W. W. Norton, 2003).

6. J. K. Hakes and R. D. Sauer, "An Economic Evaluation of the *Moneyball* Hypothesis," *Journal of Economic Perspectives* 20, no. 3 (2006): 173–185.

7. D. J. Berri, "National Basketball Association," in *Handbook of Sports Economics Research*, ed. J. Fizel (Armonk, N.Y.: M. E. Sharpe, 2006), 21–48, surveys empirical studies of discrimination in basketball. J. C. Leadly and Z. X. Zygmont, "National Hockey League," in the same volume (49–98), surveys empirical studies of discrimination in hockey.

8. C. Nardinelli and C. Simon, "Customer Racial Discrimination in the Market for Memorabilia: The Case of Baseball," *Quarterly Journal of Economics* 105, no. 3 (1990): 575–595; T. Andersen and S. J. La Croix, "Customer Racial Discrimination in Major League Baseball," *Economic Inquiry* 29, no. 4 (1991): 665–677; J. McGarrity, H. D. Palmer, and M. Poitras, "Consumer Racial Discrimination: A Reassessment of the Market for Baseball Cards," *Journal of Labor Research* 20, no. 2 (1999): 247–258.

9. The 1974 set issues an equal number of cards for each player, and the 1994 prices of these cards are far enough removed from playing careers so that speculative demand about future performance has no effect on price.

10. R. Fort and A. Gill, "Race and Ethnicity Assessments in Baseball Card Markets," *Journal of Sports Economics* 1, no. 1 (2000): 21–38.

11. *Beckett's Baseball Card Online Price Guide*, 260 (2006), http://www.beckett.com/priceguides (accessed March 15, 2008).

12. The race of a player is determined by visual inspection of baseball cards by the author in F. Slocum, *Topps Baseball Cards: The Complete Picture Collection, a 35-Year History, 1951–1985* (New York: Warner Books, 1985). The Hispanic designation was assigned to all players born in Latin American countries as listed in *The Lahman Baseball Database* 5.3 (2005), http://www.baseball1.com (accessed March 15, 2008).

13. See J. Albert and J. Bennett, *Curve Ball* (New York: Copernicus Books, 2001), for a discussion of this method.

14. J. C. Bradbury and D. J. Drinen, "Pigou at the Plate: Externalities in Major League Baseball," *Journal of Sports Economics* (forthcoming), find that batting spillovers do exist, but their magnitude is trivial.

15. See A. Schwarz, *The Numbers Game: Baseball's Lifelong Fascination with Statistics* (New York: Thomas Dunne Books, 2004), for a history of baseball statistics and sabermetrics.

16. J. Dewan, *The Fielding Bible* (Skokie, Ill.: ACTA Sports, 2006), reports a new metric that grades fielders using play-by-play video analysis with objective criteria.

17. J. Thorn and P. Palmer, *The Hidden Game of Baseball: A Revolutionary Approach to Baseball and Its Statistics* (New York: Doubleday, 1984). LWTS = (0.46 × singles) + (0.8 × doubles) + (1.02 × triples) + (1.4 × home runs) + [0.33 × (walks + hit-by-pitch)] + (0.3 × stolen bases) − (0.6 × caught stealing) − [0.25 × (at-bats − hits)]

18. Strikeouts, walks, and home runs are normalized per nine innings pitched, just as ERA is.

19. FIP = (13 × home runs) + (3 × walks) − (2 × strikeouts)/ innings pitched + 3.2. This metric was developed in T. Tango, "Defensive Responsibility Spectrum (DRS): Breaking Up the Fielders from the Pitchers" (2006), http://www.tangotiger.net/drspectrum.html (accessed October 1, 2006).

20. V. McCracken, "Pitching and Defense: How Much Control Do Hurlers Have?" *Baseball Prospectus*, January 23, 2001, http://www.baseballprospectus.com/article.php?articleid=878 (accessed March 15, 2008).

21. J. C. Bradbury, "Does the Baseball Labor Market Properly Value Pitchers?" *Journal of Sports Economics* 8, no. 6 (2007): 616–632.

22. D. J. Berri, M. D. Schmidt, and S. L. Brook, *The Wages of Wins: Taking Measure of Many Myths in Modern Sport* (Stanford, Calif.: Stanford University Press, 2006). Win Score = points + rebounds + steals + (0.5 × blocked shots) + (0.5 × assists) − field goal attempts − (0.5 × free throw attempts) − turnovers − (0.5 × personal fouls).

23. D. Oliver, *Basketball on Paper* (Dulles, Va.: Potomac Books, 2003), also presents methods for valuing performance in basketball.

Three

Sports Facilities and Urban Redevelopment: Private and Public Benefits and a Prescription for a Healthier Future

Mark S. Rosentraub

In July 2006 local governments in Sacramento, California, and Dade County, Florida, found themselves confronting the all too familiar policy conundrum of establishing a public/private partnership to build a sports facility. Leaders in both communities had labored for years to resolve the problem of building a new sports facility to retain a team, and in neither area was there any certainty if the plans would be accepted by team owners, voters, and elected officials. In both communities there was opposition to public investments in a sports facility reflecting a belief that such expenditures would be inappropriate. Team owners in each city were willing to pledge some money for a new facility but both claimed a public investment was appropriate, given the public or intangible benefits produced by the teams. The team owners also argued that they needed a subsidy to offer players competitive salaries without sustaining operating losses. The usual step of threatening to move if a subsidized facility was not built followed, and the Marlins' leadership visited cities in other states to gauge their interest in paying for a new ballpark in exchange for the team's relocation.

The new era of public-private partnerships for the building of sports facilities began almost fifteen years ago when work was initiated for Oriole Park at Camden Yards, the current home of the Baltimore Orioles. This new era has been defined by a new business model for sports facilities and the perspective that substantial public investments in the facilities through public-private partnerships was appropriate for economic and urban development. The new business model involved the creation of facilities that included numerous revenue streams that could be captured by team owners.

The idea that sports facilities would contribute to economic and urban development involved assumptions regarding the economic value of concentrating millions of fans in facilities located in or near downtown areas.

Baltimore's leadership or initiation of this era was driven by two factors. First, Baltimore lost the National Football League's (NFL) Colts to Indianapolis when the community failed to build a new stadium and elected leaders did not want to lose another team. Second, Baltimore wanted to continue to advance the development of their Inner Harbor entertainment district and downtown areas and the sports facilities appeared to be natural complements. Baltimore was attracted to the idea that sports facilities would enhance redevelopment activities, having witnessed the substantial improvements in downtown Indianapolis after it implemented a redevelopment strategy anchored by sports facilities and events.

The Orioles wanted a new ballpark with expanded retail facilities and restaurants that would generate additional income for the team. Since the public sector was paying a substantial part of the construction cost, the team's profits would be enhanced. The new ballpark also had exceptional sight lines and tiers of luxury seating, creating even more revenue from fans willing to pay higher ticket prices for these amenities. The idea that the ballpark would contribute to downtown redevelopment and enhance Baltimore's image inadvertently created a valuable tool for other team owners to use in presenting the case for their own subsidies. If a city gained new levels of development, it was argued, then the public sector should share in some or all of the expenses of building and maintaining a sports facility. While Oriole Park at Camden Yards launched an era of public investments in sports facilities, it also generated controversy about the value and appropriateness of public subsidies for professional sports teams. The question raised by many taxpayers was the same: is spending public money for a sports facility in the public's interest?

Through 2005, billions of public dollars have been spent to build new sports facilities. Even where teams paid for the complete cost of the facility and were responsible for on-going maintenance, the public sector was required to make the needed investments to address environmental and transportation infrastructure issues (Charlotte, Columbus, Los Angeles, New York City, St. Louis, and Washington, D.C.). In other areas the public sector investment ranged from paying for some portion of the cost of a facility (Arlington, Indianapolis, Philadelphia, Phoenix, and San Diego), to paying for the entire cost of the facility and then providing extremely favorable lease arrangements to teams (Baltimore, Nashville, St. Louis, and Tampa).

With this range of expenditures in mind, it is now more appropriate than ever to address the central question, "Are public investments in sports facilities just subsidies or are they investments creating community-wide benefits?" Advocates for public subsidies point to the value of sports facilities in "jump-starting" redevelopment efforts, creating new and vibrant images for cities, and improving the tax base of host communities. After fifteen years of experience in the building of sports facilities in downtown areas across North America, it is desirable to make a retrospective assessment of the impacts of sports facilities on redevelopment and identify the strategies that have produced the most success.

To accomplish these goals this chapter is organized as follows. Following the introduction is a theoretical framework to identify the private and public benefits from sports facilities. Then, based on the experiences of Major League Baseball (MLB) in four cities, I will assess the production of private and public benefits. The conclusions establish a framework for civic leaders to use to insure the creation of public benefits that reflect the level of public investment.

THE PRIVATE AND PUBLIC INTERESTS IN NEW SPORTS FACILITIES

Yankee Stadium, built in 1924 and remodeled in the 1970s, suffers from narrow aisles, antiquated restroom facilities, and location in a relatively unattractive part of the Bronx. Despite these limitations more than four million tickets were sold in 2005 and 2006. A new Yankee Stadium will open in 2009 with fewer seats than the older facility it will replace. The new Yankee Stadium will have many more revenue streams (or profit centers) than its predecessor, including tiers of luxury seating, food-service centers with expanded capacity, retail outlets offering team merchandise, expanded opportunities for advertising, and pre- and postgame entertainment options for fans. Building a new facility also creates an opportunity for the public sector to secure community-wide benefits. However, for the public sector to achieve that goal and capture some benefits for a city or community, civic leaders must first understand both what teams seek, and what can be secured for communities and the public good.

The Private Good Returns from New Sports Facilities

Owners seek new facilities—which may have fewer seats than the older ballparks they replace—to increase the quality of the fans' experience and the number of revenue streams or centers within the facility that will induce higher levels of spending from spectators. Teams can enhance the experience for fans through more comfortable seating, the provision of luxury services in special seats (suites, dugout or floor-level seats, and club areas with amenities not available to other fans), wider aisles, improved restrooms, and sight lines that offer excellent views of the playing field. Theory and management practice would suggest that facilities with these amenities would command higher ticket prices and far more spectator spending on food, beverages, and other items. The new facilities are also designed with ample opportunities for advertising and most facilities have a set of naming opportunities ranging from entrances and concourses to the entire facility. Each of these revenue streams generates greater profits for team owners. However, the quality of a fan's experience is also connected to the competitiveness of a team. It might be expected that a new facility would be successful in attracting more fans willing to pay higher prices, but to sustain attendance and spending levels, teams would also need to be competitive and that can lead to higher player salaries and team payrolls. This leads to the observation that new facilities generate important benefits for both owners and players.

The process of increasing game-day spending or of other forms of consumption (e.g., shopping for clothes) by fans can be described as the economic "Disneyfication" of sports. As stories have it, when Walt Disney saw the chaotic development of hotels, restaurants, and other recreational venues built outside of Disneyland he became attracted to the concept of building a far-larger, well-designed venue with space to include theme parks and all of the other recreational activities and spending that occurred during a visit. Disney World was the fulfillment of that strategy. While the story may or may not be true, the building of all-inclusive facilities to capture the complete range of spending associated with a recreational or tourist experience is sometimes described as the "Disneyfication" process. The new ballparks, arenas, and stadiums built since across the last two decades firmly ensconced sports in the center of Disneyfication processes involving enhanced fan experiences and the proliferation of retail and food and beverage centers within facilities.

To expand the attractiveness of sports to women (and thus create a larger market and demand for a team) the new sports facilities also increase the number and size of restrooms, giving teams the opportunity to expand their marketing to entire families. With more luxury seating the opportunities to market to businesses and wealthier individuals also increased the profitability of most teams with new facilities. These revenue possibilities make it clear how the private interest of owners is advanced through the construction of new facilities.

The private benefits from a new sports facility—especially one that enjoys a substantial subsidy from state or local governments—are relatively clear. Team owners enjoy larger revenue flows and these can lead to higher levels of annual profit or capitalized returns realized when the franchise is sold for a price that reflects the value of the new revenue streams. Players are also likely beneficiaries if team owners decide to use some portion of the new revenues to increase salaries in an effort to attract and retain the best talent and the players most likely to lead to a higher team winning percentage. While individual fans also enjoy the improved facilities and the available services, theory would suggest owners would price at market rates and not pass along any savings resulting from a public subsidy. As a result the fans may receive added enjoyment from improved sight lines and other amenities, but it is anticipated that prices will rise to market levels reflecting the value of those assets, creating no new benefits for fans. However, if an owner decided to price at lower than market rates for tickets or food and beverages to reflect the lower capital costs resulting from a public subsidy, then fans would also enjoy private benefits from the subsidy provided by the public sector.

Do these benefits actually emerge for team owners? To answer this question, and to measure the benefits, if any, received by players, information on the value of MLB franchises and players' salaries were analyzed. For brevity, this analysis was limited to franchises in MLB and their players. It is possible that assessment of outcomes for owners and players in any of the other major team sports could have yielded similar or different findings. Rising shares of total revenue for players in the NFL at the same time that franchise values have increased suggest that outcome there, as well as in the National Basketball Association, would be the same. More time must elapse under the current collective bargaining agreement between players and owners in the National Hockey League before it can be concluded if new arenas are creating the same or different levels of benefits for players and owners.

Each of the MLB teams in Table 3.1 plays in one of the new ballparks built during the last two decades and which replaced an existing facility. Excluded from this analysis were new franchises that entered MLB during these years, as each expansion franchise secured a ballpark deal as part of the MLB expansion process. The Montreal Expos/Washington Nationals was included in Table 3.1 as the increment in value reflects the ballpark plan agreed to by Washington, D.C.

Each new facility contains luxury seating, improved sight lines relative to the older facilities, and contains the outlets for enhanced revenue flows. The estimated market value for each team in 1990 is shown as well as the estimated value in 2006. These franchise values were generated by Michael Ozanian and his colleagues and are now an annual feature in *Forbes* magazine. While the estimates have been criticized they do represent a consistent measure generated from the same assumptions across sixteen years. Relative

TABLE 3.1
Team Values and New Ballparks

	Team Value (in millions US$)		Percent Change		Deviation from Mean (in millions US$)	
Teams, New Ballparks	***1990***	***2006***	***Nominal***	***Real***	***1990***	***2006***
Atlanta Braves	74	405	447	252	−23	51
Baltimore Orioles	140	359	156	65	103	5
Chicago White Sox	125	315	152	62	28	−39
Cincinnati Reds	102	274	169	73	5	−80
Cleveland Indians	75	352	369	202	−22	−2
Detroit Tigers	84	292	248	123	−13	−62
Houston Astros	92	416	352	191	−5	62
Milwaukee Brewers	81	235	190	86	−16	−119
Montreal/Washington, D.C.	74	440	495	282	−23	86
Philadelphia Phillies	130	424	226	110	33	−70
Pittsburgh Pirates	82	250	205	96	−15	−104
San Diego Padres	99	354	258	130	2	0
San Francisco Giants	105	410	290	151	8	56
Seattle Mariners	71	428	503	287	−26	74
St. Louis Cardinals	128	429	235	115	31	75
Texas Rangers	101	353	250	125	4	−1
Toronto Blue Jays	160	286	79	440	15	−68
Average	*101*	*354*	*272*	*139*	*21*	*56*

to an assessment of overall trends—especially from the impact of a new facility—errors in the value of any one franchise would not likely obscure or render meaningless the trends observed.

Team values should be expected to change in response to more than just the building of a new facility. For example, many have commented on the "honeymoon" effect, a term used to describe how long the ambiance of a new facility can be expected to affect attendance levels.[1] The "honeymoon" effect has a short duration, so after a certain point in time, if a team is not competitive, then the presence of a new facility will not sustain attendance levels and the value of a team may peak and then actually decline. The Pittsburgh Pirates provide an interesting example of this phenomenon. The value of the team after the building of a new facility increased 96 percent in real terms. However, the team has never come close to replicating the on-the-field success it had while in the older facility and as a result the team's relative value (to all franchises with new facilities) has actually declined. In 1990 the team's value was $15 million below the average of $101 million for the seventeen teams in Table 3.1. In 2006, even with a new facility, the team's value was $104 million *below* the average value of $354 million.

New ballparks do create wealth for team owners; the average real growth in value across the years was 139 percent, average rate of 8.7 percent. The Toronto Blue Jays enjoyed the lowest increase in value, 15 percent, and the value of the Seattle Mariners increased the most, 287 percent. The guarantee of a new ballpark in Washington, D.C., largely paid for by the public sector increased the value of that franchise by 282 percent. The data in Table 3.1 also include the individual deviations from the average value of all teams at each point in time. A new ballpark (coupled with the performance of the team) moved the value of the Atlanta Braves from $23 million below the mean of all teams in 1990 to $51 million above the mean in 2006. This represented a net change of $76 million, and the owners of the Houston Astros enjoyed a similar increment. The Seattle Mariners enjoyed the largest shift, $100 million, moving from $26 million below the average in 1990 to $74 million above in 2006.

It is also important to note that the average deviation in franchise value actually increased when the two time periods are considered. Average deviation from the mean was $21 million in 1990 and $56 million (an increase of 167%) in 2006. The building of new facilities did not reduce the variances in the value of teams. Rather, differences that existed prior to the building spree actually amplified. What causes the differences in team values if facilities are similar relative to revenue streams? Performance on the field clearly is a factor, but so too is the long-standing observation that the economic value or worth of an additional win for a larger market team exceeds what can be secured in smaller markets. Teams in larger markets with their greater pools of corporate and individual wealth can secure more returns for higher-quality teams and therefore the value of those franchises should be greater even if a smaller market had a new facility.[2] The experiences of the Detroit Tigers, Philadelphia Phillies, Chicago White Sox, St. Louis Cardinals, and Seattle Mariners underscore that observation. The Tigers (6.5 million residents), Phillies (5.1 million residents), and White Sox (9.3 million residents) play in large markets, but their values are far below the mean (2006) as a result of inconsistent performance. In contrast, the Cardinals (2.8 million residents) and Mariners (3.8 million residents) as a result of more consistent play (more wins) have values that exceed the average. While it is also possible that differences in valuation could be a result of different levels of subsides (meaning higher costs for teams that had to invest more in the new ballpark), the Cardinals actually invested the most for their new ballpark while the Tigers, Phillies, and White Sox benefited from far more public investment in their facilities. This again underscores the role of performance in the valuation of a team but still leaves the point that the marginal value of wins is greater in larger and wealthier markets.

In terms of individual benefits, players enjoyed a substantial increase in wages from the building of new facilities. The improved position of players can be seen on Tables 3.2 and 3.3. Table 3.2 shows the total payroll for all MLB teams, those that played in newer facilities in 2006 and playing in older ballparks. The aggregate payroll increased by 297.3 percent across the time period 1990 to 2006. From 1996 to 2006 the real increase in payroll increased by 164.8 percent. The figures in Table 3.2 include revenues from new ballparks as well as other sources available to teams playing in older ballparks but in larger markets (e.g., Boston, Chicago, Los Angeles, and New York).

Teams that played in new facilities, on average, passed along a substantial amount of the new revenues to their players. The real increase in the average payroll of these teams between 1990 and 2006 was 203.7 percent (team values rose 139 percent). Table 3.3 also includes observations for 2000 and 2003. This provides interesting views of the strategies followed by different teams. For example, the Atlanta Braves had a payroll of $115.9 million (2006 dollars) in 2003 and reduced that to $90.2 million in 2006. The team elected not to pursue higher priced free agents and not to sign some higher priced players to new contracts. The Cleveland Indians have also trimmed more than $30 million from their annual payroll after new owners paid a premium price for the franchise. With a lower annual payroll the team was still quite competitive in 2005, but then had a very disappointing season in 2006.

The extent of the private benefits from new sports facilities—illustrated for MLB team owners and players—is readily apparent. Owners enjoyed a 139 percent increase in the value of their franchises—some franchises had

TABLE 3.2
MLB Payrolls, Absolute and Constant Dollars, 1990–2006

MLB Payrolls	2006	1996	1990
		Absolute Values	
Average	139.8	45.5	26.9
Total	4,333.0	1274.3	700.7
Lowest	15.0	22.5	12.6
Highest	194.7	80.9	36.7
		Constant Dollars (2006)	
Average	139.8	58.4	41.9
Total	4,333.0	1,636.6	1,090.7
Lowest	15.0	28.9	19.6
Highest	194.7	103.9	57.2

Source: USA Today.
Note: In millions of U.S.$.

TABLE 3.3
Player Payrolls of Teams Playing in New Ballparks in or Before the 2006 Season in Selected Years

	Year, Absolute Figures				2006 Dollars		
Team	*1990*	*2000*	*2003*	*2006*	*1990*	*2000*	*2003*
Atlanta Braves	13.3	82.7	106.2	90.2	20.7	97.2	115.9
Baltimore Orioles	10.0	83.1	73.9	72.6	15.6	97.6	80.7
Chicago White Sox	9.5	31.2	51.0	102.8	14.8	36.7	55.7
Cincinnati Reds	14.8	44.2	59.4	60.9	23.0	51.9	64.8
Cleveland Indians	15.2	76.5	48.6	56.0	23.7	89.9	53.0
Detroit Tigers	18.1	61.7	49.2	82.6	28.2	72.5	53.7
Houston Astros	18.8	52.1	71.0	92.6	29.3	61.2	77.5
Milwaukee Brewers	20.2	37.8	40.6	57.7	31.4	44.4	44.3
Montreal/Washington, D.C.	16.6	33.5	51.9	63.1	25.8	39.4	56.6
Philadelphia Phillies	14.0	47.0	70.8	88.3	21.8	55.2	77.3
Pittsburgh Pirates	15.7	26.6	54.8	46.7	24.4	31.2	59.8
San Diego Padres	18.6	55	45.2	69.9	29.0	64.6	49.3
San Francisco Giants	20.9	53.6	82.9	90.1	32.5	63.0	90.5
Seattle Mariners	12.8	59.2	87.0	88.0	19.9	69.5	94.9
St. Louis Cardinals	20.9	63.1	84.8	88.9	32.5	74.1	92.5
Texas Rangers	15.1	70.8	103.5	68.3	23.5	83.2	113.0
Toronto Blue Jays	18.5	46.4	51.3	71.9	28.8	54.5	56.0
Average	16.1	54.4	66.6	75.9	25.0	63.9	72.7
Percent Change from 1990	–	–	–	203.7	–	155.6	190.8

Source: USA Today.
Note: In millions of US$.

far larger increases in values—and players saw the total amount of money spent for payrolls increased by more than 200 percent. Asset increases of more than 130 percent across a sixteen-year period might appear to be a modest return compared to other possible investments, but it must be remembered that this is not the only source of fiscal returns available to owners. Audited data on tax and income benefits from ownership are not available and one report issued by MLB itself concluded many owners were losing money.[3] There was, however, significant criticism of this report and addressing those findings is beyond the scope of this chapter. It is sufficient to note that the private benefits from new sports facilities include important if not substantial gains in the value of teams as market assets. The extent of the benefit of the new facilities for players is quite apparent even if some players would argue these benefits were long overdue relative to the earnings of owners in earlier time periods.

The Public Interest in New Sports Facilities

Where does the public interest lie in new sports facilities?

The potential exists for sports facilities to generate important benefits for governments and residents. In terms of the claims made by advocates, Table 3.4 identifies the most commonly identified or mentioned tangible and intangible benefits.

It has been suggested by proponents for new sports facilities that the presence of major-league sports teams attracts businesses, bringing new and better paying jobs to an area (higher levels of regional income). When businesses and people move to an area, the demand for land rises, leading to higher property values. Advocates for the public investment in sports facilities suggest those returns more than offset any tax increases to support the

TABLE 3.4
The Range of Possible Public Benefits from a Sports Facility That Is Home to a Sports Team

Possible Public Benefits	
Tangible	*Intangible*
Enhanced levels of regional income	Improved image
Enhanced levels of wealth in region	Enhanced identity
Higher tax revenues	New levels of civic pride
Downtown redevelopment and:	Downtown redevelopment for:
New levels of private investment	Social mixing
Relocated economic activity	Relocated economic activity

building of a facility or paying for the maintenance or infrastructure associated with a new ballpark, stadium, or arena. Based on this logic, the region raises taxes to pay for the new sports facility that initially reduces the wealth of individuals and corporations. However, as the presence of the team leads to new business attraction, income levels rise from the new demand for labor and so do property values. Those increments more than offset the investment made.

Rising property and income levels would produce higher tax revenues for the public sector even if tax rates remain unchanged. As all local governments utilize a combination of income, sales, and property taxes, if incomes and land values increase, higher tax revenues will result. It has also been argued by proponents for public investments in sports facilities that investments by governments in large-scale projects located in declining areas can attract the interest of private developers. The confidence in future development expressed by a government through its investment can thus become a catalyst for private investment that would not occur without the "pump-priming" action of a subsidized sports facility. If private investment in surrounding properties does occur, then there would be a set of tangible financial returns to a community.

The final tangible benefit identified by some sports facility advocates involves downtown redevelopment, a concern for many cities that have seen substantial levels of economic and social activity moving to suburban locations. Even in the absence of heightened levels of regional economic activity there could be substantial tangible benefits for a central city from refocusing economic activity into a downtown area. These benefits can include improved access to employment for city residents, enhanced taxed revenues for central cities (which could come at the expense of other local governments if economic activity related to recreation is simply moved from suburban locations), and reduced levels of deteriorated or abandoned properties in the downtown areas. This latter benefit was certainly at the core of proposals for new sports facilities for Baltimore, Cleveland, Dallas, Detroit, Indianapolis, Los Angeles, and St. Louis.

Sports facilities also have the potential to create important intangible benefits that while more difficult to quantify are nevertheless important. For example, new facilities in downtown areas can create a more positive image that has value in terms of the pride people have in their community or in a central city area. There is also the possibility that the building of a facility to retain or attract a team underscores that city's image as a center for sports. There could be substantial intangible benefits from hosting a team in a society that values sports as a critical social institution. Sports teams could also create feelings of pride for the residents of a city or region and establish a common regional identity. When teams are successful there is a sense of excitement in a community (at least among sports fans or people who follow teams). All of these are potential public benefits in that they accrue to those who may not attend games or even watch games. If a true public benefit were created, then its absence would represent a loss. Investing public funds to insure that a classical public good is present can represent an appropriate use of tax dollars especially if the intangible benefits can be quantified. There can also be an intangible benefit from the relocation of economic activity that stabilizes a deteriorating area. The benefit is that the area is no longer as blighted and hence leaves a more favorable impression or image of a city or community in the minds of visitors and residents.

In terms of the matrix of intangible benefits, "social mixing" refers to the role sports teams can assume in attracting people to downtown areas from the suburbs who might otherwise avoid a center city. In regions with high levels of economic class and racial segregation, the attracting of large numbers of people creates opportunities to showcase a city to people who otherwise might not visit a downtown area. This social mixing or the simple attraction of people to events in the downtown creates the potential to change the image of a downtown area.

If these benefits were created there could be a positive return on a public investment. A challenge for the public sector is that too often no investment is made to tabulate the benefits received. For example, measuring intangible benefits requires surveys of residents and those who attend sporting events. Measuring the relocation of economic activity also involves an analysis of trends and patterns with detailed models. If the required research is not performed, then a community may find itself unable to understand if the return on investment achieved any established goals or if the benefits generated exceeded the cost of the investment. It is far easier to measure the returns to the private sector by using the sales price of teams or the salaries paid to players.

Do sports facilities actually create any tangible or intangible rewards for a region that would represent a return on the use of tax dollars to build a facility?

For more than three decades the "coin of the realm" within the academic community has been and continues to be that stand-alone sports facilities that are not integrated into large-scale development plans do not generate noteworthy tangible benefits for the public sector or taxpayers. Integration into a development plan, by itself, can also lead to small or nonexistent returns for the public sector if development plans do not include large-scale private or nonprofit sector investments.[4] Noll and Zimbalist effectively summarized the state of knowledge on the role of teams and facilities in economic development labeled sports poor investments noting "Subsidized sports facilities do not exist because they are financially valuable assets. . . .

They exist, instead, because most cities have decided a subsidized team is better than no team at all, and because scarcity in the number of teams gives owners the advantage in bargaining with cities."[5] The accuracy of this observation has been sustained by another decade of research underscoring the limitations of stand-alone facilities that are not integrated in development strategies that also include robust levels of investments by entrepreneurs or the nonprofit sector.[6]

When the attention has turned to intangible benefits, some studies have found the existence of a sufficient level of benefits to justify a public subsidy. Hamilton and Kahn originally raised this issue, noting that the public subsidies used to build Oriole Park at Camden Yards and the new home for the Baltimore Ravens would be more than offset if households in the region believed the teams' presence each produced $20 per year in intangible benefits. Rosentraub and Swindell found that the intangible benefits received by Indiana residents more than offset the public's investment in new facility to retain the Indianapolis Colts.[7] Other studies indicate that intangible benefits might not sustain the entire cost of a facility for a professional sports team, but they do justify the public sector paying for a portion of the cost.

Economists have also focused on the consumer surpluses generated by sports, comparing what fans paid for tickets with the value of a team or sporting event to people who attended games. Irani found significant levels of consumer surplus for fans attending MLB games indicating that these individuals received a level of private benefits from public subsidized ballparks. It is probable, then, that a similar level of benefits existed for those who watched or listened to games involving the local home team, creating a public (nonpaying) dimension to the consumer surplus. Alexander, Kern, and Neill estimated the consumer surplus produced by teams from all of the major sports leagues and found benefits again for fans. Layson isolated the consumer surplus produced by the building of an arena for a hockey team and while the specific nature of the benefits that produced was not specified, the consumer surplus was clear. As Layson observed, "Even if liberal adjustments are made . . . the aggregate consumer surplus [from the arena] was sufficient to fully cover the income loss and debt service." In this situation, then, if benefits accrued to both spectators attending events and those who listened to events broadcasted throughout the region, a public good could be said to exist.[8]

CITIES AND SPORTS FACILITIES: CASE STUDIES

Turning to the experiences of different cities, it is also possible to learn which specific facility deals produced more public benefits from the use of tax dollars to build sports facilities. Cleveland, Indianapolis, and San Diego are examples of coordinated development programs with substantial private-sector investments that followed or were coupled to the public sector's investment in a sports facility. Can the benefits from these public investments be quantified and attributed to the presence of the sports facility? Was there in fact a positive return for the public sector? Arlington, Texas, another city that made a substantial investment in a ballpark, is a case where promised or hoped for private development never occurred at the anticipated levels.

Relying on case studies to assess at impacts is fraught with analytical traps, not the least of which is the "what for" argument. Had the public sector chosen alternative investment strategies, what other outcomes could have taken place or even been imagined? A community's corporate leadership is also the frequent champion of policies emphasizing investments in sports facilities to anchor downtown redevelopment. This generates suspicion that alternative development strategies could generate different if not higher levels of community development. Holupka and Shlay's study is representative of the research questioning the dominating role of corporate elites—members of the growth machines in numerous communities—in supporting development policies for central cities centered upon sports and entertainment.[9] There are three explicit concerns inherent in the critiques of the dominance of business leaders in redevelopment strategies. First, corporate elites frequently support an economic development agenda that provides them with substantial benefits. Those benefits some researchers argue are in conflict with the best interests of many of the residents of center cities or in conflict with longer-term development patterns likely to generate more substantial and equitable returns. Second, the focus on sports by many central cities produces too few (if any) benefits for inner-city residents. Third, the focus on sports given the scale of investment required—several hundred million dollars for construction and maintenance—leads to the inability of local governments to invest in other strategies. Imbroscio concluded that the dominance of business elites in economic policy decision-making yields an affinity for projects that, perhaps unintentionally but successfully, eliminate other potentially superior strategies from the public agenda.[10]

The argument that a bias toward sports projects obfuscates alternative strategies is raised by a number of scholars, suggesting potentially larger returns for cities from (1) neighborhood-focused urban development, (2) import substitution initiatives, (3) improved public education and labor force development, (4) the building of housing of interest to people attracted to an urban lifestyle or (5) "the development of alternative (unknown or untested) ideas about how city economies function and how best to promote local economic vitality." A cursory view of economic development strategies in U.S. cities would sustain the ubiquitous emphasis on sports and entertainment, raising the possibility that other strategies have a far lower profile or are less often tried.[11]

At the center of these concerns is the distribution of benefits when an extensive public investment is expected to build the entertainment or tourist infrastructure touted by a community's corporate interests. Squires's collection, *Unequal Partnerships*, framed the distributional and outcome issues that have been at the cornerstone of discussions of the role of elites in shaping development policy. A focus on entertainment and tourism raises the specter of substantial benefits eluding neighborhoods. Levine's observations regarding development in Baltimore vividly illustrate this point.[12]

With these criticisms in mind, and conscious of the limitations of case study analysis, the following summaries are provided to illustrate outcomes in cities that attempted to coordinate the redevelopment of downtown areas with the public sector's investment in a sports facility.

Cleveland

The city of Cleveland draws more than half of its operating budget from an earnings' tax (paid to the jurisdiction where the job is located). As the city's population dwindled from more than 950,000 in the 1950s to less than 600,000 in the 1980s, the fear that jobs would follow the cascading exodus of residents led community leaders to look at strategies to retain jobs and residents. Cleveland's policy approach emphasized large-scale projects for its downtown area, and paramount among these was new homes for the Cleveland Indians, Cleveland Cavaliers (who had left the city for the suburbs), and the Cleveland Browns (the stadium was built for the second or newly created franchise in the NFL's response to Art Modell's decision to move the original Browns franchise to Baltimore). Local governments also made investments in the Rock and Roll Hall of Fame and Museum and a new Science Center and Museum located in the downtown area.

Cuyahoga County invested $655 million in the three sports facilities (and more than $100 million in the two museums). To finance the investment in the sports facilities the county increased taxes on the consumption of alcohol and cigarettes. That tax revenue fell far short of the $46.2 million needed each year to pay for the bonds sold to fund the construction of the sports facilities. As a result the county had to rely on property taxes to meet its bond payments. Cleveland's population accounts for less than one-third of the residents of the county. In addition, Cleveland's residents have substantially lower incomes as compared to the county's residents. As a result,

Cleveland's residents pay less than 30 percent of the county's property taxes. Analyses have indicated that as much as $41 million in tax revenues is generated each year for Cleveland from the investment made in downtown Cleveland, yielding a net loss at the county level of $5.2 million in tax money. For Cleveland, however, assuming that Cleveland's residents pay 30 percent of the county's annual payment for the sports facilities, there is a positive cash flow of $26 million to the central city.[13]

If the overall tax flow is negative to the county, even if positive to the city, what other benefits were generated? In terms of image, the following review in the *New York Times* is indicative of what advocates for public investment in the sports facilities would cite:

> The Cleveland of *American Splendor*, the 2003 Oscar-nominated movie, is a dreary 1980s town of thrift stores and shambling eccentrics, a place where you'd barely care to spend 2 hours, let alone a weekend. Today, Cleveland hardly feels like the same place. In the 1990s, public-private enterprises replaced center-city blight with new sports stadiums and the lakefront Rock and Roll Hall of Fame and Museum. Meanwhile, downtown's revival spurred gentrification into forgotten enclaves along the Cuyahoga River.[14]

Analyses of private-sector investment in downtown Cleveland, as a proportion of investment in the county, show no substantial shifts after the sports facilities were built. Advocates of public investments in sports facilities would argue that simply holding investment levels constant was a substantial benefit as the city continued to lose population. However, that loss of residents after the building of the sports facilities suggests that while there are far more people living in the downtown area in close proximity to the facilities, overall population in the city has declined through 2005. For Cleveland, the returns from the sports investment involve the shifting of tax money to the city (at the expense of other cities in the county) and an improved image. It is also possible that the intangible benefits of the teams are worth the public investment. If the annual bond payments are used as a measure of the cost of the investment—assuming no positive returns—the cost of the three facilities is approximately $82 per household per year. Thus, if the combined intangible benefits of the three teams amount to $7 per month to each household, then the value of the intangible benefit of hosting three sports teams would exceed the cost of the new facilities.

Cuyahoga County's investment in three sports facilities produced improved tax receipts for Cleveland and was accompanied by successful if nascent revitalization of a downtown market for residential construction. While downtown business property continues to decline in value as a result of vacant office space, employment levels are stable, yielding dependable and slightly increasing levels of earnings taxes for the city. At the county level, however, there is a net loss of tax revenue that might be offset by the intangible value of an improved image for downtown Cleveland and of hosting three teams. However, the larger economic gains found by Carlino and Carlson and Santo are still on the region's horizon.[15]

Indianapolis

No city in North America or Western Europe has placed as substantial an emphasis on sports to redevelop a downtown center as Indianapolis. Across several decades the public sector invested more than $1.26 billion in a series of projects to create an amateur sports capital while also retaining two professional sports teams in one of the nation's smallest metropolitan areas. In 2005 the public sector agreed to build a new stadium for the Indianapolis Colts that will involve an additional investment of more than $400 million. When the sports strategy began, downtown Indianapolis was deteriorating as suburban malls, having followed people to more distant locations, virtually destroyed the retail base that had existed in downtown through the 1950s. In addition the city's population as a proportion of the region was declining even after the creation of a consolidated city/county form of government that joined many suburban areas with Indianapolis. One survey conducted in the 1970s found Indianapolis had no image in the national media or in the national consciousness.

What did the public sector get from its investment of more than $1.6 billion? Across the decades of the 1980s, 1990s, and into the twenty-first century the public investment leveraged more than $3 billion in capital commitments from the private and nonprofit sector. Led by the Lilly Endowment's investments of approximately $500 million and almost $900 million in new construction by the Lilly Corporation, downtown Indianapolis has been transformed. A new residential base has been built, a downtown shopping center continues to enjoy full occupancy, and the city is a regular destination for national sporting events. The image of the city and region has been remade, but the economic gains have not been as substantial. Median income in the consolidated city in 2000 was still lower than in the nearby counties home to Cincinnati and Columbus. The decentralization of economic activity also continues. Households in the consolidated city earned, on average, $5,000 less than households living outside of Indianapolis but within the metropolitan area. Consolidation ranked the county as the nation's fifty-fifth largest, but in terms of median income the county's rank was 729.[16]

Indianapolis's great success was in rebuilding its downtown area and image through a leveraging of funds from the private and nonprofit sectors.

For every dollar the public sector invested, at least two dollars was committed to projects by private and nonprofit sector organizations. A return of that magnitude clearly establishes an enviable benchmark. Yet, the preponderance of that money came from two organizations, both with long-term histories in the region. In addition, the Lilly Endowment—created by the family of the Lilly Corporation's founder—has a charter that urges a concentration of expenditures in central Indiana. To be sure those expenditures could have been put to a myriad of uses instead of redeveloping downtown. In that sense a case can be made that the endowment's funds were leveraged. The Lilly Endowment was an active participant and supporter of both the plans for a rebuilt downtown and some of the projects that anchored the redevelopment. The Lilly Corporation—legally independent of the Lilly Endowment—could have made decisions to invest elsewhere and to even relocate to a more suburban location. However the large role assumed by the corporation and the endowment in the rebuilding process leads to the inevitable question whether those investments would have occurred with a lower level of investment by the public sector.

Indianapolis abated more than $100 million in property taxes for projects in the downtown area. Abatements were given to the Lilly Corporation, for the new headquarters building for Simon Property Group (builders of large malls through the nation), and to American United Life for its corporate headquarters building. There is undeniable evidence of the positive nature of the outcomes from Indianapolis's downtown strategy, and the lesson to be learned is that it succeeded because of the leveraging of substantial investments from the private and nonprofit sectors. Without geographically vested partners like the Lilly Endowment and the Lilly Corporation other cities may not be able to replicate Indianapolis's success. In addition, there is no way to counter the argument that had the city not provided more than $100 million in subsidies, the investments would still have been made by the endowment and the corporation. Nevertheless, a model of success is clearly demonstrated in that leveraged private, public, and nonprofit dollars can transform a declining downtown area into one with a small and concentrated residential, retail, business, and entertainment center that is vibrant and a completely new image for a city. Coordinated activity, however, tied to a clear vision is required. And at the same time, that coordination and leveraging may not have the success hoped for in terms of creating jobs and higher wages for residents.

San Diego

Reviewing San Diego's building of PETCO Park for the Padres after considering the outcomes in Indianapolis provides another example of successful leveraging of public subsidies with private sector funds. Padres' owner John Moores wanted to move his team from a stadium designed to host football and baseball games to one with improved sight lines and numerous revenue sources. In his quest for a new ballpark he made an interesting proposal, one that responded to some of the criticisms of past sports facility deals. Instead of the usual forecast of unspecified future private sector investments—the "build it and they will come syndrome"—he guaranteed a level of investment.

While the original project became mired in political intrigue and was plagued by vacillations in Mr. Moores's fiscal solvency and concerns with his ability to fulfill the commitment, after years of delay the facility was built. Mr. Moores did guarantee that there would be a sufficient level of private investment to generate the needed property taxes to pay the bonds issued to cover the city's subsidy. John Moores and San Diego agreed—in an amendment to the original contract between the team and the city that:

> The Padres and its Master Developer will have an additional 24-month period of time after Opening Day to have on the tax rolls projects with an assessed valuation of at least $311,000,000. Except as specifically set forth herein, the obligations of the Padres and its Master Developer with regard to Phase 1 Ancillary Development remain unchanged.

How did things turn out? A *New York Times* report concluded that by 2005, $1.4 billion in new investment had taken place in the twenty-six-block area designated as the ballpark district and the area within which the team guaranteed at least $311 million of development. The development that occurred in the years immediately after the ballpark opened exceeded the guarantee by 400 percent. Relative to San Diego's financial interests, the cost of their investment in the ballpark has been completely covered by the taxes generated by this level of development. In addition, there has been an increase in property tax revenues generating a positive cash flow for San Diego.[17]

To be sure there are valid criticisms of this development deal beyond the political and fiscal intrigue that tarnished the initial concept and proposal. John Moores was made the master developer of the twenty-six-block area and given considerable latitude. While there has not been an issue of compatible land uses with the projects initiated—hotel, retail, and extensive residential development—there is a clear income-bias in that moderate- and lower-income families have been priced-out in the gentrification process. Further, it cannot be scientifically validated that the ballpark was necessary for the redevelopment and building that took place. It is possible that some if not all of the development would have occurred even if the partnership and ballpark agreements were not created. San Diego has enjoyed a substantial real estate boom, even though for the earlier years of the boom the land in the ballpark district was largely ignored in favor of more suburban and coastal locations. It is possible some development may have taken place in the future if the ballpark had not been built, but even those critics would have to acknowledge the higher present value of tax revenues accruing to San Diego if projects were built sooner rather than in some distant scenario.

Jane Jacobs's arguments regarding the recycling of land and land uses in urban areas also has to be acknowledged.[18] The ballpark agreement and the creation of a master developer effectively eclipsed the use-reuse cycle of urban land that brings with it a certain type of vitality and creativity that over time regenerates urban and neighborhood economies. To be sure the building of a ballpark and higher income housing short-circuits this process in favor of a specific, nonevolutionary direction chosen by a private-sector developer seeking to maximize immediate returns.

Those crucial criticisms not withstanding, the San Diego case, coupled with Indianapolis's experience and success, points out the clear direction toward communities working with teams to build new sports facilities. What works best for the public sector are partnerships that leverage substantial levels of private-sector investment in the same area where tax money is used to build a ballpark, arena, or stadium. When that occurs, the fiscal returns can be positive for both the private- and public-sector partners.

Arlington, Texas

A city that boasted a 2005 population of more than 300,000 residents located between Dallas and Fort Worth attracted the Washington Senators in the 1970s to play their home games at a former minor-league ballpark. Despite two sets of extensive renovations it became clear that a new facility would be needed to insure the fiscal success of the team. The Ballpark in Arlington opened in the mid-1990s with the public sector's investment funded through a sales tax increment. As Arlington is the home of several of the region's most popular shopping malls and centers, the city was able to pay off its bonds several years ahead of schedule. The city, however, had also hoped that building the ballpark would advance development in the central and north-central part of the community.

Arlington's development trend is most clearly seen in the established planning areas. Figure 3.1 illustrates the spatial distribution of recent growth in Arlington. As can be seen, the northern sector near where the ballpark is located is *not* experiencing significant changes (even though it has the

FIGURE 3.1
Growth by Area in Arlington, Texas, 2002–2003

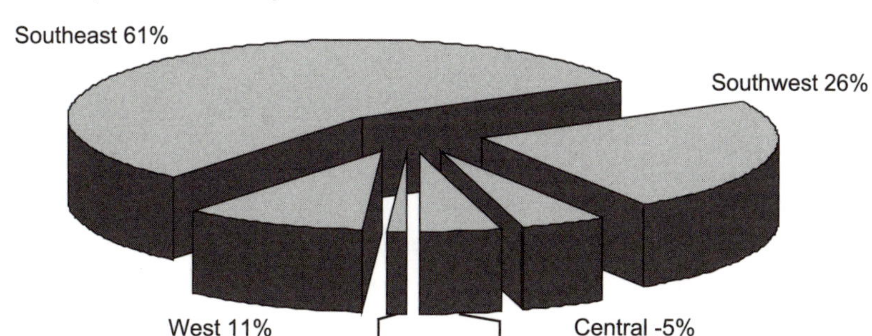

second-largest amount of developable property in the city and is across Interstate 30 from the ballpark), while the southeastern and southwestern sectors are home to the largest rates of growth. The central sector, which is adjacent to the area closest to the ballpark on the west, actually lost ground.

CONCLUSIONS: THE PRIVATE AND PUBLIC BENEFITS FROM SPORTS FACILITY DEVELOPMENT AND THE IMPLICATIONS FOR URBAN REDEVELOPMENT

Across two decades the building of new sports facilities with a range of public subsidies or investments has raised the question, "who really benefits from this use of tax money?" Sports facilities produced a range of potential private and public benefits, and from the review of other studies and the work presented here, there can be little debate that team owners and players have been substantial beneficiaries. Has the public joined them in the winner's circle?

With regard to the point of concentrated urban redevelopment changes, however, the evidence is fairly clear. Gains for the area adjacent to the sports facility and the regeneration of downtown areas are associated with firm or guaranteed levels of investment that are part of a partnership agreement. Building a facility and then hoping that development will follow is far less promising than the leveraging or partnerships that were created in Indianapolis and San Diego. The success in those areas provides clear policy direction. If a public-sector investment in a sports facility is being made as part of a redevelopment strategy, the chances for success are substantially enhanced with guaranteed private-sector investments or commitments from other organizations (nonprofit or for-profit). In both San Diego and Indianapolis, when those guarantees were in place the public sector received the benefits it anticipated. In

Arlington's case, mirrored by other cities, when facilities were built in the hope that investment would occur, there was far less success.

Underscoring the importance of commitments by the public sector, Cleveland experienced a set of fiscal gains in the central city through a substantial investment from the county, and the net public-sector position is negative. There has been a continuing level of private-sector development of downtown Cleveland, but the presence of the sports facilities did not concentrate development in the downtown area. There has not been a shift in development patterns in the decade after the sports facilities opened. While the presence of the facilities brings as many as four million visits to the downtown area, the level of redevelopment does not match the success achieved in Indianapolis or San Diego.

Even with the limited success in Cleveland, the policy lesson and direction is clear. If sports facilities are to generate a return proportionate to the private benefits created, there must be guaranteed investments by the private and nonprofit sectors. If those occur as part of a clearly articulated development plan, tangible returns can occur. In both San Diego and Indianapolis there was a clear development plan. In San Diego this was done by the master development. In Indianapolis the public and private sectors with the support of the Lilly Endowment developed the plan for a new downtown. In both instances, while there was some dissatisfaction with the level of public involvement in the planning process, there were clear plans and substantial levels of commitment from the private sector in both cities and the nonprofit sector in Indianapolis. Those commitments led to a set of tangible returns that mark the clear policy road to success for communities seeking fiscal returns on their investments in sports facilities. What must be achieved or developed is a plan that includes substantial commitments from the private and nonprofit sectors. If that does not occur, the probability that the generation of public benefits will match the private benefit levels created is far lower.

NOTES

1. Dennis Coates and Brad Humphreys, "Novelty Effects of New Facilities on Attendance at Professional Sporting Events," *Contemporary Economic Policy* 23, no. 3 (2005): 436–455.

2. Robert Sandy, Peter Sloane, and Mark Rosentraub, *The Economics of Sport: An International Perspective* (London: Palgrave Macmillan, 2004).

3. Richard C. Levin, George J. Mitchell, Paul A. Volcker, and George F. Will, *The Report of the Independent Members of the Commissioner's Blue Ribbon Panel on Baseball Economics* (New York: Office of the Commissioner, Major League Baseball, 2000).

4. Robert A. Baade and Richard F. Dye, "The Impact of Stadiums and Professional Sports on Metropolitan Area Development," *Growth and Change* 21, no. 2 (1990): 1–14; Mark S. Rosentraub, D. Swindell, M. Przybylski, and D.R. Mullins, "Sports and a Downtown Development Strategy: If You Build It Will Jobs Come?" *Journal of Urban Affairs* 16, no. 3 (1994): 221–239.

5. Roger G. Noll and Andrew Zimbalist, "Build The Stadium—Create the Jobs," in *Sports, Jobs, and Taxes*, ed. R. G. Noll and A. Zimbalist (Washington, D.C.: Brookings Institution Press, 1997), 30.

6. Mark Rosentraub, *Major League Losers: The Real Cost of Sports and Who's Paying for It* (New York: Basic Books, 1999); Dennis Coates and Brad R. Humphreys, "The Growth Effects of Sports Franchises, Stadia, and Arenas," *Journal of Policy Analysis and Management* 18, no. 4 (1999): 601–624; A. Nelson, "Prosperity or Blight? A Question of Major League Stadia Location," *Economic Development Quarterly* 15, no. 3 (2001): 255–265; Mark Rosentraub and Ziona Austrian, "Cities, Sports, and Economic Change: A Retrospective Assessment," *Journal of Urban Affairs* 24, no. 5 (2002): 549–563; Gerald Carlino and Edward Coulson, "Compensating Differentials and the Social Benefits of the NFL," *Journal of Urban Economics* 56, no. 1 (2004): 25–50; C. Santo, "The Economic Impact of Sports Stadiums: Recasting the Analysis in Context," *Journal of Urban Affairs* 27, no. 2 (2005): 177–192; Coates and Humphreys, "Novelty Effects,"436–455; Dennis Coates, Brad Humphreys, and Andrew Zimbalist, "Compensating Differentials and The Social Benefits of the NFL: A Comment," *Journal of Urban Economics* 60, no. 1 (2006): 124–131.

7. B. Hamilton and P. Kahn, "Baltimore's Camden Yards Ballparks," in *Sports, Jobs, and Taxes,* ed. Noll and Zimbalist, 245–281; Mark Rosentraub and D. Swindell, "The Value of the Indianapolis Colts to Indiana Residents and Their Willingness to Pay for a New Stadium," http://www.colts.com (accessed 2005).

8. Daraius Irani, "Public Subsidies to Stadiums: Do the Costs Outweigh the Benefits," *Public Finance Review* 25, no. 2 (1997): 238–253; Donald L. Alexander, William Kern, and Jon Neill, "Valuing the Consumption Benefits from Professional Sports Franchises," *Journal of Urban Economics* 48, no. 2 (1997): 321–337; S. K. Layson, "The Estimation of Consumer Surplus from a City Owned Multipurpose Coliseum Complex," *Journal of Real Estate Research* 27, no. 2 (2005): 221–236.

9. C. S. Holupka and A. Shlay, "Political Economy and Urban Development," in *Theories of Local Economic Development*, ed. R. Bingham and R. Mier (Newbury Park, Calif.: Sage, 1993), 175–190.

10. D. Imbroscio, "Reformulating Urban Regime Theory: The Division of Labor Between State and Market Reconsidered," *Journal of Urban Affairs* 20, no. 3 (1998): 233–248.

11. Ibid.; J. Jacobs, *The Death and Life of Great American Cities* (New York: Random House, 1961); D. Keating, N. Krumholz, and J. Metzger, "Post-populist public-private partnerships," in *Cleveland Development: A Dissenting View*, ed. Alvin L. Shorr (Cleveland: Case Western Reserve University, 1991), 53–76.

12. G. D. Squires, ed., *Unequal Partnerships* (New Brunswick, N.J.: Rutgers University Press, 1989); M. Levine, "A Third World City in the First World: Social Exclusion,

Racial Inequality, and Sustainable Development in Baltimore," in *The Social Sustainability of Cities*, ed. M. Polese and R. Stren (Toronto: University of Toronto Press, 2000), 123–156.

13. Mark Rosentraub, "The Local Context of a Sports Strategy for Economic Development," *Economic Development Quarterly* 20, no. 3 (2006): 278–291.

14. M. Gallust, "Journeys: 36 Hours," *New York Times,* May 20, 2005.

15. Carlino and Carlson, "Compensating Differentials," 25–50; Santo, "Economic Impact of Sports Stadiums," 177–192.

16. U.S. Census Bureau, 2006.

17. G. Gervey, "A Revival for San Diego's Downtown," *New York Times,* July 11, 2004.

18. Jacobs, *Death and Life of Great American Cities.*

Four

Revenue-Sharing and Agency Problems in Professional Sports Leagues

Daniel S. Mason

The credibility and success of professional sports as an entertainment product is dependent upon high levels of cooperation between teams in a league, who come together to produce the league product. However, because different teams have varying levels of support, financial resources available, and owner motivations (such as winning versus profit maximization), the opportunity arises for some teams to win more than others in the long run. While winning all the time might certainly be in the interests of fans of the winning team, in the long run interest in games as a whole is weakened. To address this problem and to allow more teams to be competitive and preserve the uncertainty of outcome of games, North American sports leagues have adopted revenue-sharing practices, where revenues are pooled and distributed to individual franchises. However, as the chapter will show, sharing revenues can also create incentive and other problems where individual team and league interests diverge.

This chapter describes how leagues are organized and how individual franchises relate to each other. It then discusses the underlying rationale behind league revenue-sharing policies and reviews how revenues are shared in the four major professional sports leagues in North America—the National Football League (NFL), Major League Baseball (MLB), National Basketball Association (NBA), and National Hockey League (NHL). Agency theory is then introduced to explain inherent problems with team and league goals, and then unique characteristics of sports leagues that exacerbate the agency relationship between franchise and league are discussed. In doing so, it is hoped that a greater understanding of the issues facing leagues in ensuring the financial and competitive success of all clubs will be achieved.

ORGANIZATION OF LEAGUES AND THE LEAGUE PRODUCT

In order to form a league, individual team owners must agree to surrender a certain degree of autonomy in order to preserve interest in and the profitability of the overall league.[1] This group of owners generally agrees on five basic elements that underpin league operations. The first relates to the format of the schedule, which typically includes a regular season followed by an elimination tournament. The second relates to hierarchy; in other words, how the league relates to other leagues within the same sport. For example, MLB and the NHL have relationships with lower leagues, used to develop players. The third element relates to multiplicity, or how many leagues exist at the same level of hierarchy. In baseball, there are two distinct leagues, the National and American, which operate at the highest level of professional baseball. The fourth element relates to membership, or the conditions that are decided upon whereby franchises may enter or exit a league. Finally, governance issues are determined, which refer to the ways in which league policies and rules are enforced.

Franchises are interested in joining leagues for several reasons. Where there are few teams to play one another, interest in games will be limited. This is related to a core element of the product—uncertainty of outcome. One of the things that makes sports events unique is that viewers cannot be sure of the final score of the game. Where no league exists, uncertainty of outcome only exists as it relates to the outcome of a single match between two teams. In addition, where independent teams exist, there may be differences in rules followed between teams. However, where teams organize into leagues, there can also be uncertainty of outcome related to a schedule of games (i.e., who will win the regular- and postseason league championship?). Leagues also codify and enforce rules, and standardize equipment.[2] These must all be agreed upon among franchises; thus the league itself and not any individual team acts as the core business unit, as leagues act as collectives of individual firms (teams) to form a single supplier to a market. Seen in this way, the league must work to preserve the uncertainty of outcome for both individual games held and the overall competition for a league championship.[3]

Leagues are usually organized as nonprofit organizations, with a constitution and bylaws developed to preserve the interests of their members (the franchises).[4] The sports product that is produced represents a joint product of the league. Teams must cooperate to produce the product—by agreeing on scheduling, locations, rules, the division of revenues, and so on—but the product itself must appear to be produced by two teams that are fiercely competing against one another to win. For this reason, it is important for teams to appear to be independent from one another; concerns over the uncertainty of game outcomes can arise where teams are too closely related or in leagues that employ a single-entity model, where a single-ownership unit controls individual franchises.[5] In the North American context, each team also retains exclusive geographic control over its home territory, and consent is required for other teams to operate within that territory. In cases where this has occurred, an indemnification fee is paid to the club already operating in the market.

Generally speaking, franchises are independently owned and managed, and come together to create a joint venture to coordinate league activities. Representatives of teams comprise a league board of directors, while a commissioner acts as the chief operating officer for the league. It is important to note that the commissioner is an employee of the owners, who control the real power in league operations. Some leagues have been organized as single entities, with virtually all power centralized through the league office. In this case, teams are not independent entities and serve more as divisions of the league business entity. As a result, the commissioner wields more power in single-entity leagues as teams and players can be added or removed at the discretion of the league office.[6]

LEAGUE RATIONALE FOR SHARING REVENUES

As mentioned above, the league is very interested in the success of all league teams. In other industries, competition will usually eliminate weaker firms. However, in the case of professional sports, teams have an interest in the health and viability of all league clubs in order to preserve both the uncertainty of outcome, and to maximize spectator interest for the league as a whole.[7] In other words, weak performing teams decrease interest in games and reduce overall revenues. For this reason, leagues will seek to share revenue among clubs in order to assist weaker teams and preserve competitive balance.[8] According to the former owner of the NFL Dallas Cowboys, Tex Schramm:

> If [any owner] can do what he feels he must, there's no structure at all. Sports leagues must be able to make rules and structure to live by. You take that away and there's no league. Competition within a league must be contrived, not natural. To compete on an equal basis you need to make that contrivance possible.[9]

Another reason why teams share revenues is to maximize profits, where the existence of revenue-sharing serves to keep player salaries lower. This occurs because revenue-sharing reduces the value of winning for individual teams.[10] By sharing revenues with weaker teams, it is hoped that they will be more likely to spend more to improve the quality of their clubs. At the same time, it may make richer teams more reluctant to spend on players, as they will have to share any increases in revenues that occur as a result of improved performance and increased revenues. If this occurs, competitive balance may increase.[11] Leagues such as the NFL have also tried to influence competitive balance by adjusting league schedules so that weaker teams face weaker opponents and stronger teams face stronger opponents.[12]

Revenue-sharing also seeks to address the small-market problem in leagues. Teams in larger markets usually have financial advantages over those in smaller ones, as they have larger populations to draw upon to increase gate attendance and television viewership, and a larger corporate base to sell premium seating and sponsorships to. In addition, teams in larger markets have a greater incentive to pay for players, as the marginal revenue generated by a win is greater in a larger market.[13] By sharing revenues, small-market teams can acquire talent to become more competitive.[14] The small-market problem has been exacerbated in the NHL, which has a number of Canada-based franchises. Fluctuations in the Canadian dollar, and higher income taxes, property taxes, and facility rental costs have led to even more disparity in revenues among league clubs in the past.[15]

In sum, leagues have a vested interest in the competitive and financial success of all league clubs. To address this, leagues share revenues among teams in order to promote competitive balance and to reduce player costs. However, the relationship between teams and the parent league remains a complex one. The following section briefly reviews how each league has chosen to share revenues.

HOW REVENUES ARE SHARED

Leagues generate revenues through two primary means—the live gate and media revenues.[16] Typically, nationally negotiated media revenues—such as ESPN's agreement with the NFL—are pooled and distributed equally, whereas each of the four major leagues has varying ways of sharing (or not sharing) gate and other local revenues. Leagues have been able to circumvent antitrust law in order to negotiate broadcasting contracts with television networks due to the Sport Broadcasting Act (1961). In doing so, leagues can get various television networks to engage in a bidding war to increase revenues, which are then distributed to individual franchises.[17] The ways in which the individual leagues have approached revenue-sharing are described in greater detail below.

The NFL shares more revenues than the other three major leagues. One reason is that television contracts are all negotiated and shared at the league level—there are no local TV revenues. Much of the success of the NFL's revenue-sharing practices has been attributed to the foresight of former commissioner Alvin "Pete" Rozelle and the NFL owners during the 1960s and 1970s, which were able to recognize that pooling revenues would benefit the league as a whole in the long run. Rozelle said:

> We were able to do it, because the owners thought League. The Maras in New York, Dan Reeves in LA, and George Halas in Chicago—the three dominant markets—agreed to share TV equally with the others, which was a major concession. They were wise enough to see the long term and they've been rewarded. All the franchises have seen their money increase from television as a consequence and the League as a whole has remained strong. All of the franchises have remained viable and have the means to compete with the rest of the League.[18]

In the early years of the NFL, a standard league agreement saw visiting teams guaranteed $1000 by the home club, with visitors receiving 40 percent of gate revenues after an initial 15 percent was deducted for stadium expenses.[19] Later, gate revenues were divided using a 60–40 home-visitor split. In 2001 the NFL amended its gate-sharing rules, placing 40 percent of gate revenues into a common pool to be shared equally among all teams. The remaining 60 percent was divided equally by the home and visiting clubs.[20]

Today approximately 60 percent of league revenues is from national television, and 20 percent is from ticket revenues. Overall, teams receive approximately $125 million per year from the NFL's central fund (shared revenues from media, licensing, and sponsorships). Most recently, the NFL has created an additional $430 million revenue-sharing pool that will be in effect until 2009. Owners who buy into the league will not have access to any funds from the pool. Around 15 NFL clubs were projected to qualify, on the condition that their player costs represented more than 65 percent of their revenue. However, high-revenue teams have raised some concerns about the eligibility of teams to receive payouts, and have suggested that low-revenue teams show that they have made a good faith effort to increase their revenues before they are eligible to receive a distribution.[21]

A recent trend in revenue-sharing among NFL teams has been through the league's willingness to assist teams in building new stadiums. Through December 2006 the NFL's G-3 program had committed $1.116 billion to

TABLE 4.1
G-3 Disbursements to Fund NFL Facilities

Date	Franchise	Amount (millions US$)
May 1999	Denver	50
May 1999	New England	150
May 1999	Philadelphia	150
May 2000	Detroit	100
May 2000	Seattle	50
October 2000	Chicago	100
October 2001	Green Bay	13
October 2001	Arizona	50
June 2005	Dallas	76.5
June 2005	Indianapolis	34
December 2006	New York Jets/New York Giants	300

Source: Adapted from data at *Sports Business Journal.*

help fund the construction or renovation of stadiums. Table 4.1 contains a list of G-3 disbursements since the program began in the late 1990s. Most recently, NFL owners voted 30–2 to allocate $300 million toward the $1.2-billion construction costs of a new stadium to be shared by both New York teams, the Giants and Jets.[22]

When the National League first started play in 1876, gate receipts were split evenly between the home and visiting clubs.[23] Eventually, gate receipts were divided in the American League using an 80–20, home-visitor split, and visiting teams in the National League received about 56 cents for every ticket sold.[24] MLB has revamped its revenue-sharing in recent years to increase the amount of revenues allocated to smaller-market teams. Major League Baseball remains the only major-league sport that does not have a salary cap, although it has developed a luxury tax system.

National television contracts have been shared in MLB, and in 1997 a luxury tax was first adopted. The tax threshold is established as a flat number—teams whose payrolls exceed that amount must pay a percentage of every dollar over the threshold as a tax. This amount varies depending upon how many times the team has exceeded the threshold in the past, as teams that repeatedly exceed the cap are penalized more. For example, the threshold was set at $117 million in 2003, $120.5 million in 2004, $128 million in 2005, and $136.5 million in 2006. The amount will rise to $178.5 million by 2011. In 2003, the tax was 17.5 percent for first-time "offenders." However, the threshold is much higher than most payrolls—the Yankees were the only team to exceed the threshold in 2003.[25]

In addition, a plan was adopted where each team contributed 20 percent of its net local revenues to a pool. Seventy-five percent of the pool was then divided equally among league clubs, with the remaining 25 percent allocated to the seven franchises with the lowest net local revenues.[26] The amount of net local revenues (NLR) shared was increased to 34 percent following the negotiation of the 2002 MLB collective bargaining agreement. Under the new plan, each club is taxed at 34 percent of its NLR, which is then distributed equally to league clubs (called the "straight pool" plan). This plan accounts for about 70 percent of revenues shared. Then, revenues are shared from national revenues, such as television rights, through a "split pool." In the latter, taxes are levied on teams above the median in revenue and distributed to teams below in proportion to how far below the median each team sits.[27]

NBA teams share national television and merchandise revenues. However, gate receipts are not shared between league clubs.[28] The league features a "soft" salary cap that penalizes teams (a luxury tax) for exceeding the cap. The salary cap for the 2007/08 NBA season was set at $55.63 million and is determined by Basketball Related Income (BRI).[29] Teams that exceed a payroll of $67.865 million must pay a luxury tax of $1 for every dollar that exceeds that amount. This provides a deterrent for teams to exceed the cap and also serves as a form of revenue-sharing by distributing revenues from teams exceeding the cap to teams that cannot afford high payrolls. During the 2006/07 season, five teams exceeded the cap. For example, the New York Knicks paid a luxury tax of over $45 million for the 2006/07 season. This is an anomaly, as the second highest-paying franchise was Dallas, which paid out over $7 million. The remaining twenty-five teams whose payrolls remained under the cap received one-thirtieth of the luxury tax, which amounted to approximately $1.9 million per team.[30]

In early 2007 the NBA began exploring reconfiguring its revenue-sharing program and increasing the funds available.[31] A comprehensive market analysis of each franchise has been undertaken by an independent business consulting firm since 2003, in order to determine the distribution of revenues to franchises considered to be in "competitively disadvantaged markets." These teams then receive revenues left over from the league's escrow fund of player salaries, which have typically amounted to $2 to $6 million per team. However, the NBA was approached by several team owners regarding reexamining this process.[32]

Like the NBA, the NHL shares national television contracts and licensing revenues, but does not share local gate revenues. The NHL differs from the other three major professional sports leagues, in that it truly has a North American presence with six franchises located in Canada. During the mid- to late 1990s, the weak Canadian dollar hurt these clubs, who paid player salaries out in U.S. funds. As a result, the NHL created the Supplemental Currency Equalization Plan. Canada-based teams in the bottom half of league revenues were eligible to receive up to US$5 million if they either had revenues that were 80 percent of the league average or sold a defined number of season tickets, skyboxes, and other in-arena advertising. In addition, Canadian teams were eligible to receive financial assistance to match contract offers made to their players by U.S.-based teams. The most recent collective bargaining agreement also features a new revenue-sharing formula, where teams in the bottom half of league revenues in markets of fewer than 2.5 million are eligible to receive funds from the league.[33]

AGENCY THEORY

The discussion above examined the motivations behind revenue-sharing practices in professional team sports in North America and the ways in which individual leagues have elected to pool and disperse these revenues. However, some fundamental agency problems exist within the sports league model which has led to behavior by individual teams that has compromised the interests of the league as a whole. In order to examine this further, the following section uses agency theory to better understand some of the inherent conflicts of interest within professional sports leagues.

Agency theory has its roots in organizational economics; an agency relationship involves a contractual agreement between a principal and an agent (or agents).[34] Typically, the agent performs some type of service on behalf of the principal. Within this context, it is assumed that conflicts arise within the principal-agent relationship because the interests of the two parties can diverge.

In order to deter divergent behavior, an implicit or explicit contract is negotiated between the agent (in this case the team) and principal (the professional league).[35] In this case, a single-principal, multiple-agent relationship exists. The "contract" can be either implicit or explicit; an implicit contract might be the mutual agreement of teams to unite with other clubs to produce the league product on behalf of the league. In contrast, an explicit contract would be the terms set out by a league's constitution and bylaws that determine the conditions under which the teams interact. This is critical, as each agent's output is directly affected by the output of the other teams.[36]

Although leagues are typically organized as nonprofit organizations, their goal is to act entrepreneurially to maximize the combined wealth of all teams. An agency problem arises when the entrepreneur is the agent and not the principal.[37] While some entrepreneurial team behavior may result in an increase in wealth to the league as a whole, others will result in an increase in wealth to the agent at the expense of the league. The league, as principal, then has two ways to address this problem. First, it can monitor agent behavior in order to deter opportunism. Second, it can contract on the outcome of agent behavior.[38] These two solutions are not mutually exclusive; the degree to which either will be pursued will be dependent upon the cost-effectiveness of each in any given principal-agent scenario.[39]

In addition, agency theorists suggest that sharing in the total wealth will reduce diverging interests; quite simply, interests are aligned when increasing the profitability of the league as a whole results in increases in profitability of each individual club. As a result, revenue-sharing would seem to be an appropriate mechanism to reduce opportunism for sports leagues as each team would have a greater interest in the financial well-being of other clubs. Leagues attempt to regulate the behavior of individual teams through league executive committees (LECs), where each individual club is represented. Rules and decisions are then voted upon; depending upon the league and the rule involved, decisions by the executive committee typically require a majority or greater in order to be passed. Thus, a sports league's executive committee acts as a corporate board that is chaired by the league's commissioner. The LEC will attempt to align the interests of the different franchises in order to avoid opportunism, maximize league-wide revenues, and maintain the integrity of league contests.

Despite the efforts of leagues through their respective LECs, teams can and do act opportunistically in a way that furthers the interests of the franchise to the detriment of the league as a whole. Perhaps the most prominent example of this occurs where teams relocate to new cities. In many ways, the threat of relocation benefits all league clubs; by keeping the number of franchises artificially low and maintaining a number of markets interested in acquiring a league club, existing teams are able to extract more lucrative lease and other facility agreements within their existing communities. However, this works where the league can oversee—and approve of—franchise movement. For example, an existing club may be interested in moving to a new market in order to generate greater revenues. However, the new market might be an ideal expansion site, which can generate a large expansion fee that would be divided amongst league clubs. In addition, the relocation of a team might undermine the interest in, or reputation of, the league as a whole, as the LEC seeks stability among its franchises and does not want to alienate fans in existing markets.

Notable examples where this has occurred are found in franchise moves in the National Football League over the past twenty-five years. In the NFL, the Raiders moved from Oakland to Los Angeles and back to Oakland, the Rams from Los Angeles to St. Louis, and the Cleveland team to Baltimore. The Raiders and Rams moves are particularly troublesome from the NFL's perspective, as they have resulted in a void in Los Angeles for NFL football, the second-largest television market in the United States. St. Louis agreed to pay the league a $29-million relocation fee; however, the absence of a team in the Los Angeles market makes the television rights to NFL games less desirable from the perspective of television networks, and these revenues are also divided evenly among teams.

INHERENT AGENCY PROBLEMS IN SPORTS LEAGUES

This section describes characteristics of the sports industry that will lead to additional agency problems. With increased revenue-sharing, small-market (i.e., weaker revenue) teams may lose the incentive to improve their team's performance. In this case, they will rely on larger-market teams to generate revenues, which are then allocated to the weaker teams through revenue-sharing. Profit-maximizing weaker teams will then avoid increasing payrolls to improve team performance and improve competitive balance.[40] In doing so, the weaker team's share of revenues remains the same, but that team will make greater profits by spending less on playing talent.[41] To discourage this behavior, leagues with salary caps will also set a minimum amount teams must spend on payroll. From an agency theory perspective, the above scenario creates a problem between the team and the league. The league seeks to maximize league-wide profits. However, the weaker-market team may compromise this in trying to maximize individual franchise profits. In fielding a weaker club, demand for the league product may be diminished as teams are perennially out of contention for a league championship.

To see how this has occurred in practice, consider again the discussion of revenue-sharing in MLB, where in 2006 the richest thirteen clubs subsidized the weakest seventeen clubs. Eight of the latter teams received in excess of $20 million. However, it would appear that several weaker teams are not spending on playing talent to improve their club's performance. For example the Toronto Blue Jays received $33 million in shared revenues, and the team spent $72 million on their team payroll; clearly the Jays are reinvesting their shared revenues on playing talent. In contrast, the Florida Marlins spent only $15 million on payroll despite receiving $31 million in shared revenue. Thus, while the New York Yankees have a payroll that nears $200 million annually, five of the seventeen clubs receiving shared revenues have invested less than $40 million on payroll.

This suggests that the revenue-sharing plan in MLB discourages low-revenue teams from improving performance (and therefore increasing competitive balance). As a result, a new program has two straight pool components; the first lowers the "luxury" tax to 31 percent (based on NLR) and accounts for 65 percent of shared funds. The second component uses NLR from previous seasons to project NLR, which does not vary with local revenues. This provides an incentive for teams to increase local revenues, as they will not have to share them with other clubs. In 2006 $326 million was shared from this pool, with the amount projected at $350 million in 2007. Teams such as the Yankees pay in excess of $70 million, the Red Sox over $50 million, and the Chicago Cubs over $30 million. In total, the top thirteen teams subsidized the bottom seventeen, with Tampa Bay, Toronto, Florida, and Kansas City each receiving $30 million or more.[42]

In basketball, similar concerns have resulted in proposed changes to the revenue-sharing plan for the NBA. Recently, eight low-revenue teams have requested that the NBA increase its revenue-sharing to assist these teams. In addition, to avoid having teams simply collect shared revenues and not improve team performance, a formula has been devised which grades the effectiveness of each team's business operations and then distributes revenues based on those teams that are considered play in disadvantaged markets. In other words, teams that are losing money but are not performing to the potential of their respective markets may not receive any shared revenues.[43]

Another agency problem that arises from revenue-sharing relates to teams reporting revenues. With MLB sharing 31 percent of net local revenues, franchises now have an incentive to "hide" local revenues to avoid having to share them with other league clubs. This leads to related-party transactions where revenues are underreported or favor other business interests that the franchise owner might possess. A notable example of this occurs with the Tribune Corporation, which owns the Chicago Cubs and TV station WGN. When WGN enters into a contract to televise Cubs games, it benefits the Tribune Corporation to undervalue this agreement so that WGN makes more profits (which do not have to be shared). As a result, critics have noted that the agreement between the Cubs and WGN is for a much lower amount that would be found if the two entities were owned by different parties.[44] Similarly, the Florida Marlins reported losses of $30 million in 1997, the year that team won the World Series. However, revenues from luxury suites, naming rights, parking, merchandising, and concessions were all attributed to the stadium and not the team (which was also owned by the same party). Revenues from these sources were valued at $36 million and were not deemed part of net local revenues.[45]

THE SPORTSMAN EFFECT

Another issue that can significantly undermine the ability of a league to maximize revenues is the "sportsman effect." In many cases, team owners are not interested in simply maximizing profits; rather, some owners would rather see their teams win at the expense of some profitability, or even go so far as to spend to win at all costs. The sportsman effect occurs where an owner sacrifices financial value by expanding the talent of the club beyond the team's profit-maximizing level.[46] This can cause significant problems for other teams when overall salaries escalate as some owners overpay to assemble winning teams. "Thus the universal problem in professional sports leagues is to set up and police a structure that maximizes joint profits in spite of the interests of individual owners in either individual profit maximization or in utility maximization."[47]

In this scenario, the league must work with member clubs that act as either profit maximizers or utility maximizers. Unlike profit maximizers, utility maximizers may be willing to bear long-term financial losses, pay players more that they are worth, and even stockpile more players than are necessary. In general, team owners likely fall somewhere on a continuum of profit maximizing to utility maximizing—most owners would be willing to sacrifice some profits to win a championship. By way of comparison, it has been suggested that teams in North America are more profit maximizing, while European professional sports teams are more utility maximizing.[48]

The fact that some teams are utility maximizers may actually help increase competitive balance. For example, with extensive revenue-sharing, a profit-maximizing weaker revenue franchise would have the incentive to keep payrolls low and maximize profits, but this would lead to competitive imbalance due to a consistently weak franchise. In contrast, a utility-maximizing weak-revenue team that receives revenue-sharing will be more likely to invest that shared money to improve the quality of the team, and thus improve competitive balance.[49]

THE LARGE-MARKET PROBLEM

A common concern across sports leagues remains the prominence of large-market teams, who tend to dominate leagues in terms of profitability and winning. All things being equal, large-market teams can generate more revenues than smaller-market teams, which can lead to competitive imbalance if the large-market teams invest in playing talent. Historically, teams in larger markets win more often than smaller-market teams. As this chapter has shown, revenue-sharing seeks to have larger markets subsidize smaller ones in order for the latter to become more competitive, which is in the best interests of the league as a whole. However, depending on how the revenue is shared (luxury tax, shared local revenues) and at what levels, large-market teams will still have an incentive to spend more on playing talent: "Every single unit of talent hired produced winning that was more valuable to the large-market team. Therefore, it hires more talent and wins more. It is this important feature that leads us to the conclusion that competitive imbalance is a fact of life as long as there is revenue imbalance."[50]

In addition, despite being taxed and sharing revenues with smaller markets, the need to accumulate talent in order to maximize individual franchise profits may drive large-market teams to continue to build winning teams. Because teams in larger markets can generate more revenues than smaller markets from each win, large-market clubs will continue to stockpile talent. This occurs in MLB, where in the absence of a salary cap large-market teams have spent ten times as much on player salaries as small-market teams. As a result, a situation called the "Yankee paradox" arises, where "the accumulation of talent in the singular pursuit of maximum profit by individual clubs may lead to significant externalities and a self-defeating dominance of the league by large-market clubs."[51]

In addition, even where salary caps limit the amount that large-market clubs can spend on players, there will still be a tendency for players to migrate to larger markets, where the players can earn greater revenues from endorsements and other off-field activities.[52] This is exacerbated by the fact that players may not be profit maximizers and may want to play for teams that have a greater chance of winning championships, which not coincidentally tend to be in larger markets. Finally, because larger-market clubs generate more revenues from winning, large-market teams may have an incentive to violate or circumvent cap rules in order to acquire players.[53]

Larger-market clubs may also have an incentive to circumvent league licensing and sponsorship agreements. In some case, owners of popular teams feel that shared revenues are not commensurate with the total revenues that the franchise generates for the league. An example might be in the sale of licensed apparel, where some teams sell a disproportionate number of jerseys and other apparel. In addition, these same teams may feel that they are losing out on other local revenues as a result of league-wide contracts. This occurs when teams receive a share of revenues from businesses that contract to become "official" league sponsors. Prominent examples include the New York Yankees' $92-million agreement with Adidas and the Dallas Cowboys' agreement with Pepsi to give the soft drink company official pouring rights at Texas Stadium, home of the Cowboys. This undermined the NFL, who had agreed to a lucrative pact with Coca Cola to be the official soft drink of the NFL.[54] As a result, Cowboys owner Jerry Jones sought to maximize his team's revenues at the expense of the league as a whole.

CONCLUSION

This chapter has explored revenue-sharing in professional team sports in North America. Leagues can justify revenue-sharing on the grounds that each team has the interests of other teams in mind as they come together to produce the league product.[55] However, leagues have an incentive for larger market teams to win more often, as this increases the network television audience and therefore the value of the television contract. Thus, when leagues consider policies that affect the location of teams and the strength of franchises, they will tend to favor larger markets.[56] However, leagues recognize that the long-term interest in their product will depend to a great degree upon competitive balance.

As this chapter has shown, interactions between the league and individual teams are also influenced by the degree to which teams are utility maximizers or profit maximizers. "Within the typical team-and-league structure the teams have individual interests (depending on the owner these might lean toward profit maximization or toward win maximization) and the league has a collective interest in overall profit maximization."[57] When we consider the issue of utility versus profit maximization, and small versus large markets, we see that competitive balance will be highest where small-market teams are utility maximizers and large-market teams are profit maximizers.[58] In this scenario, small-market teams may be willing to spend more to field a competitive team, while large-market teams will not drive up player salaries by overspending. However, there is no reason to believe that team owners in smaller markets are likely to be utility maximizing to a greater degree than those found in larger markets.

The NFL generates the most revenues of the four major sports and is widely considered the most successful financially. It has the most comprehensive revenue-sharing program, and has also implemented measures to increase competitive balance, such as an imbalanced playing schedule. Teams from smaller markets tend to win the Super Bowl more frequently than do teams from smaller markets in other leagues.[59] MLB has seen increased parity along with increased revenue-sharing in recent seasons. In fact, there were seven different World Series champions over seven years from 2000 through 2006.

In basketball, the NBA recently announced a plan to increase revenue-sharing, with a new supplemental pool to provide teams up to a maximum of $5 million annually. The total amount available will be $30 million. In the previous year, the amount available from the luxury tax and escrow fund was $14.8 million, which was distributed to eight teams.[60] The NHL has increased its revenue-sharing with the advent of the most recent collective bargaining agreement in 2005.

Clearly, the four leagues recognize how increasing revenue-sharing can assist low-revenue teams in remaining financially viable, and allow them to compete for players. However, incentives must be created so that profit-maximizing small-market teams do not simply realize greater profits through revenue-sharing and avoid trying to improve the quality of their teams. This certainly is an agency problem where the interests of the team and the league diverge, despite the fact that both league and team are profit maximizing. As a result, each league will continue to experiment with revenue-sharing models with the hopes of maximizing overall league revenues while acknowledging that individual clubs will have varying market sizes and goals.

NOTES

1. T. A. Piraino Jr., "A Proposal for the Antitrust Regulation of Professional Sports," *Boston University Law Review* 79 (1999): 923.
2. Gerald W. Scully, *The Market Structure of Sports* (Chicago: University of Chicago Press, 1995), 22.
3. G. R. Roberts, "Professional Sports and the Antitrust Laws," in *The Business of Sports,* ed. P. D. Staudohar and J. A. Mangan (Urbana: University of Illinois Press, 1991), 144; P. Downward and A. Dawson, *The Economics of Professional Teams Sports* (London: Routledge, 2000), 31, 37.
4. John Barnes, *Sport and the Law in Canada,* 3rd ed. (Toronto: Butterworths, 1996), 181.
5. G. D. Daly, "The Baseball Player's Labor Market Revisited," in *Diamonds Are Forever: The Business of Baseball,* ed. P. M. Sommers (Washington, D.C.: Brookings Institution Press, 1992), 17, 18.
6. R. G. Noll, "The Organization of Sports Leagues," *Oxford Review of Economic Policy* 19 (2003): 540.
7. P. J. Sloane, "The Regulation of Professional Team Sports," in *Transatlantic Sport: The Comparative Economics of North American and European Sports,* ed. C. P. Barros, M. Ibrahimo, and S. Szymanski (Cheltenham: Edward Elgar, 2002), 51.
8. Piraino, "Proposal for the Antitrust Regulation," 931.
9. David Harris, *The League: The Rise and Decline of the NFL* (New York: Bantam Books, 1986), 598.
10. J. Vrooman, "The Economics of American Sports Leagues," *Scottish Journal of Political Economy* 47 (2000): 373.
11. Andrew Zimbalist, "Sport as Business," *Oxford Review of Economic Policy* 19 (2003): 507 ("In addition, gate-sharing has unexpected negative consequences for players. Because it is winning-elastic and diminishes the marginal revenue product of each player for each team, gate-sharing induces profit-maximizing teams to reduce their salary offers to players."); Marc Lavoie, "Economics and Sport," in *Handbook of Sport Studies,* ed. J. Coakley and E. Dunning (London: Sage, 2000), 165.
12. Noll, "Organization of Sports Leagues," 548.
13. Scully, *Market Structure of Sports,* 83–84.

14. Lavoie, "Economics and Sport," 164. An alternative is to have a salary cap, which reduces the ability of larger market clubs to outbid smaller markets for players. It has been argued that, despite the best efforts of leagues to influence player movement and influence competitive balance, that players will eventually be distributed as they would in a free market. This notion was pioneered by economist Simon Rottenberg.

15. D. Whitson, J. Harvey, and M. Lavoie, "Government Subsidization of Professional Sports Franchises: A Risky Business," in *The Commercialization of Sport*, ed. T. Slack (London: Routledge, 2004), 75.

16. Other revenue sources include the sales of licensed merchandise, but this figure is not as high as the aforementioned two sources of revenues

17. A. Zimbalist, *Baseball and Billions* (New York: BasicBooks, 1992), 152.

18. Harris, *The League,* 14–15.

19. R. Fort and J. Quirk, "Cross-subsidization, Incentives, and Outcomes in Professional Team Sports Leagues," *Journal of Economic Literature* 33 (1995): 1286.

20. D. Howard and J. Crompton, *Financing Sport,* 2nd ed. (Morgantown, W.V.: Fitness Information Technology, 2004), 41).

21. Daniel Kaplan, "NFL Execs Optimistic on Revenue Sharing," *Sports Business Journal,* August 1, 2005, 3; Andrew Zimbalist, "Lesson in Capitalism Would Be Instructive for Some NFL Owners," *Sports Business Journal,* March 19, 2007, 56; Daniel Kaplan, "Exception Could Hurt Value of Some Teams," *Sports Business Journal,* April 2, 2007, 26.

22. Daniel Kaplan, "NFL Owners Give $300M for N.Y. Stadium," *Sports Business Journal,* December 11, 2006, 3.

23. Fort and Quirk, "Cross-subsidization, Incentives, and Outcomes," 1286.

24. D. Marburger, "Baseball's New Collective Bargaining Agreement: How Will It Affect the National Pastime?" in *Sports Economics: Current Research,* ed. J. Fizel, E. Gustafson and L. Hadley (Westport, Conn.: Praeger, 1999), 195.

25. R. A. Kaplan, "The NBA Luxury Tax Model: A Misguided Regulatory Scheme," *Columbia Law Review* 104 (2004): 1627, 1630.

26. Marburger, "Baseball's New Collective Bargaining Agreement," 196.

27. Andrew Zimbalist, "New MLB Labor Deal Corrects Earlier Flaws, Lays Foundation for Growth," *Sport Business Journal,* November 6, 2006, 27.

28. John Lombardo, "NBA Set to Boost Revenue Sharing, Adjust Formula," *Sports Business Journal,* February 12, 2007, 1.

29. The NBA also has caps set on individual player salaries.

30. Cleveland Cavaliers, "NBA Announces Salary Cap for 2007–2008," http://cavscourt.wordpress.com/2007/07/11/nba-announces-salary-cap-for-2007-2008 (accessed March 15, 2008); Marc Stein, "Knicks Top List of Teams to Pay Luxury Tax," ESPN.com, http://sports.espn.go.com/espn/print?id=2935728&type=story (accessed March 15, 2008).

31. Lombardo, "NBA Set to Boose Revenue Sharing," 1.

32. John Lombardo, "NBA Taking Fresh Look at Revenue Split: Eight Owners Asked Stern for change," *Sports Business Journal,* December 11, 2006, 1.

33. Whitson, Harvey and Lavoie, "Government Subsidization of Professional Sports Franchises, 81; A. Cocco and J. C. H. Jones, "On Going South: The Economics of Survival and Relocation of Small Market NHL Franchises in Canada," *Applied Economics*

29 (1997): 1549; M. J. Greenberg and J. T. Gray, *The Stadium Game* (Milwaukee: National Sports Law Institute, 1996), 11; Lombardo, "NBA Taking Fresh Look," 1.

34. See M. C. Jensen and W. H. Meckling, "Theory of the Firm: Managerial Behaviour and Ownership Structure," *Journal of Financial Economics* 3 (1976): 305–360.

35. See C. W. L. Hill and T. M. Jones, "Stakeholder-agency Theory," *Journal of Management Studies* 29 (1992): 131–154.

36. See S. E. Atkinson, L. R. Stanley and J. Tschirhart, "Revenue Sharing as an Incentive in an Agency Problem: An Example from the National Football League," *RAND Journal of Economics* 19 (1988): 27–43.

37. G. R. Jones and J. E. Butler, "Managing Internal Corporate Entrepreneurship: An Agency Theory Perspective," *Journal of Management* 18 (1992): 733–749.

38. See K. M. Eisenhardt, "Agency Theory: An Assessment and Review," *Academy of Management Review*, 14, (1989): 57–74.

39. See M. Beccerra and A. K. Gupta, "Trust Within the Organization: Integrating the Trust Literature with Agency and Transaction Costs Economics," *Public Administration Quarterly* 23 (1999): 177–203.

40. Barros, Ibrahimo, and Szymanski, eds., *Translatlantic Sport*, 5.

41. R. D. Fort, *Sport Economics* (Upper Saddle River, N.J.: Prentice-Hall, 2003), 160.

42. Zimbalist, "New MLB Labor Deal," 27; Eric Fisher, "Fresh Approach to Talks Keeps MLB on the Field," *Sport Business Journal*, October 30, 2006, 1.

43. Lombardo, "NBA Set to Boost Revenue Sharing," 1.

44. Andrew Zimbalist, *May the Best Team Win: Baseball Economics and Public Policy* (Washington, D.C.: Brookings Institution Press, 2003), 62.

45. Howard and Crompton, *Financing Sport*, 33.

46. Vrooman, "Economics of American Sports Leagues," 386.

47. R. Sandy, P. J. Sloane, and M. S. Rosentraub, *The Economics of Sport: An International Perspective* (New York: Palgrave MacMillan, 2004), 25.

48. Ibid.; R. G. Sheehan, *Keeping Score: The Economics of Big Time Sports* (South Bend, Ind.: Diamond Communications, 1996), 8; Lavoie, "Economics and Sport," 162.

49. Zimbalist, "Sport as Business," 506.

50. Fort, *Sport Economics*, 26, 191.

51. Vrooman, "Economics of American Sports Leagues," 370.

52. See ibid.

53. Fort and Quirk, "Cross-subsidization, Incentives, and Outcomes," 1281.

54. B. L. Grusd, "The Antitrust Implications of Professional Sports' League-wide Licensing and Merchandising Arrangements," *Virginia Journal of Sports and the Law* 1 (1999): 15.

55. Sheehan, *Keeping Score*, 198–199.

56. R. G. Noll, "Professional Basketball: Business and Economic Perspectives," in *The Business of Sports*, ed. Staudohar and Mangan, 33.

57. Sandy, Sloane, and Rosentraub, *Economics of Sports*, 25.

58. Zimbalist, "Sport as Business," 506.

59. Sandy, Sloane and Rosentraub, *Economics of Sports*, 170–171.

60. Lombardo, "NBA Set," 1.

Five

New Developments in Stadium Financing

Dennis Zimmerman

Debate over the public financing of stadiums for professional sports teams has been ongoing for the last fifteen years. The economics literature suggests a stadium does not generate sufficient economic development and incremental tax revenue to pay for the public's share of stadium cost (Coates and Humphreys, 1999, and Baade, 1994). As a result, conflict arises over whose taxes will be raised or which public services reduced to pay the public subsidy. Should those costs be borne by sports fans or nonfans, high-income or low-income citizens, wages or capital income, city or suburbs?

As a general principle, when many benefits of a publicly provided service accrue to identifiable individuals and groups, and collectively consumed benefits are of secondary importance, it is best to utilize the benefit principle of taxation as a guide to financing that service. Each person's tax payment should be a function of the benefits received. Not only is that thought to be equitable, it is also efficient because relating the price a person pays to the benefits received discourages excess demand and over consumption of the service.

Professional sports stadiums seem to fit that description. The direct beneficiaries include fans who attend the games and watch them on television; owners and players who divide the rents provided by the team's monopoly; and some related businesses whose property values rise or whose customer demand increases. Proponents argue that civic pride is an important collective consumption benefit, but the great majority of cities that have professional sports teams already have substantial civic pride and the incremental intangible benefit from a team has not been measured.

General sales taxes, income taxes, property taxes, lotteries, rental car charges, and hotel/motel taxes are not well targeted to taxing only the groups receiving the direct benefits. Ticket taxes, personal seat license fees, excise taxes on food and souvenirs sold at the stadium, special taxing jurisdictions, and assorted franchise fees are better. Unfortunately, state and local governments do not often utilize the benefit principle of taxation to structure the financing of their share of stadium costs. They use such revenue sources as general sales taxes, car rental and hotel/motel charges, and lottery revenue. Furthermore, they often apply the taxes only to residents and businesses in the central city in which the stadium is located, even though many of the fans live in suburbs beyond the reach of the city's tax authority.

Several factors account for the willingness of local communities to subsidize stadiums and to finance that subsidy with general tax revenue. First, professional sports leagues are monopolies. As such, they maintain excess demand for their franchises by restricting entry into the league and suppressing the number of franchises. Cities must bid against each other for one of those franchises, and that price is their willingness to pay the cost of the team's major capital cost, a stadium. Second, the debate over the economic impact of a stadium is generally misleading and one-sided. Proponents (call them the dominant political coalition) argue the stadium will pay for itself and utilize misleading pseudo-economic studies to justify their position (Compton, 1995). That coalition is well financed because its relatively few members expect to receive benefits that greatly exceed their cost. The opposing coalition is composed of many more people who each would receive very small benefits relative to his or her costs and, not surprisingly, usually is poorly financed. And third, almost every stadium is financed with tax-exempt bonds whose interest costs are subsidized by the federal government, and the federal tax law that controls access to that subsidy is structured in a way that discourages the use of the benefit principle of taxation.

The monopoly and coalition issues are not easily remedied. The former issue would require a change in the antitrust exemption for Major League Baseball (MLB) and a reexamination of antitrust enforcement policy for all professional sports leagues. The latter issue would require local governments to reexamine and adjust the legislative and administrative processes that control stadium projects. In contrast, the perverse incentive structure of the tax-exempt bond law could be corrected quite easily with a few changes to the federal income tax code.

Accordingly, this chapter focuses on the role of tax-exempt bonds in stadium finance. It is divided into four parts. The first part explains tax-exempt bonds: their economic rationale, how they are structured, and how the subsidy is provided. The second section provides a history of the federal tax law and relevant regulations as they pertain to the use of tax-exempt bonds for stadium finance, and explains how its incentive structure evolved from 1968 through 2006. The third section describes how the 2006 developments might be viewed as good or poor policy depending upon one's policy objective. The fourth section suggests a series of changes to the federal tax-exempt bond law that might control the federal revenue loss and encourage state and local governments to utilize the benefit principle of taxation to finance their share of the cost for professional sports stadiums.

THE SUBSIDY PROVIDED BY TAX-EXEMPT BONDS

Section 103 of the Internal Revenue Code (the Code) exempts the interest income on debt issued by state and local governments from federal income taxation. The exemption causes the interest rate on tax-exempt bonds to be lower than the interest rate on taxable bonds of equivalent risk and maturity that are issued by corporations and the federal government. The explanation for that lower interest rate is straightforward. A potential bond purchaser focuses on the after-tax return earned on a bond. Purchase of a taxable bond paying 8 percent interest by a taxpayer with a 25 percent federal marginal tax rate provides that taxpayer with a 6 percent after-tax return. That taxpayer is indifferent between that taxable bond and a bond issued by a state and local government with a 6 percent interest rate on which no tax is paid. In effect, the state-local government can issue its bonds at the lower interest rate because the federal government provides the bond purchaser with a reduced tax liability to compensate for the 2 percent difference in the interest rate.

Some argue tax-exempt bonds are necessary to satisfy claims of intergovernmental tax immunity and the Tenth Amendment of the U.S. Constitution, but the concept does have an economic rationale. Some of the benefits of a local or state government's construction of public facilities (such as for sewage waste treatment or a hospital) accrue to people outside the jurisdiction; that is, the benefits spill out of the jurisdiction. Since local taxpayers are reluctant to pay for those spillover benefits, state and local investment in capital facilities is likely to be too low. Thus, the subsidy's economic purpose is to encourage more investment in public facilities by compensating local taxpayers for the cost of providing benefits to those outside the jurisdiction.

The provision of any subsidy is accompanied by a persistent danger. Businesses and individuals whom legislators did not intend to subsidize have an incentive to try to take advantage of it. Economists call it rent seeking, and it is a primary cause of the unintended consequences that so frequently accompany well-intentioned government policies. This chapter tries to explain how a subsidy intended to reduce the cost to local taxpayers of providing collectively consumed public facilities has been used to finance billions of dollars of stadiums for privately owned franchises in professional sports leagues, most recently the issuance of more than a billion dollars of tax-exempt bonds for two baseball stadiums in New York City. It then discusses policy options to control that rent seeking that would simultaneously reduce the use of the subsidy and make the state and local financing packages for stadiums more faithful to the benefit principle of taxation.

HISTORY OF TAX-EXEMPT BONDS FOR PROFESSIONAL SPORTS STADIUMS

Since 1968, three different sets of tax rules have governed the use of tax-exempt bonds for financing professional sports stadiums. Those rules provide differing incentives and economic effects. This section provides a brief history of those bond rules. Zimmerman (1991) provides a more detailed history up through 1990.

1968 to 1986

Prior to 1968, the Code did not constrain state and local officials from issuing tax-exempt debt and using the proceeds to finance investment projects for individuals and privately owned businesses. Any constraints that existed arose from state and local constitutional and statutory restrictions, usually in the form of limits on outstanding debt as a share of the issuing jurisdiction's assessed property value or a requirement to submit proposed bond issues to voters for comment and approval. In the 1960s the volume of debt issued for private activities started to grow. Elected officials learned to make the debt service payments (principal and interest) on bonds dependent upon the revenue generated by the private facility being built rather than on general taxes, thereby reducing the effectiveness of the state and local constraints on bond issuance.[1] Those revenue bonds carried slightly higher interest rates than did general obligation bonds that pledged the tax capacity of the issuing government to pay for the debt service. However, the interest rate on a tax-exempt revenue bond was still considerably lower than the interest rates on taxable debt, and the use of the bonds for private purposes continued to grow.

Some state and local governments complained that those tax-exempt revenue bonds were driving up interest rates for general obligation tax-exempt debt issued to finance public facilities, and federal policymakers became increasingly concerned about the federal revenue loss and the role of state and local officials in allocating the nation's supply of savings. As a result, the Revenue and Expenditure Control Act of 1968 placed curbs on tax-exempt debt issued for private purposes.

The Act defined an industrial development bond (IDB) as one that had two characteristics. First, more than 25 percent of the bond proceeds was used by a nongovernmental entity. Second, more than 25 percent of debt service payments was paid directly or indirectly by property used in a trade or business.[2] Those percentage rules have come to be known as the private use test and the private security test. Bonds that exceeded both of those 25 percent limits were declared to be taxable and not eligible for tax exemption. Bonds for professional sports stadiums usually violated both those 25 percent rules: a privately owned team used 100 percent of the bond proceeds; and most of the debt service was paid from stadium-related revenue (property used in a trade or business) such as ticket taxes and sales taxes on food and souvenirs sold in the stadium. However, Congress provided a list of activities for which tax-exempt IDBs could be issued, and stadiums were on that list.

Allowing professional sports teams to finance their capital costs with tax-exempt IDBs did have two advantages. First, it meant that more than 25 percent of the debt service on those bonds (usually far more than 25 percent) was paid from stadium-related revenue which is likely to be paid by those who benefit directly from the stadium (owners, players, fans, some related businesses), thereby implementing the benefit principle of taxation. In effect, the cash flow from the stadium was used to pay principal and interest on the bonds. In contrast, the debt service on stadium bonds that exceeded the 25 percent use-of-proceeds test but did not exceed the 25 percent debt service test was financed at least 75 percent by generally applicable taxes such as income, sales, and property taxes that are paid by many people not receiving direct benefits from the stadium. Second, when debt service is paid from general governmental revenue, neither the principal nor the interest is paid with franchise-generated revenue. All the cash flow from the stadium remains with the team. In contrast, when stadium-related revenue is used to pay debt service, the subsidy is limited to the reduction in interest costs because team revenue is use to pay the principal and the (lower) interest cost.

1986 to 2005

Those IDB restrictions proved to be too weak and the volume of tax-exempt debt issued for private purposes continued to grow until the Tax Reform Act of 1986 made significant changes. The 25 percent rules were reduced to 10 percent. Bonds that satisfied at least one of the 10 percent rules were renamed "governmental" bonds and could be issued without limit. Bonds that exceeded both of the 10 percent rules were called taxable "private-activity" bonds, terminology that better reflected the diverse list of private activities than did IDBs.[3] In addition, private activities that would still be eligible to issue tax-exempt bonds even though they exceeded the two 10 percent tests (tax-exempt private-activity bonds) were subjected to an annual limit (volume cap) on the amount issued by all entities within each state.

However, stadiums were removed from the list of activities eligible to use tax-exempt private-activity bonds. The expectation was that the use of tax-exempt debt for financing stadiums would wither because local governments, given their state and local statutory and constitutional constraints on borrowing, would be reluctant to issue governmental debt that would require general tax revenue to pay the debt service. Two forces operated to frustrate that expectation. First, those who benefit most from stadiums (owners of teams, players, fans, some related businesses) learned how to utilize pseudo-economic studies to argue that the economic benefits from stadiums generated sufficient additional tax revenue to pay for the public subsidy, a proposition that runs counter to an extensive economics literature. Second, the monopolistic structure of professional sports leagues maintains excess demand for franchises, forcing cities to compete for a limited number of franchises with offerings of stadium subsidies. As a result, many stadiums were built and financed at least 90 percent with general taxes paid by local taxpayers, many of whom receive limited benefits.

2006

Some stadium projects have been thwarted by the unwillingness of local taxpayers to pay 90 percent of the debt service for a professional sports team's capital facilities, and many others have been long delayed in obtaining that approval.[4] Thus, stadium proponents have continually sought creative ways to eliminate the requirement that 90 percent or more of tax-exempt debt service must be paid with generally applicable taxes and in effect make stadiums eligible for tax-exempt private-activity bond. If one is unable to induce local taxpayers to finance all of your capital costs and to induce the federal government to reduce the interest portion of those capital costs by about 25 percent, the consolation prize is to at least obtain the federal government's reduction of interest costs.

In 2006 the Internal Revenue Service approved one of those creative efforts when it issued two letter rulings that allowed the tax-exempt bond financing of two New York City stadiums. Those rulings occurred after New York taxpayers had indicated a substantial reluctance to finance the stadiums with general tax revenue. In effect, the IRS ruled that stadium-related revenue could be used to pay the debt service on governmental debt (Internal Revenue Service, 2006, July 6, and 2006, July 11). Since 1986, payment of more than 10 percent of debt service with stadium-related revenue would make the bonds taxable private-activity bonds. But IRS ruled that stadium-related revenue is actually payments in lieu of taxes (PILOTs). As such, those payments qualify as generally applicable taxes and do not count against the 10 percent limitation on using revenue arising from private business activity to pay for debt service. Suddenly, private-activity bonds, as they have been understood since 1986, can be used to finance stadiums because the 10 percent debt service rule has been eviscerated. In effect, taxable private-activity bonds have been reclassified as tax-exempt governmental bonds.

IS THE PILOT RULING GOOD OR BAD POLICY?

Whether the IRS ruling and the current state of tax-exempt stadium financing is desirable depends upon whether one's goal is to eliminate federal subsidy of professional sports stadiums or to promote economic efficiency by making stadium financing more closely approximate the benefit principle of taxation (Zimmerman, 1997).

PILOTs as Poor Policy

If one's goal is to eliminate federal subsidy of stadiums, the PILOT ruling is undesirable. It reduces the burden on local taxpayers because cash flow from the stadium substitutes for general taxes in the financing of debt service. It reduces the need to raise general taxes, which is likely to reduce local taxpayer resistance to public financing of stadiums. Less local taxpayer resistance means more stadium bonds issued and more federal revenue loss.

Even worse, renaming business-related revenue as PILOTs might open the door for widespread tax-exempt governmental bond financing of private investment projects not currently on the list of activities that are exempt from the private-activity bond 10 percent rules. In effect, any private investment project potentially could be eligible for tax-exempt financing, not as an eligible private-activity bond but as a governmental bond. And unlike tax-exempt private-activity bonds, private activities financed with governmental bonds would not be subject to a volume cap. Issuance could be unlimited. The rulings raise the prospect of making elected officials into commercial bankers in charge of allocating ever-larger portions of the nation's scarce supply of savings, a role that the 1986 tax act was designed to curb.

A straightforward way to eliminate federal subsidy of professional sports stadiums would be to add a prohibition against the use of tax-exempt governmental bonds for stadiums to the existing prohibition against use of private-activity bonds. Former senator Daniel Moynihan championed that approach when he introduced the Stop Tax-exempt Arena Debt Issuance Act (STADIA) in 1996. The simplest way to accomplish that objective would be to eliminate the 10 percent private-security test for stadiums and subject them only to the 10 percent private-use test. A professional sports stadium would always use more than 10 percent of the bond proceeds, thus failing the 10 percent private-use test. A professional sports stadium would always be classified as a taxable private-activity bond and, assuming stadiums remained absent from the list of private activities eligible to use tax-exempt debt even when classified as private-activity bonds, it would be impossible to use tax-exempt financing.

Such outright prohibition of state and local use of tax-exempt financing for governmental debt is rare. Two prior instances have occurred: a prohibition against its use to finance public takeover of investor-owned utilities; and a prohibition against its use to finance the acquisition of rental properties outside the boundaries of the jurisdiction issuing the bonds. But if one's objective is to eliminate the federal subsidy of professional sports stadiums, outright prohibition is clearly the most effective tool.

Outright prohibition is consistent with the view that federal taxpayers receive no economic benefit from their subsidy of stadiums, even should state and local governments receive some benefit. The effect of fiscal policy on the size of the nation's employment pie is determined by the spending, revenue, and deficit totals in the federal budget. Those totals determine the effect of the budget on national output, which in turn determines the number of jobs in the economy. Once those budget totals have been established in the congressional budget resolution, the congressional budget process mandates that any proposal to expand a specific program or cut a tax must be offset by a change elsewhere in the budget. Thus a change in any individual program or tax has a zero effect on job creation and economic activity unless it is able to alter the structural elements of the economy affecting the natural rate of unemployment. To reduce the natural rate of unemployment it is necessary to decrease the levels of structural and frictional unemployment through such programs as job training, relocation assistance, and better information about job availability, or increasing productivity through net increases in investment in physical capital and research (Gravelle, Kiefer, and Zimmerman, 1992, and Courant 1994).

Tax-exempt bonds do not accomplish that objective. The net economic benefits from a stadium diminish as the geographic span of the subsidizing unit of government increases (Noll and Zimbalist, 1997). Unless the fans attending games come from foreign countries, all spending is made by residents of the political jurisdiction providing the subsidy; the United States of America. Except for those few U.S. residents who will reduce their savings to attend games, all of this spending is offset by reductions in spending on alternative entertainment or other activities.

Thus, to federal taxpayers, very few economic benefits are created to offset the cost of the subsidy. The subsidy is only worthwhile to federal taxpayers if they value spending and associated jobs and public consumption in one location more than they value them in another location. If that is the case, it is only this differential valuation that should be included in taxpayer benefits. But it is unlikely that federal taxpayers value stadiums differently according to their locations: the subsidy is not approved for some locations and disapproved for others. It is, in effect, an entitlement program without regard to the location of the spending and associated jobs.

PILOTS as Good Policy

If one's objective is to implement the benefit principle of taxation that would require those who receive benefits from the stadium to pay its costs, the PILOT ruling might be beneficial. Some argue that society overinvests in stadiums because the dominant political coalition that pushes for stadiums receives most of the benefit while others in society pay most of the cost. The IRS PILOT ruling promotes the benefit principle of taxation. In effect, it would allow stadium-related revenue to be used to pay debt service and would reduce the pressure to finance stadiums with general tax revenue. Stadium-related revenue is generally paid by those receiving direct benefits from the stadium, whereas generally applicable taxes such as income, property, and sales taxes are poorly related to stadium usage and the receipt of benefits. It would be efficient because it would bring the dominant political coalition's benefits and costs into better balance, thereby rationalizing prices and discouraging over consumption of stadiums.

However, one must balance that improvement in economic efficiency against the danger that the PILOT precedent will lead to its general application across the spectrum of private business activity, as discussed in the previous section.

AN ALTERNATIVE POLICY

A four-step compromise is available that could advance both policy objectives: eliminate the 10 percent security interest test for stadium bonds; add stadiums to the list of private activities eligible for tax-exempt financing;

subject stadium bonds to the private-activity bond volume cap; and wipe the PILOT precedent off the books.

First, subject stadium bonds only to the 10 percent use-of-proceeds test. That would classify bonds for professional sports stadiums as taxable private-activity bonds. How the debt service is financed is irrelevant; since virtually 100 percent of all the proceeds from a stadium bond issue is used to finance property used in a business, the bonds are taxable private-activity bonds. Second, include stadiums on the list of private activities eligible for tax-exempt financing. That would make it possible for state and local governments to finance debt service with cash flow from the stadium. That stadium-related revenue would be far more likely to implement the benefit principle of taxation than would financing from general tax revenue. Third, require stadium projects to compete for scarce private-activity bond volume cap with other eligible private activities such as mortgage revenue bonds, small-issue industrial development bonds, and student loan bonds. That would force state and local governments to think more carefully about their fiscal priorities and would minimize the federal subsidy. Fourth, eliminate the PILOT precedent. Requiring PILOTS to be classified as trade or business-related revenue would prevent the indiscriminate application of the PILOT rulings to a broad range of private activities and would control elected officials' role of commercial bankers.

ACKNOWLEDGMENT

The view expressed are the author's and do not represent those of the American Tax Policy Institute.

NOTES

1. Most important were a series of state court rulings that revenue bonds are excluded from the constraint that limited debt issuance to a fixed share of the issuing jurisdiction's assessed property value (Zimmerman, 1991).

2. The meaning of direct is obvious—any revenue produced by the facility that is funded by the bond proceeds or by other private property and that is used to pay debt service. For example, a team owner cannot use ticket revenue from the stadium or revenue from his other businesses to pay the debt service. Indirect means paying the governmental entity with revenue produced by the facility or the owner's other businesses while the governmental entity uses its other revenue to pay the debt service. The tax law views the payment to the governmental entity as a replacement for the governmental funds and thus an indirect payment of the debt service.

3. As of 2007, twenty-one activities are eligible for tax-exempt private-activity bond financing. Among the eligible private activities are airports, docks, wharves, and mass

commuting facilities; low-income residential rental multifamily housing; mortgages for owner-occupied housing; small-issue bonds for certain manufacturing facilities; student loans for investment in higher education; green buildings and sustainable design projects; redevelopment bonds; and New York Liberty Zone and Gulf Opportunity Zone bonds.

4. Among stadiums that were not publicly financed are the San Francisco Giants' baseball stadium, the Washington Wizards/Washington Capitals basketball/ice hockey arena, the Washington Redskins football stadium, and the Philadelphia Flyers/76ers ice hockey/basketball arena.

REFERENCES

Baade, R. A. (1994). Stadiums, professional sports, and economic development: Assessing the reality. Heartland Policy Study no. 62.

Coates, D., and B. Humphreys. (1999). The growth effects of sport franchises, stadia, and arenas. *Journal of Policy Analysis and Management,* 18.

Courant, P. N. (1994, December). How would you know a good economic policy if you tripped over one? Hint: don't just count jobs. *National Tax Journal*, 47.

Gravelle, J. G., D. W. Kiefer, and D. Zimmerman. (1992, September 8). Is job creation a meaningful policy justification? Library of Congress, Congressional Research Service Report 92-697 E.

Internal Revenue Service. (2006, July 11). Private Letter Ruling PLR 2006400001.

———. (2006, July 19). Private Letter Ruling PLR 200641002.

Noll, R. G., and A. Zimbalist. (1997). The economic impact of sports teams and facilities. In R. G. Noll and A. Zimbalist (Eds.), *Sports, jobs, and taxes* (pp. 1–54). Washington, DC: Brookings Institution Press.

Zimmerman, D. (1991). *The private use of tax-exempt bonds: Controlling public subsidy of private activities.* Washington, D.C.: Urban Institute Press.

———. (1997). Subsidizing stadiums: Who benefits, who pays? In R. G. Noll and A. Zimbalist (Eds.), *Sports, jobs, and taxes* (pp. 119–145). Washington, DC: Brookings Institution Press.

Six

Economics of Incentives in Individual Sports

Peter von Allmen

"You can lead a horse to water but you can't make him drink," goes the old saying. The same is true with people. You can take an athlete to a track meet or a football game, but you can't force him to run his fastest or play his best. This chapter is about incentives and tournaments. Its purpose is to describe how individuals respond to incentives and how these responses are considered when designing compensation schemes for professional athletes. In the end, my hope is that this chapter will help answer a series of questions:

- Why do athletes compete?
- What makes them want to win?
- Are humans naturally competitive or must we offer either a carrot or a stick in order to induce them to perform their best?
- What might the implications be of a poorly constructed compensation scheme?

Before we discuss human behavior, let's briefly reconsider the case of the horse. Although we take it for granted that horses run as fast as they can in races, why should this be so? Horses have no stake in the winnings. Perhaps the answer lies in negative reinforcement for running slowly: the jockey's crop, or whip. It may be the crop of the jockey, though it seems just as plausible that the horse would respond to being whipped by simply throwing the jockey off the horse. It may also be that horses run fast to try to prove their prowess to their peers. An alternative strategy for animal racing is the case of greyhound racing, in which the animals have a "carrot" or source of positive reinforcement in the form of an artificial "rabbit" lure instead of a whip.

Can we expect the same for people? Must there be some form of extrinsic reward or penalty in order to induce top performances? Amateur athletes may compete simply for the pride in demonstrating their prowess to their peers. Yet, for professional athletes, the carrot of large payoffs is the norm. In this chapter I focus specifically on professional athletes. Although the effort that some amateurs devote to their sports is extraordinary, there are essentially two reasons why professional athletes receive compensation for their efforts—one on the supply side and one related to demand.

On the supply side, athletes are like all workers in that they consider opportunity costs when making decisions. The time devoted to one activity cannot be also devoted to some other activity. Thus, an income-maximizing worker will spend time training and competing in professional athletics only if that person could not earn more by devoting those hours to pursuing some other activity. Individuals who compete at the professional level devote countless hours—often beginning at a very young age—to learning and practicing their craft. Once they achieve professional status, the effort required to remain at that level requires compensation sufficient to prevent the individual from switching to another occupation.

At this point you might be thinking $5 million per year (roughly the National Basketball Association [NBA] average salary) is a lot more than it would take to keep most people from switching jobs! Thus, we must also consider the demand side of the equation. Professional sports teams do not operate as competitive firms in a perfectly competitive industry. Each team can best be thought of as a member of a cartel, and the league as that cartel. As such, teams have the opportunity to earn substantial economic rent. Economic rent is the difference between the income earned from the use of a factor of production (i.e., labor) and minimum cost of obtaining the resource. Given that the product or output of a team is based almost completely on the players, it follows that the source of this rent is the athletes. Athletes are not homogeneous workers in that professional players possess skills that are extremely rare (and desirable when it comes to winning). In the case of profitable leagues, players generate very substantial economic rent. The question then, is who should receive this rent? If the players are powerless to negotiate, the owners may keep all rent as profits. If the players are able, they will negotiate to be paid some of the earned rent. The more fans are willing to pay, the more revenue firms will earn, and the greater will be the rents. In sum, players receive high salaries in part to keep them employed in their current profession, and in part as a negotiated share of the rents that they generate.

Relative to team sports, individual sports have very different compensation schemes (discussed later in the chapter), yet the same general rules governing behavior still apply. In individual sports such as tennis or golf, players are only paid if they are among the best. Thus, weaker players who typically do not finish "in the money" will end up pursuing other activities because the opportunity cost of entering tournament after tournament will be too high. The size of the prize pool is a function of the rents that the tournament organizer can generate. If fans will pay to watch the best professional players play tennis or golf, then those rents may be substantial and the best players will want to capture some of the rents that they can generate.

Based on the concepts of opportunity costs and economic rent, the difference between amateur and professional sports is straightforward. Amateurs compete for pride and other intrinsic rewards because the opportunity costs of becoming and remaining a professional are too high, and/or the economic rents that they can generate as individuals (as marginally talented players) or their teams can generate in sports with low fan appeal are insufficient to make a living. For the remainder of this chapter, unless specifically stated otherwise, I refer only to professional athletes.

INCENTIVES AND BEHAVIOR

Economics focuses on the impacts of small changes at the margin because most of the changes we observe—such as wage changes—are of this nature. If a worker's wage increases by a small fraction, how will he respond? In the case of sports compensation, the appropriate question is: what types of incentives might make a player improve his performance at the margin? To answer this question, economists use models to describe how individuals make decisions about their behavior. Economic models allow us to describe and make predictions about complex human interactions. All economic analysis rests on assumptions that are necessary to simplify the real world. When economists model human behavior, we typically assume that people are rational and that they are utility maximizers. Rationality within economics has a special and limited definition. Rationality refers to consistency. As long as an individual acts or responds in a consistent manner with respect to maximizing her well-being, we would say that she is rational. For example, although you might say that a letter courier who rides a bicycle through busy New York City streets is irrational to ride so aggressively, she may well be acting rationally if she believes that to do so maximizes her income.

By assuming a model of maximizing behavior on the part of both athletes (income) and contest organizers (profit), we dramatically simplify the task of designing a reward system for athletes. While maximization is the standard behavioral assumption, there are other assumptions we could make about behavior. For example, suppose a student was to perform just well enough to earn a C in a class even though he could have earned an A by devoting an extra hour of study each night. Economists call this behavior "satisficing." *Satisficing* means performing just well enough to meet a current need or standard, rather than as well as possible. We certainly observe instances of satisficing in sports and we will discuss such instances in some detail later in the chapter. However, unless we specifically note otherwise, we will assume that athletes respond rationally to incentives by attempting to maximize their utility (satisfaction or well-being), and that income is an important component of satisfaction. Other rewards may figure prominently in athletes' decisions regarding their work and careers, such as fame (which, like pay, is extrinsic) and internal satisfaction and pride of achievement (which is intrinsic), but to simplify the discussion, I assume that these other rewards are strongly related to earned income, and not strong enough to overwhelm the effects of monetary compensation. The model of labor supply also assumes that, all else equal, there is disutility associated with increases in work or effort. That is, individuals will shirk rather than work unless they have some incentive to do otherwise.

The next section describes the most common compensation schemes and the reasons that an employer might choose them. The third section discusses the conditions that exist in a professional athletic employment relationship and discusses which compensation scheme(s) might be optimal and the potential pitfalls of inefficient choices. The fourth section concludes the chapter and offers thoughts on the future of compensation relationships.

COMPENSATION SCHEMES

In this section, we consider three commonly observed compensation schemes: piece-rate or commission pay, hourly pay, and fixed salary.[1] Each of these schemes is found in a variety of occupations in the United States. We take it as given that workers are compensated to produce output. As it relates to our discussion of athletes, there are three relevant sources of variation in output (risk). The first risk is associated with fluctuations in output beyond the worker's control (exogenous variation). An example of exogenous risk in golf would be changes in the weather. The other two potential sources of variation are worker quality and output, which may vary if workers shirk instead of work. As we will see below, the choice of compensation scheme impacts directly on who bears the risks associated with these variations. Before turning to each, a bit more terminology regarding shirking will be useful.

An important determinant of the employer's choice of which scheme to use with a given occupation depends on the employer's ability to control or monitor the worker's activity, what economists call the *principal-agent problem.* The principal-agent problem exists when the well-being of one party (the principal) is dependent on the behavior of another (the agent). In an employment relationship, the employer's profits are dependent on the behavior of the employee (the agent). Yet, as we noted at the very outset of this chapter, the principal has no way to directly control the behavior of the agent. Depending on the production technology, the principal may or may not be able to solve the principal-agent problem by simply monitoring the workers' productivity. In some occupations, monitoring may be difficult or impossible. In these cases, the principal must attempt to construct a maximization problem for the agent such that when the agent acts to solve his own maximization problem (e.g., utility maximization) he also in turn supports the goals of the principal.

Piece-Rate Compensation

When worker activity is easy to monitor, piece rates can be an effective compensation scheme. For example, in the case of agricultural workers picking vegetables, worker effort is directly observed through the weight of the vegetables picked. In this case, the owner of the farm maximizes profits by paying workers by the pound. Commission sales of items such as furniture, automobiles, and suits work in the same way. In order to be paid, workers must demonstrate their effort by producing output. In this scheme, solving the principal-agent problem is reduced to finding the piece-rate wage that will elicit an efficient level of effort from the workers. With the correct rate set, the employer maximizes profits with little or no need to monitor workers' activities. A simple count of output is all the monitoring needed.

Even if employees do produce a physical product that can be readily counted, piece rates are not likely to be optimal when workers efforts are interdependent. For example, even though one could add up the touchdowns scored by a football team, it would be problematic to compensate each member of the offensive line based on points he helped the team to score. The productivity of the running game for any team is the combined efforts of the linemen and the running back. If any one lineman were to shirk, the blocking schemes would often fail despite the best efforts of the others.

An important feature of this form of compensation is that workers bear the risk of variations in output for whatever the reason because pay varies directly with actual output. If output falls for some reason that the worker cannot control, wages fall. For example, if an employer hires workers to fish for trout on a piece-rate basis, the workers bear the risk of bad fishing conditions. Workers may also earn lower wages than the average worker if they are not as skilled at fishing. Finally, if the employee exerts no effort (shirks), employers observe no output, and workers receive no compensation. In each case, it is the employee who suffers the loss of income. The employer does not pay for output that is not produced. Employers are strongly insulated against losses in this model because payment is made *ex-post*. That is, workers are not paid until after the output is produced. Pure piece-rate compensation as described here is not utilized in professional sports, although performance bonuses paid for reaching specific milestones (such as scoring fifty goals or pitching a certain number of innings) are a form of piece-rate compensation that is often incorporated into the contracts of professional athletes.

Hourly and Salary

When monitoring of individual employee effort is difficult, workers are often compensated using some form of salary scheme. In such a payment scheme, workers are paid a fixed salary per time period, agreed upon at the start of the period, regardless of output, assuming that effort, however imperfectly observed, does not fall below a specified minimum. The simplest form of pay under this scheme is hourly pay, in which workers are paid a fixed hourly rate for each hour worked independent of the output produced during that time period. In professional and managerial full-time work occupations, the time period for the fixed payment typically extends over the course of an entire year and is not calibrated to a specific number of hours worked. Thus, while an hourly worker may earn less if she leaves work early or more is she stays late, a salaried worker would not. Because hourly pay schemes are not utilized in professional sports, I instead focus on the annual salary model.

As an example, full-time college professors are paid using a salary model. In this profession, output is extremely difficult to quantify, much less monitor. The two principal activities of such a person are to teach students and produce research. Neither is readily measurable using counting, and research may require many months of work with no output at all despite intense effort that will eventually yield a significant publication. As long as professors meet their classes, receive satisfactory evaluations, and make some measurable progress on publication over the course of a year, they are typically renewed to work again the following year. Salary compensation is also commonly used when worker efforts are interdependent. If a research team made up of scientists with complementary skills works together in a laboratory over many months to successfully develop a new vaccine, the cost of monitoring activity in the lab closely enough to determine the value of individual input to the project may be prohibitive.

The costs of the risks in an hourly or salary scheme are shared but, depending on how difficult it is to monitor effort, they may be concentrated on the employer. In a straight salary model, the employer bears much of the risk of shirking. Workers may choose to satisfice and exert just enough effort to avoid being dismissed. As long as the employer has set the salary at a level such that satisficing will not result in losses, the firm stays in business, but profits are not maximized if an alternative compensation scheme could induce maximizing behavior at lower average cost of output. If workers shirk to the point where effort levels are below the minimum standard, employers bear that cost until they are exposed as shirking and dismissed. Given that in some occupations the interdependence of worker effort and the inherent difficulty in monitoring make individual contributions to output unobservable over short time periods, the costs of shirking may be substantial. Clearly, solving the principal-agent problem in the case of difficult monitoring is more challenging than when monitoring is easy. When workers are paid a fixed salary to perform work that for whatever reason results in output that cannot readily be measured (lack of a physical output, worker interdependence), employers are left with no good system by which to offer the carrot and no way to know when to use the stick.

Solving the Principal-Agent Problem in Team Sports

In the context of most team sports, worker effort is by definition interdependent. Thus, monitoring worker contribution to output is inherently difficult. In an ice hockey game, the left wing can make a perfect pass to the center directly in front of the net, but he only receives an assist on the play if the center shoots and scores. The same scenario occurs routinely in the course of an NBA game. In the National Football League (NFL), a quarterback can throw a pass right into the hands of a wide-open receiver in the end zone, but will only receive credit for a touchdown if the receiver catches the ball. Baseball is the one exception to this rule, in that although some productivity is interdependent (a double play usually requires two or three players), other productivity (home-run hitting) is independent of one's teammates. Nonetheless, the general structure of athlete compensation is similar across all four sports.

THE STRUCTURE OF COMPENSATION

The parameters of professional athletes' compensation are determined *ex ante* through contractual negotiation.[2] Contract lengths may be for one season or may cover many seasons. Because each contract is different, there is no single formula we can use to describe them all. That said, we can set up a general formula that contains each of the elements that are typically found in a contract.

There are three main components to professional athlete compensation in team sports: The signing bonus, the base salary, and incentive payments, also known as performance bonuses. A *signing bonus* is paid to a player at the time that the contract is signed. These payments represent advance payments on the base salary. The larger the bonus paid at the time the contract is signed, the greater the risk to the team. If the player fails to perform or is injured and cannot play, the team bears the cost without receiving the benefit. The *base salary* is an amount paid to the player for the season independent of how well or even how often the player actually plays. The only exception here is that in the case of nonguaranteed salaries (which are common in the NFL) the player must actually make the team to receive the salary. If the payment is guaranteed, the player receives the payment from the team (or a new team in the event of a trade) whether the player actually plays or not. In the context of our discussion above, both signing bonuses and base salary represent salary payments. Finally, *performance bonuses* are paid to the player for achieving certain productivity milestones. As such, they represent a form of piece-rate payment in that the team is only obligated to make the payment to the player if that player reaches the agreed-upon goal. These goals vary widely from position to position and across sports.

For example, a quarterback might receive a bonus for throwing a certain number of touchdown passes. This type of payment most closely resembles a piece-rate payment because it is directly related to output. Even so, it is not a pure piece-rate payment unless the quarterback is paid a bonus *for each touchdown pass*. Another type of incentive payment is a payment made for achieving a specific recognition, such as winning the scoring title, making the All-Star team, and being voted Most Valuable Player or some other league-wide award. These payments are different from bonuses based on productivity milestones in that they often rely on subjective judgment of peers or fans (as in the case of MVP or All-Star voting) and they are relative to one's peers rather than absolute. For example, only one player can win the MVP trophy and to do so requires that the player receive more votes than his peers. Yet, productivity milestones are independent of how well others play, even at the same position.

In the context of the principal-agent problem, incentive pay is used to motivate players to give their best effort given that the team coaches and owners are not able to fully monitor them. For example, the coach of an NFL team cannot tell with certainty whether a player tried his best to run the best route, break free from his defender, and then catch a pass in the end zone. He only observes the outcome. He does not have the ability to fully monitor or acquire knowledge pertaining to the off-season training, practice in season, study of the playbook, and the effort on the play. If the player wants to shirk, it may be very hard to detect. If the player contract calls for all guaranteed payments or signing bonuses, the owner has very limited ability to respond even if the player admits to shirking. In his first game as a Philadelphia Eagle, Ricky Watters essentially admitted to not going all out to catch a pass thrown to him late in a game that the Eagles went on to lose. In response to a question about the play, Watters responded by asking "For who? For what?" This represents a classic example of the principal-agent problem. If Watters's contract had been structured such that he was paid by the catch with sizable increases in payments for touchdown catches, he may have responded quite differently. More generally, if players receive incentive bonuses based on desirable contributions to team success, much less monitoring is needed. The player solves his own maximization problem by working his hardest to earn the bonus, while at the same time maximizing the utility of the owner who wants to win the game.

Table 6.1 shows the compensation packages for three prominent NFL players. As the table indicates, although each player earned at least $5 million in 2005, the structure of their individual contracts varied widely. Tom Brady signed a new six-year contract in 2005. As part of the agreement, he received a very substantial signing bonus of $14.5 million, much larger than his base pay. Brady's contract also includes very modest (by NFL standards) incentive bonuses. In the remaining years of Brady's contract, the signing-bonus column would be $0. As such, his pay is very strongly "front-loaded." Thus, the risk of a drop-off in Brady's productivity falls heavily on his team,

TABLE 6.1
Compensation of Selected Players in the NFL, 2005

Player	Signing Bonus	Base Pay	Other Bonuses[a]	Total Compensation
Tom Brady (QB)	$14,500,000	$1,000,000	$154,180	$15,654,180
Jevon Kearse (DE)	$0	$890,000	$2,125,000	$3,015,000
Shaun Alexander (RB)	$0	$6,323,000	$0	$6,323,000

[a]Includes all incentive payments including "roster, report, workout and other bonuses, plus any likely-to-be-earned bonuses."

Source: USA Today Salaries Databases (Football) at http://asp.usatoday.com/sports/football/nfl/salaries/default.aspx?Loc=Vanity (accessed March 15, 2008).

the New England Patriots. By contrast, Jevon Kearse's contract is made up of a smaller base salary and a very large bonus payment, shifting much of the risk of injury to the player. This is particularly notable given that in 2006 Kearse suffered a serious injury early in the season and did not play again that year. Finally, Shaun Alexander's contract contains no incentive payments at all. Alexander earned MVP honors in 2005. Although he did not receive a bonus for doing so, he was rewarded by the Seattle Seahawks with an eight-year contract valued at $62 million, over $15 million of which was guaranteed.[3]

Although teams that offer bonus-laden contracts do risk having high payroll costs if the bonuses are met, teams also make these payments knowing that they have received the productivity already. Another way to think about the difference between contracts that contain large signing bonuses and guaranteed annual salaries and contracts that offer small base salaries and large bonus opportunities is that the former are *ex-ante* payments in hopes of receiving the productivity to justify them later. The latter are *ex-post* payments that require that the player's productivity to be "in hand" before the payment is made. Before we move on to discuss league specific rules about contract structure, we must resolve the question of why the contracts in Table 6.1 (and indeed all pro contracts) look so different from one another. Given that every player is playing the same sport, it seems as though they should all have similarly constructed contracts.

Limits on Incentive Pay

In professional team sports, athletes are represented by unions in negotiations with the league. The National Hockey League Players Association (NHLPA) represents players in the NHL; the National Basketball Players Association (NBPA) represents NBA players; the Major League Baseball Players Association (MLBPA) represents baseball players; and the NFLPA represents NFL players. In each sport, the players' associations bargain collectively with team owners on behalf of the players over issues such as health and pension benefits, personal conduct and disciplinary rules, drug-testing programs, general working conditions, and contingencies regarding injury. The resulting contracts are known as collective bargaining agreements (CBAs). Unlike most union CBAs, the player associations and the league representatives do not bargain over individual player salaries or salaries based on occupation or tenure within the organization. Each player (usually through an agent) individually negotiates a salary agreement with the team. However, each CBA does specify important parameters regarding salaries such as identifying the types of incentive clauses that are allowable, minimum salaries, and in some cases maximum allowable payments are stipulated in the agreements.

In the NHL, no team performance bonuses are allowed. In the context of the principal-agent problem, such a clause makes sense in that a single player on an excellent team may be able to shirk and still achieve team bonuses. Allowable bonuses are divided into two categories. Category A bonuses include statistical milestones such as goals, assists, plus/minus rating, and ice time, as well as awards such as selection to the All-Star team or the all-rookie team. Bonuses in this category are paid from the team to the player. Category B bonuses are paid for league-wide awards and league-wide achievements in scoring and goaltending. These payments are not actually part of the individual contract with the team as these payments are made directly from the league.[4]

In the NFL players can earn performance bonuses in four ways. In contrast to the NHL, the NFL does allow team performance-based bonuses. Team bonuses can be earned for offensive categories such as points scored, defensive categories such as points allowed and special teams categories such as punt-return average.[5] In addition to team bonuses, players may also earn individual performance bonuses based on statistical measures such as yards, tackles, touchdowns, and field-goal percentage. Third, players can receive bonus payments for earning league-wide awards and honors, such as being named to the Pro Bowl. Finally, the NFL has a performance pay system that is unique to its league based on playing time. The NFL Performance Based Pay System was designed to reduce pressure on league minimum salaries, but also reward those players who receive the most playing time. Under this system, each team distributes payments from a central pool to players based on their playing time. The system is weighted to reward lowest-paid players the most.

> Under the system, Performance Based Pay is computed by using a 'Player Index.' To produce the index, a player's regular season playtime (total plays on offense, defense and special teams) is divided by his adjusted regular season compensation (full season salary, prorated portion of signing bonus, earned incentives). Each player's index is then compared to those of the other players on his team to determine the amount of his pay.[6]

In MLB, the CBA allows players to earn individual performance bonuses and award bonuses such as Most Valuable Player. The NBA CBA allows for achieving league-wide honors and for individual performance bonuses with the stipulation that they be based on some absolute performance measure rather than relative.

> By way of example and not limitation, an amendment agreed upon . . . may provide for the player to receive a bonus if his free-throw percentage exceeds 80%, but may not provide for the player to receive a bonus if his free-throw percentage improves over his previous season's percentage.[7]

Empirical Evidence of Performance Changes Related to Contract Form

We began by noting that players have two types of motivating factors: intrinsic and extrinsic. Theory predicts that if players are strongly motivated by extrinsic incentives (income), teams will need to set contract terms carefully given the principal-agent relationship that exists between player and team. Based on the discussion thus far, it seems that there are two general classes of problems that may arise from the multipart contracts common to North American professional team sports. The first is that incentive clauses may be set inefficiently. The second is that the guaranteed nature of base salaries and signing bonuses may lead to variation in effort across the contract cycle—players may work extra hard the year before they are eligible to negotiate a new contract and then shirk once the guaranteed payment is received.

First, consider the potential problems of payments set at inefficient levels. Payments for achieving productivity milestones may be either too high or low. Assume that players do respond to incentives with changes in effort (a question we return to shortly). If payments are systematically too high (for example, the team could have motivated player X to score thirty goals with a $100,000 bonus instead of $200,000), the result would be that players would elicit maximum effort, but team profits would be lower than if the bonuses were harder to achieve. If bonus payments are systematically too low, players would not elicit maximum effort, performance would decline, and team profits would be lower. To detect this type of inefficiency would be very difficult given that we can only observe the payments that players actually receive and cannot run a series of repeated trials.

The second problem—the potential for changes in intensity of effort over the contract cycle—has been empirically tested using data from baseball and basketball. Whether players with guaranteed contracts will shirk, while those nearing the end of their contract cycle will increase the intensity of their effort, represents a direct test of principal-agent effects. Theory predicts that effort will vary and shirking will occur. Anthony Krautmann and coauthors have published several studies that conclude that baseball players do not shirk following contract negotiations.[8] While others have found that effort does vary across the contract cycle, we can only say that the results are mixed.[9] In a separate study using data from basketball, the conclusion regarding whether players shirk or not is dependent on the measure of productivity employed.[10] Thus, it seems that we cannot definitively say that the theoretical prediction is sound. Players may have intrinsic sources of motivation that outweigh any income effects.

PLAYER AND OWNER PREFERENCES

While theoretical predictions and the empirical tests that follow do not present a clear and consistent story regarding how players respond to incentives, when a player and an owner meet to negotiate a contract, perceptions and preferences matter. Which type of contract is most preferable to players? What about the owners? These might seem like simple questions with obvious answers—the player would prefer the guarantees and the owners would prefer the incentives. Keep in mind that these contracts are always made at a time when both sides only know for certain only what has happened in the past. Either or both sides may have some information about the future outlook for the team or the health of the player that they do not share with the other party (asymmetric information). Thus, neither can say for sure what will happen next season.

Suppose that an owner believes that a player is near the end of his productive career and, given a history of nagging injuries, is unlikely to be able to contribute much to the team. The owner may only be willing to offer a salary close to the league minimum of a few hundred thousand dollars if the player insists on an all guaranteed contract. If the player believes that he has finally resolved his injury problems and is ready to make a major contribution, he may not want to push for a guaranteed contract. Instead, he may be willing to accept a contract from the owner with a very low base salary and the opportunity to make significantly more in the event that he remains healthy and contributes. For example, entering the 2006 baseball season, Frank Thomas had suffered previous injury problems with his left foot. The Oakland A's offered Thomas a contract in which his base pay of $500,000 could increase by $2.6 million with payments on May 1, June 15, July 15, and August 15 on the roster and achieved various plate appearance incentives.[11] In this case, Thomas was confident enough that he could achieve the incentive milestones offered that he was willing to take a base salary that was a small fraction of what he had earned in recent years. The A's were happy to receive his added productivity, though once Thomas proved his health and value, he subsequently signed with the Blue Jays after the 2006 season.

In summary, player contracts typically include three forms of payment: signing bonuses, which are guaranteed; base salaries, which are not contingent on any specific level of productivity; and incentive bonuses, which are similar to piece rates. In theory, the principal-agent relationship that exists between players and owners implies that contracts must be constructed carefully in order for owners to obtain maximum effort (and so maximum profits). Empirical studies offer conflicting evidence on whether players do alter effort levels across the contract cycle. Team and player preferences for assuming risk vary, as indicated by the observed variations across contracts. Although incentive-laden contracts may be an effective mechanism to solve the principal-agent problem, guaranteed salary payments may offer lower costs to teams if players like to avoid the risk of missing incentive levels. Salary payments also offer cost certainty to teams.

REWARD SCHEMES IN INDIVIDUAL SPORTS

Up to this point, the focus has been completely on team sports in which players are employed by an owner who attempts to maximize profits by, in turn, maximizing player effort. Individual sports such as golf, tennis, and bowling are organized in a fundamentally different way. When athletes compete in individual sports, players enter tournaments with known prize structures and play (apply talent and exert effort) based on prize distribution (and intrinsic rewards). In this case, the principal is the tournament organizer. In one sense, this is a much simpler problem than the case of an owner offering a multiyear contract to a player on a baseball team. There are no multiyear or even multitournament contracts for earnings in individual sports. With few exceptions, winning or placing well in one event is unrelated to what one might win in the next or any subsequent event. An individual golfer is not under a season-long contract with the PGA Tour. Each tournament is a separate event that offers prize money based on revenues from television, sponsors, and attendance.[12] As the entertainment value of the tournament rises, revenue from attendance, sponsorship, and television ratings also increases. To maximize profits, organizers must try to maximize the entertainment value of the tournament for any given expenditure level. What are the challenges for the PGA Tour as it attempts to accomplish this goal?

A defining characteristic of golf and tennis tournaments, auto and foot racing, as well as other individual sports, is that the winner is determined based solely on the order of finish as opposed to margin of victory. As such, all performances are relative to one's competitors and measuring actual productivity is impossible. Although a tennis tournament is played as a sequence of rounds and a golf tournament requires that each player simultaneously beat all others, entrants must only beat the second-best performance in order to win. Tiger Woods may win the Masters with a combined four round score of 278 one year, but place third the following year with an even better score of 276. It depends on how well his opponents play.

In cases where only the rank order of finish matters, tournament organizers must be concerned with eliciting high levels of effort from contestants to ensure that the event attracts fan demand. Yet, with no clear way to determine effort levels because monitoring is not possible, none of the compensation mechanisms discussed to this point will ensure efficient levels of effort. For instance, it is not hard to imagine that in a tournament in which there is no top prize but instead each player is paid the same hourly wage for the amount of time spent on the course, the contestants will not care much if they win or not. In 1981 Edward Lazear and Sherwin Rosen published a seminal paper titled "Rank Order Tournaments as Optimum Labor Contracts."[13] In this paper, the authors show that when effort and productivity are unobservable and performance is relative to peers, the most efficient compensation scheme may be one in which rewards increase rapidly as a player increases his or her position in the final standings. For example, all PGA Tour tournaments have the same weighting on the prizes, independent of the absolute size of each prize. Table 6.2 shows the percentage prize distribution for professional golf tournaments. These reductions in the share of the prize received as finish order declines result in dramatic differences in earnings even among the top two places. In a tournament with a total prize pool of approximately $5.55 million, the winner receives $1 million, while the runner-up receives only $600.000.

TABLE 6.2
Compensation in Professional Golf Tournaments

Final Place	Percentage of Purse
1st	18.0
2nd	10.8
3rd	6.8
4th	4.8
5th	4.0
6th	3.6
7th	3.35
8th	3.1
9th	2.9
70th	0.2

Source: Stephen Shmanske, *Golfonomics* (Hackensack, N.J.: World Scientific, 2004), 243.

The motivation for players is clear. Lack of substantive effort in the form of training or tournament play results in dramatic reductions in earnings as the player slips in the standings. As such, rank-order tournament compensation schemes seem to solve the principal-agent problem in a very straightforward way. No effort leads to no prize, but the returns to maximum effort can be extraordinary.

Unfortunately, the solution is not as simple as it might seem as important challenges remain for the organizer. When the value of the prize(s) is (are) predetermined, the organizer must choose a single prize distribution for a heterogeneous field. It is unrealistic to assume that every player will respond to incentives in the same way. For those who place a very high value on income, steeply sloped winnings profiles will provide strong incentives to play better. For those who place high value on the intrinsic value of winning, such a structure will be overly generous. Thus, the task that remains for tournament organizers is to determine the depth and breadth of the prize pool. At one extreme, the organizer could offer a winner-take-all format. At the other, each player could receive equal payments simply for entering. How might an inefficient prize distribution affect player behavior?

First, suppose that the prize pool offered is too shallow. That is, there are only prizes for a few finishers, and the remaining participants receive nothing. There are two principal effects here: limits on entry and giving up. As an extreme example, assume that the tournament payout scheme is winner-take-all. For players who believe they have little chance to win, they are not likely to even enter the tournament if there are large talent differences and/or entry requires up-front costs or effort. The result is a small pool of contestants. For those that do enter, they may simply quit trying once they realize that they are no longer in a position to win. It follows that the lack of entry and giving up effects will be exacerbated as the variation in talent increases. Such a tournament would likely elicit little demand from fans. There is another potential pitfall of a distribution in which prizes are weighted to heavily toward top finishers: players may exert excessive effort in ways that negatively impact the competition itself such as cheating, sabotage, or reckless behavior.[14]

If, on the other hand, the prize pool is very deep or relatively equally split among contestants, players who have little or no chance to win the tournament may enter in hopes of at least earning something. That is, we end up with too many players because the field contains players who are not in contention to actually win. In addition, entrants may shirk, knowing that they are assured of some level of payout and the chances of obtaining a top prize are small. In the limit, if prizes are distributed too equally, contestants may shirk (similar to the case of offering prizes to too many contestants).

Assuming fans want to see high-level competition between a wide field of high-quality contestants, wide-scale failure to enter or giving up (shirking) in a tournament again leads to low entertainment value for spectators.

Although the preceding discussion makes it clear that setting up rank-order tournaments that elicit an efficient level of effort from contestants is multidimensional and difficult, they remain the standard in sports in which only order of finish matters. As long as players respond to financial incentives (or organizers believe that they do) rank-order tournaments will continue to offer prize structures that are highly skewed toward the winner.[15]

CONCLUSION

We began this chapter with a series of questions. As we conclude, it is appropriate to revisit those questions to summarize the discussion. Professional athletes compete by investing substantial training and game effort in order to earn income, which we assume to be an important component of utility maximization. Although some athletes compete as amateurs, the talent and sustained effort required to maintain professional-level play represent substantial opportunity costs for which the player seeks compensation. Compensation over and above this level represents a sharing of gains from owners to players. Although some individuals are inherently competitive, the rewards that are available to professional athletes create the incentive to maximize performance. A principal-agent relationship exists because the principal, which is the league/team or tournament organizer in this case, cannot force the athlete to play. Thus, a primary function of rewards in professional sports is aimed at solving the principal-agent problem. Rewards that are too high can result in destructive behavior by contestants. Rewards that are too low can result in shirking. As the U.S. professional sports industry moves forward, a continuing challenge for owners and contest organizers is to set compensation limits at levels that maximize profits by creating the enjoyable viewing events at the lowest possible cost. Given the strong demand for U.S. professional team sports as well as for major individual sports such as golf and tennis, a related and equally challenging issue to address is the sharing of monopoly rents.

NOTES

1. Those interested in a rigorous theoretical comparison of piece rates and salaries may refer to Edward P. Lazear, "Salaries and Piece Rates," *Journal of Business* 59, no. 3 (1986): 405–431.

2. In this section, all salaries are taken from the *USA Today* online salary database, at http://www.usatoday.com/sports/salaries/index.htm (accessed March 15, 2008).

3. Len Pasquarelli, "MVP Agrees to Eight-Year Deal to Remain with Seattle," http://sports.espn.go.com/nfl/news/story?id=2355855 (accessed March 15, 2008). Although Jevon Kearse and Shaun Alexander show no signing bonus for the current year, they may have received a signing bonus in a previous year as part of the same contract.

4. For a complete description of the NHL A and B bonus system, see Exhibit 5 of the NHL Collective Bargaining Agreement, pp. 260–265, at http://www.nhlpa.com/CBA/index.asp (accessed March 15, 2008).

5. Bonus categories for the NFL are found in the 2006 amended collective bargaining agreement, at http://www.nflpa.com/pdfs/Agents/CBA_Amended_2006.pdf (accessed March 15, 2008). See Exhibits A through D, pp. 69–83.

6. "Performance-based Pay for NFL Players Up Nearly 80 Percent," NFL.com, http://www.nfl.com/news/story/8317559 (accessed March 15, 2008).

7. NBA Collective Bargaining Agreement Article 2, section 3, part (b), http://nbpa.org/cba_articles/article-II.php (accessed March 15, 2008).

8. See Anthony C. Krautmann, "Shirking or Stochastic Productivity in Major League Baseball," *Southern Economic Journal* 56, no. 4 (April 1990): 961–968; Krautmann, "Shirking or Stochastic Productivity in Major League Baseball: Reply," *Southern Economic Journal* 60, no. 1 (July 1993): 241–243; Anthony C. Krautmann, Joel G. Maxcy, and Rodney D. Fort, "The Effectiveness of Incentive Mechanisms in Major League Baseball," *Journal of Sports Economics* 3 no. 3 (August 2002): 246–255.

9. Daniel R. Marburger, "Does the Assignment of Property Rights Encourage or Discourage Shirking?" *Journal of Sports Economics* 4, no. 1 (February 2003): 19–34.

10. David J. Berri and Anthony C. Krautmann, "Shirking on the Court: Testing for the Incentive Effects of Guaranteed Pay," *Economic Inquiry* 44 no. 3 (July 2006): 536–546.

11. Jorge Ortiz, "'Big Hurt' Finds Healing in Oakland," USAToday.com, http://www.usatoday.com/sports/baseball/al/athletics/2006-09-25-frank-thomas_x.htm (accessed March 15, 2008).

12. According to Tom Clavin, as of 2006, total television revenue for the PGA Tour was estimated to be $270 million, an amount equal to the total purses in all PGA tournaments. See Tom Clavin, "Brave New World for Golf on TV," Hamptons.com, April 13, 2006. Http://Hamptons.com/hamptons_article_magazine_1533.htm (accessed January 22, 2007).

13. Edward Lazear and Sherwin Rosen, "Rank Order Tournaments as Optimum Labor Contracts," *Journal of Political Economy* 89 (1981): 841–864.

14. For example, Peter von Allmen, "Is the Reward System in NASCAR Efficient?" *Journal of Sports Economics* 2, no. 1 (February 2001): 62–79; and Craig A. Depken II and Dennis Wilson, "The Efficiency of the NASCAR Reward System: Initial Empirical Evidence," *Journal of Sports Economics* 5, no. 4 (November 2004): 371–386, consider the possibility of accidents created by overly generous payout schemes in the case of auto racing.

15. For more on this phenomenon, including applications outside the sports industry, see Robert Frank and Philip J. Cook, *The Winner-Take-All Society: Why the Few at the Top Get So Much More Than the Rest of Us* (New York: Penguin, 1996).

Seven

The Measurement of Efficiency in Sports Organizations

Carlos Pestana Barros and Mário Teixeira

The analysis of efficiency of sport organizations is a growing theme in contemporary sport economics. The intention behind efficiency studies is to benchmark the units under analysis in order to help the inefficient to catch up with the frontier of management "best practices." Despite its intuitive and obvious importance, there is a paucity of research into this aspect of sport management. Recent exceptions are Fizel & D'Itri (1997), Dawson, Dobson, & Gerrard (2000), Barros (2003), and Haas (2003a, 2003b). Following Farrell (1957), researchers analyzing efficiency adopt the frontier estimation techniques represented a bounding technology function that reflects best-practice production, defined in terms of the maximum real output technologically possible to produce given available inputs. Normally two scientific frontier methods are used to analyze efficiency quantitatively: the econometric frontier (Khumbhakar & Lovell, 2000) and data envelopment analysis (DEA) (Cooper, Seiford, & Tone, 2000). Both have their advantages and drawbacks. Unlike the econometric stochastic frontier approach, the DEA does not impose any functional form on the data; neither does it make distributional assumptions for the inefficiency term. Both methods can handle multiple outputs and assume that the production function of the fully efficient decision unit is known. In practice, this is not the case and the efficient isoquant must be estimated from the sample data. Under these conditions, the frontier is relative to the sample considered in the analysis.

An important advantage of the econometric frontier is that there are a number of well-developed statistical tests to investigate the validity of the model specification—tests of significance for the inclusion or exclusion of factors, or for the functional form. The accuracy of this hypothesis depends to some extent on the assumption of normality of errors, which is not always fulfilled. A second advantage of the econometric frontier is that if a variable that is not relevant is included, it will have a low or even zero weighting in the calculation of the efficiency scores, so its impact is likely to be negligible. This is an important difference from DEA, in which the weights for a variable are usually unconstrained. A third advantage of the econometric frontier is that it allows the decomposition of deviations from efficient levels between "noise" (or stochastic shocks) and pure inefficiency, whereas the DEA classifies the whole deviation as inefficiency.

In this chapter, we perform an efficiency analysis of sport organizations using an econometric frontier model to analyze training programs for referees, trainers, and managers of Portuguese sports federations. Using a sample of the latter, which apply for public financing to help support the development of their training programs, technical efficiency is estimated for the period 1998–2002. This analysis uses the determinants of training costs of publicly financed sport federations to identify the level of efficiency, identify the change in efficiency over time, and determine if the Olympic cycle drives training costs. This permits us to derive policy implications to improve the efficiency of publicly funded Portuguese sport federations. The results are mixed. While the mean efficiency score is high and equal to 0.9788, signifying a small level of inefficiency equal to $(1 - 0.9788 = 0.0212)$ it does not vary during the period. In a dynamic world, the efficiency frontier shifts over time and therefore should lead to time-varying efficiency scores. These results will help the Sports Regulatory Council to insist on improvements in training activities as a criterion for subsidy allocation, encouraging the federations to implement a best-practice management procedure in their training activities. We analyze only publicly financed sport federations. Therefore the football federation, the sole private competitive sport federation in the country, is excluded from the analysis.

EXISTING RESEARCH ON SPORT EFFICIENCY

Sports efficiency is infrequently analyzed due to the lack of adequate data for this purpose (Slack, 1997). There are two contemporary approaches to measure efficiency: the econometric or parametric stochastic frontier approach and, the nonparametric or DEA approach. If one compares the stochastic frontier model with the DEA model, it is clear that both methods have their advantages and drawbacks. Unlike the stochastic frontier approach, DEA permits the use of multiple inputs and outputs, does not impose any functional form on the data, and does not make any distributional assumptions for the inefficiency measure. Both methods assume that the cost function of the fully efficient decisionmaking unit is known. In practice, this is not the case, and the efficient isocost frontier must be estimated from the sample data. Under such conditions, the frontier is measured relative to the sample considered in the analysis. An important advantage of the econometric approach is that there are a number of well-developed statistical tests designed to investigate the validity of the model specification—tests of significance for the inclusion or exclusion of factors, or for the functional form. The accuracy of these hypotheses depend to some extent on the assumption of a normality of errors, a condition that is not always fulfilled. A second advantage of the econometric approach is that if an irrelevant variable is included it will have a low or even zero weighting in the calculation of the efficiency scores, so that its impact is likely to be negligible. This is an important difference from the DEA method, where the weights for a variable are usually unconstrained. A third advantage of the econometric frontier approach is that it allows for the decomposition of deviations from efficient levels into "noise" (or stochastic shocks) and pure inefficiency, while the DEA method classifies the whole deviation as inefficiency.

The efficiency estimate, also known as the efficiency score, measures the difference between the frontier of best practices and the performance of each federation. With an efficiency score equal to 1, the federation is on the frontier of best practices and is therefore efficient. With an efficiency score lower than 1, the sport federation is inefficient, and is more inefficient the lower the value of the efficiency score. Table 7.1 lists the characteristics of published papers applying both methods.

This highlights several questions. First, it can be verified that sports economics adopts either the parametric approach of the stochastic frontier model or the nonparametric approach of the DEA. Second, the application cited encompasses almost all types of sports. Third, all the papers cited use what is now out-of-date frontier models. Recent innovation in frontier models such as the random frontier model (Greene, 2001, 2005), the latent frontier model (Orea & Kumbhakar, 2005), the Bayesian frontier models (Griffin & Steel, 2007) and the bootstrapped DEA model (Simar & Wilson, 2007) have not been so far published in sport economics. Fourth, the applications are restricted to the United States and Europe. Fifth, there is no consensus on the use of inputs and outputs because the availability of the data determines the variable choice. Finally, the identification of the causes of inefficiency is sometimes restricted due to the so-called black-box effect of the standard cost function (Valverde, Humphrey, & del Paso, 2007).

TABLE 7.1
Literature Survey of Frontier Models Applied to Sports

DEA Frontier Models					
Paper	**Method**	**Units**	**Inputs**	**Outputs**	**Prices**
Barros & Santos (2004)	DEA-CCR Model and DEA-BCC model	13 Portuguese first-division soccer clubs, 1999/2000 to 2001/02	Supplies and services expenditure, wage expenditure, amortization expenditure, other costs.	Match receipts, membership receipts, sponsorship receipts, TV receipts, gains on players, financial receipts, points won, tickets sold.	—
Haas (2003a)	DEA-CCR and DEA-BCC model	12 U.S. soccer clubs observed in year 2000	Players' wages, coaches wages, stadium utilization rate.	Points awarded, number of spectators and total revenue.	—
Haas (2003b)	DEA-CCR	20 English Premier League soccer clubs observed in one season, 2000/2001	Total wages, coach salary, hometown population.	Points, spectators, and revenue.	—
Barros & Santos (2003)	DEA-Malmquist index	18 training activities of sports federations, 1999–2001	Number of trainers, trainers' remuneration, number of administrators, administrators' remuneration and physical capital.	Number of participants, number of courses, number of approvals.	
Barros (2003)	DEA-Allocative model	19 training activities of sports federations, 1998–2001	Number of trainers, number of administrators, physical capital.	Number of participants, number of courses, number of approvals.	Price of trainers, price of administrators, price of capital.
Fizel & D'Itri (1997)	DEA-CCR model in first stage and regression analysis in second stage	147 college basketball teams, 1984–1991	Player talent, opponent strength.	Winning percentages.	—
Fizel & D'Itri (1996)	DEA-CCR model	Baseball managers	Player talent, opponent strength.	Winning percentages.	—
Porter & Scully (1982)	A linear programming technique (probably DEA-CCR)	Major League baseball teams, 1961 to 1980	Team hitting and team pitching.	Team percent wins.	—

Econometric Frontiers

Paper	Method	Units	Inputs	Outputs	Prices
Carmichael, Thomas & Ward (2001)	System of production functions by mach.	English soccer Premier League, by match, 1997–1998	15 variables such as goals scored, etc.	Points as percentage of the maximum possible.	—
Dawson, Dobson & Gerrard (2000)	Stochastic Cobb-Douglas frontier model	Sample of English soccer managers, 1992 to 1998	Player age, league career experience, career goals, number of previous teams, league appearances in the previous season, goals scored, player divisional status.	Winning percentages.	—
Hadley, Poitras, Ruggiero & Knowles (2000)	Deterministic frontier model	National football league teams, 1969/70 to 1992/93	24 independent variables describing offense and defense.	Team wins.	—
Audas, Dobson & Goddard (2000)	Hazard functions	English professional soccer, 1972/73–1996/97, match level data	Match results, league position and manager age, manager experience, player experience.	Duration (measured by the number of league matches played).	
Hofler & Payne (1997)	Stochastic Cobb-Douglas production frontier	27 National Basketball Association teams, 1992–1993	Ratio of field goal percentage, ratio of free- throw percentage, ratio of offensive rebounds, ratio of defensive rebounds, ratio of assists, ratio of steals.	Number of wins.	—
Scully (1994)	Deterministic and stochastic Cobb-Douglas frontier model	41 basketball coaches, 1949/50–1989/90	Team hitting and team pitching.	Win percent.	—
Zak, Huang & Siegfried (1979)	Cobb-Douglas deterministic frontier model	National Basketball Association teams	10 variables of pitch performance such as ratio of steals, ratio of assists.	Ratio of final scores.	—

This literature survey reveals that, to our knowledge, there are no published papers analyzing the efficiency of public sport federations with a stochastic frontier model. Moreover, this review is, in our view, included too few papers for such an important issue in sport, and many of the existing papers rely on old techniques, such as the deterministic frontier model, or the DEA methodology. The present chapter seeks to expand the existing literature alongside Dawson et al. (2000) and Hoeffler & Payne (1997), and to call the attention of other researchers to this neglected aspect of sports management.

METHODOLOGY

This chapter adopts the stochastic cost econometric frontier approach to illustrate the analysis of sport organizations efficiency. This approach, first proposed by Farrell (1957), came to prominence in the late 1970s as a result of the work of Aigner, Lovell, & Schmidt (1977), Battese & Corra (1977), and Meeusen & Van den Broeck (1977). In the stochastic econometric frontier, the method "floats" a piece-wise linear surface on top of the observations. This hyperplane defines the efficiency cost frontier, and the degree of inefficiency is quantified and partitioned by a series of measures of various distances from the hyperplane. In a cost frontier, the units on the frontier are efficient and the units above the frontier are inefficient. The zone below the frontier is unattainable, since the most production-efficient unit lies on the frontier. For clarity, frontier models normalize the efficiency scores in order for them to be equal to 1 for the best performing federation, and less than 1 for the inefficient federations. The econometric approach estimates the efficiency frontier econometrically and measures the difference between the inefficient units and the frontier by the residuals.

This is an intuitive approach. However, when it is assumed that the residuals have two components (noise and inefficiency), the result is the stochastic frontier model. Therefore, the main issue in econometric frontier models is the decomposition of the error terms. The model is defined by a general frontier cost function, dual to the production function proposed by Aigner et al. (1977) and Meeusen & van den Broeck (1977). The key feature of this approach is that the error term, which captures unobservable factors that affect costs, can be decomposed into two components: one that is traditionally found in econometric models, assumed to be independently and identically distributed, representing the effect of random shocks (noise) and a second term that captures technical inefficiencies and is assumed to be positive and distributed normally with zero mean and constant. The inefficiency component is assumed to be positive and represented by a half-normal independent distribution truncated at zero, signifying that each sport federation's actual cost must lie on or above its cost frontier. This implies that any deviation from the frontier is caused by management factors controlled by the sport federation. This signifies that the decomposition of error term describes more accurately the reality when compared with a cost function that aggregates both error terms.[1]

Because standard estimation procedures of the cost function yield merely the usual regression residual ε, rather than the inefficiency term, inefficiency in this model must be observed indirectly (Greene, 2003). In the case of panel data, such as that used in this chapter, Battese & Coelli (1988) used a conditional expectation of the inefficiency factor, conditioned on the realized value of the composite error term as an estimator of the inefficiency term. In other words, the mean "productive inefficiency" for the ith federation at any time t. See Kumbhakar & Lovell (2000) and Coelli, Prasada & Battese (1998) for details.

CONTEXT AND DATA

The Portuguese public sports sector, chosen to illustrate the use of frontier models to analyze efficiency in sports organizations, consists of a diverse variety of competitive sports, usually organized in leagues and managed centrally by a federation and locally by associations. The organizational structure of all sport in Portugal is vertical, headed by the Ministry of Sport. Below this, but without formal ties, is the National Confederation of Sport, which serves principally as a lobbying organization and interlocutor between its sixty-seven member-federations and the government. The next formal tier below the Ministry comprises the national federations of each sport, which are then hierarchically subdivided into regional associations covering the entire country. The latter serve as the local interfaces for the sports clubs and individuals involved as competing practitioners of the sports. Sport federations are politically influential and usually have some power when negotiating with the regulatory sport agency.

The government finances the federations on an annual basis as a means of carrying out sports policy. The annual allocation of public resources by the regulatory agency to the federations is based on an annual evaluation program in which sport activities are listed and quantified. Activities are only partially government-funded, but this is sufficient to fulfill the sports policy objectives. However, despite the follow-up inspection procedure carried out by the Sports Regulatory Council, based on ratios, auditing or feedback regarding the federations' activities is still imprecise and the regulatory agency ratios are based in information reported by the sport federations.

This, in turn, implies that the government is, at best, underinformed as to the return on its spending since incorrect or misleading information may be provided by the federations. From this it can be inferred that the federations are free to set their own private agendas, bypassing the public objectives that they are assumed to pursue and that would be in common with the government's declared policy goals.

Table 7.2 lists the funds allocated for training purposes to our sample of federations in 1998 and 2002. At present, there are ninety sports federations in Portugal, sixty-seven of which currently apply for public funds in order to promote training. Those that applied successively in 1998, 1999, 2000, 2001, and 2002 are listed in Table 7.2.

To estimate the cost frontier, a panel data set is used for the years 1998 to 2002, obtained from the public sports regulatory agency, on nineteen sport federations for five years (i.e., 19 units × 5 years = 95 observations). The federations that are considered in the analysis are those listed in Table 7.2. The regulatory agency registers the data for internal control.

TABLE 7.2
Public Funds Allocated to Sports Federations for Training, 1998–2002 (in Euros)

Federations	1998	1999	2000	2001	2002
Handball	23,443	24,939	21,049	49,879	51,375
Athletics	74,460	77,563	62,349	67,337	69,020
Badminton	10,692	11,023	8,514	12,469	12,743
Basketball	88,647	90,920	82,281	94,771	96,856
Cycling	42,617	44,393	39,903	27,299	27,900
Corfeball	19,947	20,670	34,915	39,903	40,781
Gymnastics	61,686	64,933	62,349	62,115	63,482
Judo	59,379	62,504	42,313	62,274	63,644
Wrestling	11,846	12,469	7,935	14,629	14,951
Swimming	33,169	34,915	42,253	43,599	44,558
Orienteering	32,995	34,915	34,791	34,287	35,041
Roller Hockey	12,275	13,058	14,963	17,457	17,841
Rowing	35,029	37,464	32,132	33,274	34,006
Rugby	21,313	22,435	24,939	14,694	15,017
Tennis	13,723	14,445	12,469	10,803	11,041
Table Tennis	48,778	50,029	29,593	35,045	35,816
Triathlon	2,418	2,493	2,678	2,946	3,011
Volleyball	23,941	24,939	21,049	49,879	50,976
Chess	75,236	77,563	62,349	67,337	68,818
	691,594	721,670	638,824	739,997	756,878

Frontier models require the identification of inputs (resources) and outputs (transformation of resources). Several criteria can be used in their selection. First, one empirical criterion is availability. Second, the literature survey is a way to ensure the validity of the research and hence, another criterion to take into account. The last criterion for measurement selection is the professional opinion of sports managers. This analysis follows all these three criteria.

A generalized stochastic Cobb-Douglas cost function is estimated. The variables in this model are defined in Table 7.3. This table also shows

TABLE 7.3
Descriptive Statistics of the Data, 1998–2002

Variable	Description	Minimum	Maximum	Mean	Standard deviation
Log costs	Logarithm of operational cost (euro) at constant price 1999=100	12.230	14.294	13.273	0.459
Log Pstudent	Logarithm of price of student measured dividing total subsidy allocated to the student by the number of students	0.200	1.400	1.310	0.033
Log Pinstructor	Logarithm of price of instructor, measured by dividing instructor's total salary by the number of instructors	3.957	4.220	4.075	0.045
Log Porganization	Logarithm of price of the organization, measured by dividing total subsidy allocated to secretaries and managers by the number of secretaries and managers	4.321	5.124	5.120	0.532
Log Pcapital	Logarithm of the price of capital, measured dividing the rents paid by the premises used to teach by the estimated square meters	1.352	2.381	2.014	0.058
Log courses	Logarithm of the total number of courses	3.180	4.289	3.895	0.202
Log passed	Logarithm of the total number of students passed	11.700	14.700	13.408	0.618
Olympic	Dummy variable which is one if the federation won an Olympic medal in the period and zero otherwise	0	1	0.150	0.281

summary statistics for these variables, and transformations made to these variables are described in the "Description" column. The traditional log-log specification is adopted to allow for the possible nonlinearity of the frontier.

The range of the frontiers is narrow, indicating that the federations in the sample are of similar dimension in terms of inputs and outputs. A justification for the inclusion of the Olympic dummy variable is needed. Its inclusion captures additional investment due to the Olympic cycle, which is an expenditure independent from training costs of federations, but may be indirectly related to these costs.

RESULTS

This study estimates a stochastic generalized Cobb-Douglas cost function with three input costs (cost price of students, measured by dividing total subsidy allocated to students by the number of students; cost price of instructors, measured by dividing the instructor's total salary by the number of instructors; and cost price of the organization, measured by dividing total subsidy allocated to secretaries and managers by the number of secretaries and managers), two outputs (courses offered and students passed), and a dichotomous variable to account for winning Olympic medals. Regularity conditions require that the cost function be linearly homogenous in input prices, nondecreasing in input prices, and concave, (Cornes, 1992). The traditional requested propriety of cost prices is that they are homogenous and linear (Varian, 1987). This is achieved by dividing money values by the price of the input capital. Table 7.4 presents the results obtained for the stochastic frontier using the software Frontier 4.1 from Coelli (1996), and adopting a half-normal distribution specification.[2]

The variables have been defined and characterized in Table 7.3. Table 7.4 presents the estimated results for the stochastic frontier. It is verified that the Cobb Douglas cost function specified above fits the data well, as the R-squared from the initial ordinary least-squares estimation that was used to obtain the starting values for the maximum-likelihood estimation is in excess of 93 percent and the overall F-statistic is 264.44. It is also verified that the variables have the expected signs, with the operational cost increasing with the price of students, the price of instructors and the price of organization, number of courses passed. Moreover, the total cost increases also with the Olympic dummy. The frontier parameters are all significant with the exception of eta (η), signifying that there are no statistically significant time-varying parameters in the sample. However, mu (μ) is positive, indicating that statistically significant, time-invariant, technical inefficiencies exist. Therefore the classical production frontier is not adequate to describe statistically the data used in the analysis. Therefore it can be concluded that the

TABLE 7.4
Stochastic Cobb Douglas Panel Cost Frontier (Dependent Variable Log of Total Cost)

Variables	Coefficients (t-ratio)
Constant	−0.921 (−1.126)
Log (Pstudents)	0.265 (4.588)[a]
Log (Pinstructors)	0.203 (2.532)[a]
Log (Porganization)	0.298 (4.910)[a]
Log (Courses)	0.985 (1.079)
Log (Passed)	0.094 (1.453)
Olympic	0.451 (4.631)[a]
$\sigma^2 = \sigma_V^2 + \sigma_U^2$	0.4401 (2.588)[a]
$\gamma = \frac{\sigma_U^2}{\sigma^2}$	0.16 (4.027)[a]
μ	0.170 (2.286)[a]
η	0.190 (0.510)
Log (likelihood)	87.653
Observations	95

[a]Significant at 1 percent level.
t Statistics in parentheses are below the parameters.

estimated model reads the data adequately either statistically and according to the economic theory. The efficient scores are not time varying, signifying constancy along the period, but are statistically significant.

Efficiency Rankings

Table 7.5 presents the results of the time-invariant efficiency scores computed from the residuals. Technical efficiency is achieved, in a broad economic sense, by the unit that allocates resources without waste and thus, the concept refers to a position on the best-practice production frontier. A position above the frontier represents wastage.

TABLE 7.5
Average Efficiency Scores, 1998–2002

Federation	Efficiency Scores
Orienteering	1.0000
Wrestling	0.9923
Rugby	0.9923
Basketball	0.9918
Cycling	0.9911
Gymnastics	0.9907
Roller hockey	0.9902
Athletics	0.9876
Judo	0.9872
Handball	0.9870
Rowing	0.9862
Tennis	0.9862
Swimming	0.9851
Badminton	0.9795
Chess	0.9763
Corfeball	0.9734
Triathlon	0.9566
Table tennis	0.9262
Volleyball	0.9173
Mean	0.9788
Median	0.9870
Std dev.	0.0221

The mean score is 98.8 percent. This score suggests that sports federations could reduce their input costs by 1.2 percent without decreasing their output, which, in this case, is the number of training courses held and the numbers of students passed. The maximum sports federation efficiency score was naturally 1, while the minimum score was 91.7 percent. The median was 98.7 percent and the standard deviation was 2.2 percent. These scores are average in comparison with those estimated for other activities. Low-efficiency scores are consistent with public-financed activities. High-efficiency scores are consistent with competitive activities, such as sports. Therefore the average result stays in the middle of these two possible extreme results. Our results demonstrate that the efficiency score is high but does not vary across the sample period.

DISCUSSION

The significance of the results of this research is clearly mixed. Overall, training costs increase with the price of students, with the price of instructors, with the organizational price, with the number of courses, and the number of students passed. These findings are intuitive for sports training, similar to what is observed in education (Abbot & Doucouliagos, 2003), and follows the economic theory stating that costs increase with activity.

In addition, training costs increase in the case of federations with Olympic medal winners. This reflects the larger investments needed to achieve sporting success at the highest level. Moreover, the larger Portuguese federations, measured by the number of federated athletes, are on average more efficient than their smaller counterparts, confirming previous research on this issue (Barros, 2003; Barros and Santos, 2003), despite these papers using different variables and different techniques. Conventional sports, such as athletics, also receive more funding than the minor sports, confirming previous research undertaken with another technique (Barros and Santos, 2003).

The general conclusion is that the current incentive regulation is not leading to productive efficiency for almost any of the federations. Why can we conclude that incentive regulation is not leading to the desired increase in efficiency? Because the average efficient score is 0.9872 and is not varying over time, therefore efficiency is not improving. Based on the results, the least efficient federations have room to improve, in order to reach the frontier of best practices, by using the subsidies allocated in an efficient way. Consequently, amendments to the regulation along the lines explained below are called for in order to enforce the achievement of productive efficiency.

On the basis of the estimated results, it can be affirmed that the main reason for time-invariant efficiency is derived from the political process of allocating subsidies, with the regulatory agency not linking the subsidies awarded to efficiency. In this context, the federations active in this field maintain their position independently of their performance, signifying that there is no incentive for these federations to change their level of efficiency over time. Furthermore, training costs increase with all factors, including with the Olympic dummy variable, which signifies that the sport federations are funding the Olympic cycle with training funds. Since there is separate funding for the Olympic cycle, this signifies that public funds allocated to sport federations may not be achieving sport policy aims, but rather finance the federation's priorities. While this funding mechanism seems a reasonable managerial practice, it also highlights the absence of adequate auditing practices by the regulatory agency.

Considering the results, the managerial implications of this chapter are as follows: (1) The government should establish a direct relationship between subsidies and sport performance. (2) The regulatory agency must upgrade its follow-up inspection procedure regarding the sports federations' activities in order to provide more explicitly binding incentives for increasing productive efficiency. (3) The regulatory agency must expand the scope of the data collected in the follow-up inspection to include contextual factors beyond managerial control, since it is not clear if different federations have the same operating environment. (4) The data gathered must be published and posted on the Internet, establishing a transparent data set, so that stakeholders have access to all data, including data not presented in the federation's annual report. (5) A benchmark analysis should be carried out with the data and published in order to enforce an efficient adjustment of the least-performing federations. (6) The benchmark should be based on competitive allocation of sport subsidies, based on performance.

Benchmarks based on European comparisons should be part of the policy agenda, since, in the context of a European market, this will be of most relevance for all units. A rationale to adopt this procedure is the poor performances of Portuguese athletes in the Olympic Games, in contrast to those of other countries of similar development levels, for example, Greece.

These measures will define an organizational governance environment with accountability, transparency, and efficiency incentives, which explicitly oblige the sport federations to achieve efficiency in their training activities. These recommendations seek to establish a governance framework within the federations, with the aim of improving organizational efficiency. Moreover, the savings that will result for the government will prevent waste and can be diverted toward alternative public uses.

CONTRIBUTION, LIMITATIONS, AND EXTENSIONS

At this juncture, it is appropriate to consider the contribution of the chapter to sports management, as well as its limitations and the possible extensions. The key contribution to the literature is the estimation of a stochastic cost frontier model in order to calculate efficiency scores of Portuguese federations that reflect the management of their training programs. Moreover, an extended literature survey is presented which clarifies the relative contribution of this chapter. Finally, the paper departs from previous papers in this field (Barros & Alves, 2003; Barros, 2003), which employed DEA and did not link efficiency in management with sporting performance. Compared with previous research, which was based on a smaller sample period, the results are somewhat similar, but the statistical results allow a clear interpretation of the determinants of costs and the statistical measurement of inefficiency in the production process.

The first limitation of this research concerns the data set and the second stems from the method. With reference to the data set, the panel data used is somewhat short. However, it can always be claimed that the data is short, and therefore, a quality analysis equally could not be carried out. The short data set implies that the conclusions are limited. In order for the latter to be more generalized, we would need to have a larger panel data set. Regarding the method, the homogeneity of the sports federations used in the analysis is questionable, since we compare units with different dimension.

A variety of extensions to this chapter could be undertaken. First, depending on the future availability of data, more sports performance measurements and nondiscriminatory inputs could be included. Second, input distance functions can be used to assess the efficiency scores.

CONCLUSION

This chapter has proposed a simple framework for the evaluation of sport federations and the rationalization of their operational activities. The analysis is based on a stochastic frontier model. Benchmarks are provided for improving the operations of less performing federations. Several interesting and useful managerial insights and implications from the study are raised. The general conclusion is that the majority of the federations analyzed are efficient, while a number of them have inefficiencies to be overcome. For the latter group, adjustment is needed in order to achieve the efficiency frontier. More investigation is needed to address the limitations mentioned.

NOTES

1. The total variance is defined as $\sigma^2 = \sigma_V^2 + \sigma_U^2$. The contribution of the error term to the total variation is as follows: $\sigma_V^2 = \sigma^2 /(1+\lambda^2)$. The contribution of the inefficient term is as follows: $\sigma_U^2 = \sigma^2 \lambda^2 /(1+\lambda^2)$. Where σ_V^2 is the variance of the error term v, σ_U^2 is the variance of the inefficient term u and λ is defined as $\lambda = \frac{\sigma_U}{\sigma_V}$, providing an indication of the relative contribution of U and V to ε.

2. The model is as follows:

$$Log\frac{TC_{it}}{Pcapital} = \beta_0 + \beta_1 Log\left(\frac{Pstudents_{it}}{Pcapital}\right) + \beta_2\left(\frac{Pinstructors_{it}}{Pcapital}\right)$$
$$+ \beta_3 Log\left(\frac{Porganization_{it}}{Pcapital}\right) + \beta_4 Log(Courses)_{it}$$
$$+ \beta_5(Passed_{it}) + \beta_6 Olympic + (V_{it} + U_{it})$$

REFERENCES

Abbot, M., & Doucouliagos, C. (2003). The efficiency of Australian universities: A data envelopment analysis. *Economics of Education Review, 22*(1), 89–97.

Aigner, D. J., Lovell, C. A. K., & Schmidt, P. (1977). Formulation and estimation of stochastic frontier production function models. *Journal of Econometrics, 6,* 21–37.

Barros, C. P. (2003). Incentive regulation and efficiency in sports organizational training activities. *Sport Management Review, 6*(1), 33–52.

Barros, C. P., & Alves, F. P. (2003). Human capital theory and social capital theory on sports management. *International Advances in Economic Research, 9*(3), 218–226.

Barros, C. P., & Santos, A. (2003). Productivity on sport organizational training activities: A DEA study. *European Sport Management Quarterly, 1,* 46–65.

Battese, G. E., & Coelli, T. J. (1988). Prediction of firm-level technical efficiencies with a generalised frontier production function and panel data. *Journal of Econometrics, 38,* 387–399.

Battese, G. E., & Corra, G. S. (1977). Estimation of a production frontier model: With application to the pastoral zone of Eastern Australia. *Australian Journal of Agricultural Economics, 21,* 169–179.

Coelli, T. J. (1996). A guide to FRONTIER version 4.1: A computer program. For stochastic frontier production and cost function estimation. Working Paper no. 7/96, Centre for Efficiency and Productivity Analysis. University of New England, Armidale, Australia.

Coelli, T. J., Prasada, R., & Battese, G. E. (1998). *An introduction to efficiency and productivity analysis.* Amsterdam: Kluwer Academic Press.

Cooper, W. W., Seiford, L. M., & Tone, K. (2000). *Data envelopment analysis.* Boston: Kluwer.

Cornes, R. (1992). *Duality and modern economics.* Cambridge: Cambridge University Press.

Dawson, P., Dobson, S., & Gerrard, B. (2000). Stochastic frontier and the temporal structure of managerial efficiency in English soccer. *Journal of Sports Economics, 1*(4), 341–362.

Farrell, M. J. (1957). The measurement of productive efficiency. *Journal of the Royal Statistical Society,* Series A, *120*(3), 253–290.

Fizel, J. L., & D'itri, M. P. (1997). Managerial efficiency, managerial succession and organizational performance. *Managerial and Decision Economics, 18*(4), 295–308.

Greene, W. (2001). New developments in the estimation of stochastic frontier models with panel data. Efficiency Series Paper 6/2001, Department of Economics, University of Oviedo, Spain.

Greene, W. (2005). Reconsidering heterogeneity in panel data estimators of the stochastic frontier model. *Journal of Econometrics, 126,* 269–303.

Greene, W. H. (2003). *Econometric analysis* (5th ed.). Upper Saddle River, N.J.: Prentice-Hall.

Griffin, J. E., & Steel, M. F. J. (2007). Bayesian stochastic frontier using winbugs. *Journal of Productivity Analysis, 27*(3), 163–176.

Haas, D. J. (2003a). Financial efficiency in the major league soccer. *Journal of Sport Economics, 4*(3), 203–215.

Haas, D. J. (2003b). Productive efficiency of English football teams—a data envelopment approach. *Managerial and Decision Economics, 24*, 403–410.

Hoeffler, R. A., & Payne, J. E. (1997). Measuring efficiency in the National Basketball Association. *Economic Letters, 55,* 293–299.

Khumbhakar, S. C., & Lovell, C. A. K. (2000). *Stochastic frontier analysis.* New York: Cambridge University Press.

Meeusen, W., & Van den Broeck, J. (1977). Efficiency estimation from a Cobb-Douglas production function with composed error. *International Economic Review, 18,* 435–444.

Orea, L., & Khumbhakar, S. (2004). Efficiency measurement using stochastic frontier latent class model. *Empirical Economics, 29,* 169–183.

Simar, L., & Wilson, P. W. (2007). Estimation and inference in two-stage, semi-parametric models of production processes. *Journal of Econometrics, 136,* 31–64.

Slack, T. (1997). *Understanding sport organizations—The application of organizational theory.* Champaign, Ill.: Human Kinetics.

Valverde, S. C., Humphrey, D. B., & del Paso, R. L. (2007). Opening the black box: Finding the sources of cost inefficiency. *Journal of Productivity Analysis, 27*(3), 209–220.

Varian, H. R. (1987). *Intermediate microeconomics: A modern approach.* New York: Norton.

Eight

New Franchise Location in Major- and Minor-League Baseball

Michael C. Davis

Since 1961 Major League Baseball (MLB) has expanded by an average of about one team every four years. It has been a number of years since the last MLB expansion (1998), but eventually due to congressional pressure or the threat of a lawsuit from a spurned suitor of a team, the American or National League will expand again. While MLB has only seen one team move in the last thirty years, many teams have threatened relocation in that period and those threats continue today with the Florida Marlins. Some indication of which cities would be next in line for an expansion or a relocated team is useful. By examining the factors that determine which cities currently have MLB teams, we can help potential cities determine whether they are truly in the hunt for a future team.

In addition, minor-league baseball will have to expand at the same time to provide farm clubs for the major leagues. Also, almost all of the cities that are under consideration for major-league teams currently have minor-league teams that would need to find new homes if a major-league team moves into their territory. This chapter will therefore identify possible minor-league cities for future expansion teams. Finally, while major-league relocations are rare, franchises change homes in the minor leagues every year. The cities that are suggested for minor-league expansion teams will also be good suggestions for franchise shifts.

Following an introduction to the professional baseball market in North America, we examine past studies of the locations and attendance for major- and minor-league baseball teams. Factors that are considered are demographics, league rules, geography, team success, and interest in baseball. After examining all of the various factors and how they should affect particular teams and cities, we examine cities identified as the best homes for future baseball teams.

INTRODUCTION TO THE PROFESSIONAL BASEBALL MARKET

Professional baseball can be divided into three groups for examining how teams move. The three groups are the major leagues, affiliated minor leagues, and the independent minor leagues. A complete listing of all leagues can be found in Table 8.1.

TABLE 8.1
Professional Baseball Leagues in the United States and Canada

League	Level	Number of Teams	Location
National	Major	16	Entire USA
American	Major	14	Entire USA/Toronto
Pacific Coast	AAA	16	Western Half and parts of South
International	AAA	14	Eastern Half
Eastern	AA	12	New England/Mid-Atlantic
Southern	AA	10	Gulf States/Tennessee/Carolinas
Texas	AA	8	Texas and Southern Plains
Florida State	High A	12	Florida
California	High A	10	California
Carolina	High A	8	Mid-Atlantic/South Atlantic
South Atlantic	Low A	16	South Atlantic/Mid-Atlantic/ Eastern Midwest
Midwest	Low A	14	Midwest
New York–Penn	Short-Season A	14	Massachusetts/New York/ Pennsylvania/Vermont
Northwest	Short-Season A	8	Pacific Northwest
Appalachian	Rookie	10	North Carolina/Tennessee/ Virginia/West Virginia
Pioneer	Rookie	8	Idaho, Montana, Utah, Wyoming
Gulf Coast	Rookie	13	Florida
Arizona	Rookie	9	Arizona
American Association	Independent	10	Great Plains/Texas/Louisiana
Atlantic	Independent	8	Mid-Atlantic/Connecticut
Can-Am	Independent	8	New England/Mid-Atlantic/ Quebec
Frontier	Independent	10	Midwest
Golden Baseball	Independent	6	Arizona/California/Nevada
Northern	Independent	8	Midwest/Alberta/Manitoba
United	Independent	6	Texas/Louisiana

The major leagues comprise two leagues, the National and American, with a total of thirty teams. The major leagues have a great degree of stability, as there has only been one franchise shift since 1973 (Montreal to Washington in 2005). In addition, the number of teams has risen from twenty-four in 1970 to thirty in 1998.

The affiliated minor leagues are made up of teams that are subject to a player development agreement with the major-league teams. The major-league teams control most, if not all, baseball operations associated with the minor-league teams, including the assignment of players and coaches to the teams. There are sixteen affiliated minor leagues, with 182 teams.[1] There are six levels of minor leagues (from highest to lowest): AAA, AA, High-A, Low-A, Short-Season-A, and Rookie. The playing talent is generally higher in AAA than in AA, in AA than in High-A and so forth. Also the stadiums tend to be bigger at the higher levels leading to higher attendance totals. Each major-league team is affiliated with one team in each of AAA, AA, High-A, and Low-A, and with one to three teams from Short-Season A or Rookie.

There is less stability in the affiliated minor leagues than in the major leagues. Over the last few years approximately five franchises per year on average have moved in the affiliated minor leagues. Expansion generally precedes or follows the major-league expansions, so those are fairly rare for the leagues.[2] The affiliations are constantly changing, even if the teams do not move.

The last group to discuss consists of teams found in the independent leagues. The independents are professional baseball leagues not associated with the major-league teams in any way. The independent leagues have substantially more freedom in choosing their own players, since they are not assigned by the major-league teams. There are more independent-league teams in major cities since they do not have to abide by the restrictions that major- and minor-league teams can place on other affiliated teams moving into their territories. The independent leagues are much less stable than either the major leagues or the affiliated minor-league teams. Whereas teams frequently change locations in the affiliated minor leagues, whole independent leagues frequently come into existence and fold.

FACTORS AFFECTING THE LOCATIONS OF TEAMS

Demographic Factors

In 2003, the Shreveport Swamp Dragons left their longtime home for Frisco, Texas, a suburb of Dallas. The stadium in Shreveport, Louisiana, was only sixteen years old and there was a lot of tradition associated with the city. Shreveport was a city with a metropolitan area of approximately 420,000, whereas Frisco could draw from the large population base of Dallas with almost 6 million. While the market is shared with the major-league Texas Rangers, there is still plenty of population for a successful minor-league baseball team in the area as well.

Demographic variables that could be important determinants of major-league baseball include population, income, population growth and income distribution. While the other demographic variables are important, population overwhelms all other variables.[3]

Table 8.2 shows a comparison of the number of teams in each U.S. metropolitan area in North America's four major sports.[4] Table 8.3 presents a similar list of metropolitan areas in Canada.[5] The baseball teams are more closely tied to population than the other three. MLB has occupied almost all of the larger markets with the exception of Montreal and Vancouver, markets that have been ignored (with the exception of the NHL) by the other leagues as well. The NFL has teams in small cities such as Jacksonville, Buffalo, and New Orleans, and does not have any teams in Los Angeles.[6] The NHL has teams in a number of smaller cities like Ottawa, Calgary, Edmonton, and Raleigh, while lacking a team in larger cities such as Houston, Seattle, and San Diego. The NBA has teams in Memphis, New Orleans, and Salt Lake City, but no teams in San Diego, St. Louis, and Montreal.

TABLE 8.2
Combined Statistical Areas Ranked by Population for American Metropolitan Areas Major-League Sports Teams

Rank	City	Population	MLB	NFL	NHL	NBA
1	New York	21,899,042	2	2	3	2
2	Los Angeles	17,481,473	2	0	2	2
3	Chicago	9,610,038	2	1	1	1
4	Washington-Baltimore	8,050,560	2	2	1	1
5	San Jose–San Francisco-Oakland	7,148,000	2	2	1	1
6	Philadelphia	5,949,976	1	1	1	1
7	Dallas–Fort Worth	5,927,494	1	1	1	1
8	Boston	5,802,063	1	1	1	1
9	Detroit	5,424,253	1	1	1	1
10	Miami	5,355,903	1	1	1	1
11	Houston	5,277,455	1	1	0	1
12	Atlanta	5,121,741	1	1	1	1
13	Seattle	3,766,678	1	1	0	1

(*continued*)

TABLE 8.2 (*continued*)

Rank	City	Population	MLB	NFL	NHL	NBA
14	Phoenix	3,713,291	1	1	1	1
15	Minneapolis–St. Paul	3,434,066	1	1	1	1
16	Cleveland	2,938,607	1	1	0	1
17	San Diego	2,935,190	1	1	0	0
18	St. Louis	2,829,371	1	1	1	0
19	Denver	2,605,861	1	1	1	1
20	Tampa–St. Petersburg	2,586,417	1	1	1	0
21	Pittsburgh	2,490,915	1	1	1	0
22	Sacramento	2,157,974	0	0	0	1
23	Cincinnati	2,099,045	1	1	0	0
24	Charlotte	2,067,297	0	1	0	1
25	Portland	2,062,109	0	0	0	1
26	Kansas City	1,994,720	1	1	0	0
27	Indianapolis	1,934,621	0	1	0	1
28	Orlando	1,923,655	0	0	0	1
29	Columbus	1,917,450	0	0	1	0
30	San Antonio	1,852,508	0	0	0	1
31	Milwaukee	1,707,181	1	1	0	1
32	Las Vegas	1,686,210	0	0	0	0
33	Virginia Beach–Norfolk–Newport News	1,641,671	0	0	0	0
34	Providence	1,627,194	0	0	0	0
35	Salt Lake City	1,559,957	0	0	0	1
36	Greensboro–Winston-Salem	1,472,050	0	0	0	0
37	Nashville	1,469,698	0	1	1	0
38	Raleigh-Durham	1,466,593	0	0	1	0
39	Austin–Round Rock	1,411,199	0	0	0	0
40	New Orleans	1,362,086	0	1	0	1
41	Louisville	1,332,300	0	0	0	0
42	Grand Rapids	1,305,498	0	0	0	0
43	Hartford	1,297,440	0	0	0	0
44	Memphis	1,248,492	0	0	0	1
45	Buffalo	1,236,788	0	1	1	0
46	Jacksonville	1,223,741	0	0	1	0
47	Oklahoma City	1,210,109	0	0	0	0
48	Greenville	1,172,838	0	0	0	0
49	Birmingham	1,160,814	0	0	0	0
50	Richmond	1,156,849	0	0	0	0

Source: Bureau of Economic Analysis.

Note: All major-league teams are accounted for except Canadian teams (see Table 8.2) and the Green Bay Packers. The Green Bay metropolitan area has a population of approximately 295,000.

TABLE 8.3
Canadian Metropolitan Areas Major-League Sports Teams Ranked by Population

Rank	City	Population	MLB	NFL	NHL	NBA
1	Toronto	4,682,897	1	0	1	1
2	Montreal	3,426,350	0	0	1	0
3	Vancouver	1,986,965	0	0	1	0
4	Ottawa	1,063,664	0	0	1	0
5	Calgary	951,395	0	0	1	0
6	Edmonton	937,845	0	0	1	0
7	Quebec	682,757	0	0	0	0
8	Winnipeg	671,274	0	0	0	0
9	Hamilton	662,401	0	0	0	0
10	London	432,451	0	0	0	0

Source: Statistics Canada.

Two reasons might explain these differences. The first is that MLB is dependent upon a larger fan base, as MLB teams have eighty-one home games with stadiums that hold around 40,000 people. The NBA and NHL have fewer home games (forty-one) and smaller arenas (~25,000). While NFL teams have much larger stadiums (~70,000) they only have eight home games a year. The other three sports are dependent upon a dedicated small fan base, whereas baseball is more dependent upon a large group of fans. Therefore they need a larger base to draw from. A related issue is stadium quality. In particular, NFL teams get to keep a larger portion of their revenues from luxury boxes than from regular seats. An NFL team would be more interested in stadium quality than in the size of the surrounding population, which can be seen from its lack of having a team in Los Angeles.

Population is such a key factor in determining the location of a major-league baseball team in a particular metropolitan area that it prevents a statistical analysis of other factors. Even the exceptions to the correlation between population and presence of a major-league team can be explained by the presence of large nearby cities. A comparison of Milwaukee (the smallest metropolitan area with a team) and Sacramento (the largest metropolitan area without a team) can shed light on this phenomenon. Milwaukee is about ninety-two miles from Chicago and Sacramento is about eighty-two miles from Oakland. Both the San Jose–San Francisco–Oakland and Chicago metropolitan areas have two MLB teams. However, metro Chicago has a population of approximately 9.2 million and metro San Jose has a population of approximately 7.1 million. The difference between the populations in secondary markets could greatly outweigh the small difference in population in the primary market.

Population is the key variable to determine the particular level of minor-league baseball present in a metropolitan area. Figure 8.1 graphs the predicted probabilities of having different types of minor-league teams for various population levels. For low population levels, the predicted probabilities for having no team are almost 100 percent, but once we pass 1,000,000 people, it is much more likely that the city will have a team in High-A, AA or AAA. Also, the middle levels peak in their probability of having a team at the middle values of population. Low-A has the highest probability of having a team at approximately 500,000.

Tables 8.4 and 8.5 list cities underrepresented or overrepresented in terms of the minor-league baseball teams in those cities.[7] These tables can be used to identify idiosyncratic factors missed in the estimation of the team level and to identify future entries into team levels.

We now have three years of franchise movements to examine since the creation of the data set used to produce the tables in this chapter. Austin now has a AAA franchise that moved there from Edmonton. Allentown, Pennsylvania (fifteenth among those without a AAA team and thirty-sixth

FIGURE 8.1
Predicted Probabilities of Level of Minor-League Baseball for Different Populations

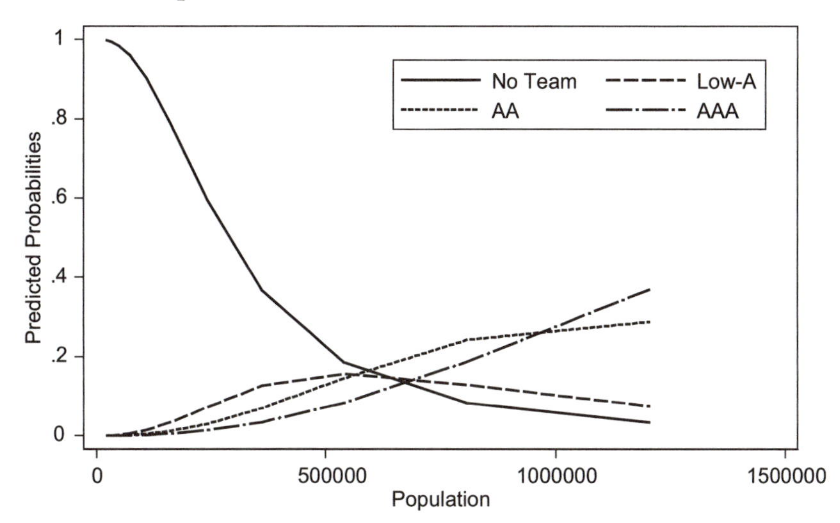

Source: M. C. Davis, "Called Up to the Big Leagues: An Examination of the Factors Affecting the Location of Minor League Baseball Teams," *International Journal of Sport Finance* 1, no. 4 (2006): 253–264.
Note: Figure graphs predicted probabilities of having team at a particular minor-league level, when all other values are set to their mean values. Probabilities are calculated at set intervals of log (population) but described in levels, with linear interpolation between points. Independent, Rookie/SS-A and High-A are included in the model but excluded from the graph for clarity.

TABLE 8.4
Top 10 Cities with Highest Probabilities to Have Team at Particular Level That Do Not Have Team at That Level or Higher

	AAA	AA	High A	Any Team
1	San Antonio (7)	Greensboro, N.C. (4)	Honolulu (2)	Honolulu (29)
2	Orlando (8)	Grand Rapids, Mich. (7)	Grand Rapids, Mich. (3)	Springfield, Mass. (47)
3	Hartford, Conn. (17)	Albany (8)	Albany (4)	Anchorage (49)
4	Jacksonville (18)	Dayton, Ohio (10)	Dayton, Ohio (5)	Lafayette, La. (57)
5	Greensboro, N.C. (20)	Honolulu (12)	Allentown, Pa. (6)	Gulfport, Miss. (59)
6	Grand Rapids, Mich. (21)	Springfield, Mass. (19)	Springfield, Mass. (8)	Fayetteville, N.C. (65)
7	Austin (22)	Charleston, S.C. (20)	Charleston, S.C. (9)	Reno, Nev. (69)
8	Albany (24)	Allentown, Pa. (21)	Baton Rouge (10)	Madison, Wis. (77)
9	Birmingham (26)	Baton Rouge (22)	Boise (11)	Lancaster, Pa. (83)
10	Tulsa (27)	Boise (23)	Jackson, Miss. (12)	Santa Barbara, Calif. (87)

Source: M. C. Davis, "Called Up to the Big Leagues: An Examination of the Factors Affecting the Location of Minor League Baseball Teams," *International Journal of Sport Finance* 1, no. 4 (2006): 253–264.

Note: Number in parentheses represents rank for particular level or above excluding teams that have a team at higher rank. The Any Team is rank among all locations. Example: Excluding cities with major league teams, Greensboro had the twentieth-highest probability of having a team at the AAA level, but Greensboro does not have a AAA team. Of the nineteen cities in front of Greensboro, fifteen of them had AAA teams. Excluding cities with major and AAA teams, Greensboro had the third-highest probability of having either a AAA or AA team.

TABLE 8.5
Top 10 Cities with Lowest Probabilities to Have Team at Particular Level That Do Have a Team at That Level

	AAA	AA	High A	Any Team
1	Scranton, Pa. (59)	Altoona, Pa. (226)	Kinston, N.C. (336)	Clinton, Iowa (459)
2	Colorado Springs (53)	Jackson, Tenn. (153)	Vero Beach, Fla. (114)	Richmond, Ind. (417)
3	Tucson (46)	Erie, Pa. (110)	Lynchburg, Va. (87)	Oneonta, N.Y. (416)
4	Syracuse (45)	Binghamton, N.Y. (93)	Myrtle Beach, S.C. (71)	Burlington, Iowa (410)
5	Des Moines (44)	Norwich, Conn. (84)	Visalia, Calif. (68)	Kinston, N.C. (369)
6	Toledo (38)	Midland, Tex. (77)	Wilmington, N.C. (60)	Rome, Ga. (354)
7	Fresno, Calif. (35)	Reading, Pa. (52)	Roanoke, Va. (57)	Martinsville, Va. (330)
8	Albuquerque (34)	Mobile, Ala. (40)	Port St. Lucie, Fla. (52)	Helena, Mont. (306)
9	Omaha (31)	Huntsville, Ala. (35)	Modesto, Calif. (46)	Jamestown, N.Y. (280)
10	Oklahoma City (30)	Chattanooga (33)	Lakeland, Fla. (36)	Great Falls, Mont. (279)

Source: M. C. Davis, "Called Up to the Big Leagues: An Examination of the Factors Affecting the Location of Minor League Baseball Teams," *International Journal of Sport Finance* 1, no. 4 (2006): 253–264.

Note: Number in parentheses represents rank for particular level or above excluding teams that have a team at higher rank. The Any Team is rank among all locations. Example: Des Moines has a AAA team; however, according to the model it only had the thirty-seventh highest probability of having a AAA team and there were five cities with lower probabilities that have AAA teams.

overall), will get a AAA franchise (moving from Ottawa) for the 2008 season. These moves would be predicted by the model.

However, some recent moves that have taken place would not be consistent with the cities listed in Table 8.4. Three AA franchises that changed homes can be used as examples. In the Texas League, El Paso (ranked twenty-seventh likely for a AA team) moved to Springfield, Missouri (ranked seventy-first), and recently it was announced that Wichita (ranked eighteenth) would be moving to Springdale, Arkansas (ranked eighty-sixth). Also a Southern League franchise moved from Greenville, South Carolina (ranked fourteenth), to Jackson, Mississippi (ranked twenty-fifth). According to the results presented in Table 8.4 these would all be suboptimal moves. In each case the city the team was moving to either had recently built a new stadium or agreed to build a new stadium. Springfield had the advantage of becoming affiliated with the St. Louis Cardinals. The Fayetteville-Springdale-Rogers metropolitan area is one of the fastest growing in the country. The population there grew 39 percent between 1993 and 2003, compared to an 8 percent growth rate for Wichita. The northwestern Arkansas area might be one of the most appealing markets in years to come, and the first franchise there would be able to restrict other teams from invading their territory. Jackson, Mississippi, would have been an attractive market for a Southern League team to move into. The much greater appeal of the stadium in Jackson could easily have made up for the smaller population of the area relative to Greenville.

Market size also has a positive effect on minor-league baseball attendance. The larger the market size, the greater the attendance.[8] However, the effect seems most prevalent at the middle levels of minor-league baseball: AA, High A and Low-A.[9]

League Rules and Regulations

In 1991 Steve Bryant dreamed of bringing a minor-league baseball team to Raleigh, North Carolina.[10] At the time, there was already one minor-league team in the metropolitan area, the Durham Bulls. Also the National Association of Baseball Teams granted geographical rights that prevented a team from moving within thirty-five miles of an existing one. The owner had intended to place the team in Raleigh, but that was within the thirty-five-mile exclusion zone. The owner chose a spot exactly thirty-five miles away from the Durham Bulls, and the Carolina Mudcats had a stadium built in Zebulon, North Carolina.

The rules of MLB and Minor League Baseball are important for the location of teams. The current major-league rules grant each major-league team a series of counties within which they retain exclusive rights, or in some cases shared rights with another major-league team. In addition, they have a fifteen-mile buffer beyond the county zone from which they can restrict teams.

These rules have a particularly important impact on markets that are large enough to have multiple teams. The New York metropolitan area has about 22 million people. A team looking to relocate in the absence of any rules would seriously consider a move to that metropolitan area, but would not be allowed to do so under the current rules.

There are five metropolitan areas with two major-league teams. Four of these situations came into existence when the two major leagues were less cooperative with each other than they are now. The exception shows the difficulty in a team relocating into another team's market. When the Nationals moved into Washington in 2005, the Baltimore Orioles had to be given a great deal of compensation for the entry into their market. This demand for compensation may have been well grounded, though over-dramatized, as it has been estimated that a team in northern Virginia would cost the Orioles $861,502 a year from lost attendance.[11] Additional losses would come from competition in television, radio, and merchandising.

The current minor-league rule is that a team cannot enter into a county that borders a county that already has a team. This is less of an issue since the cities that typically have populations large enough to support multiple minor-league baseball teams also have populations large enough to support a major-league team. However, these rules can make a difference on occasion, as was shown with the Carolina Mudcats example. Under the current rules the Bulls would not only have been able to restrict the Mudcats from Raleigh, but would also have been able to keep the Mudcats out of Zebulon, as Zebulon's county (Wake) borders Durham County. To get around the current rules would have required the Mudcats to move an additional five miles away from Durham but, more important, away from the population base in Raleigh.

Additional rules that will affect the feasibility of certain locations obtaining a AAA team in the short term are the minimum requirements for stadiums for that level. The current rules require that AAA franchises have a stadium capable of holding a minimum of 10,000 fans. A city considering an AAA team must have a stadium already capable of holding 10,000 people, have a stadium expandable to 10,000 people, or be willing to build a new, larger stadium. Both the major- and minor-league rules will strongly influence the feasible placement of future expansion teams or existing teams looking for new homes.

Geographic Factors

On August 15, 2006, the Chicago Cubs were tied entering the seventeenth inning of their away game with the Houston Astros. The Cubs had gone through their entire bullpen and most of their starters. The only remaining pitcher was the scheduled starter for the next day, and the Cubs used this pitcher for two innings and won the game. Although they had just finished a late game and they were scheduled to play the next day at 2:20; the Cubs were fortunate that their AAA affiliate, the Iowa Cubs, was playing at the Astros' AAA affiliate in Round Rock, a suburb of Austin. The Cubs called up Iowa's scheduled starter for the next day and had him pitch the game instead of any of their tired pitchers from the night before. Thanks to an outstanding pitching performance from their emergency starter, the Cubs won that game as well.

The above anecdote, while in this case benefiting the away team and being an extreme example, shows an advantage of having a nearby minor-league affiliate to the major-league teams. Teams can call on those players when needed, whether the reason is injury, pitcher fatigue, or strategy. If the Iowa Cubs had been playing in Tacoma, the manager of the Chicago Cubs might have felt constrained to keep the original starter in reserve for the next game, which would have reduced the team's chances of winning the first game. A close farm team increases the likelihood of this eventuality having a positive result.

In addition to influencing the affiliations of the AAA teams, distance from major-league affiliates might influence the location of teams in smaller markets that are closer to major-league teams. Table 8.5 shows the ten teams with the lowest predicted probabilities to have a AAA league team yet actually have one. Five of the top six provide logistical advantages of having a relatively nearby team that larger more distant markets could not provide. The five are Scranton for Philadelphia, Colorado Springs for Colorado, Tucson for Arizona, Des Moines for the Chicago Cubs, and Toledo for Detroit. One of the appealing features of the AA Eastern League is that it provides nearby affiliate teams for the major-league teams in the Northeast.[12]

As the distance from a major-league team increases, so does the likelihood of having a minor-league baseball team at a higher level, because there is a competition factor involved.[13] A similar effect exists for nearby major-league teams as well, as there is a small effect on the attendance of major-league teams in neighboring cities.[14]

While major-league teams have no problem traveling great distances, none of the minor leagues encompass the entire nation. Lower travel costs would explain why the lower the level of baseball the more close-knit the leagues are. In trying to determine where future minor-league baseball teams end up, we should realize that the Florida State League is not going to put a team in Barrow, Alaska.

Team Success

"First in War. First in Peace. Last in the American League." During the 1950s the Washington Senators often finished last in the American League in the standings and last in the American League in attendance. The fans simply showed no interest in supporting a team that was never in a pennant race. In 1960 the team left Washington for Minnesota where their fortunes improved as the team was more successful and the attendance was much higher. The team was replaced in Washington with a new Washington Senators team that had similar success in the stands and on the field as the first incarnation. In only one season did the team finish above .500, and in that season the team also was in the top half of the American League in attendance. After eleven seasons of futility, the team left for Texas.

When Washington was mentioned as a possible site for the Montreal Expos, the fact that the first two teams left was held against Washington as a prospective site. However, if the new team is capable of attaining success on the field it might also be able to draw fans to the stands as well.

A number of studies have shown that attendance for baseball is correlated with team success. This finding is not surprising given that attending a sporting event is a lot more fun if the team you are rooting for is winning. Even casual fans will get more enjoyment as the fans around them are more excited.

Fans also want the outcome of the game to have uncertainty; otherwise the excitement is lessened. The optimal winning percentage for the home team in order to maximize attendance is between .60 and .66.[15]

While success would seem to be of obvious importance to fans of major-league teams, the team success might not be as important to minor-league fans. Minor-league pennant races are not nearly as important, and the teams rely on casual fans for their support. However, everyone would prefer to see a higher quality product, and a more successful minor-league team would be more likely to provide that. Winning affects attendance positively for at least some minor-league teams.[16]

Since success is important for attendance, a team that consistently loses will not draw many fans. The lack of fans will cause the team to lose money and then begin to look for a more profitable location. So even though team success is tied to factors that are mostly independent of location, it can be associated with team movements.

Interest in Baseball and Other Entertainment Options

Ottawa would seem to be an optimal location for AAA baseball. The metropolitan area has approximately 1 million people, about the right size and near the mean value for AAA teams. There is a fifteen-year-old state-of-the-art stadium built specifically for baseball and to the current specifications of AAA baseball. While not having won any pennants recently, the Ottawa team has usually finished over .500. However, in 2008 the Ottawa Lynx of the International League will be moving to Allentown, Pennsylvania. While Allentown seems like a logical site for a AAA team, especially with a brand-new ballpark being built and its proximity to Philadelphia, there are only about 780,000 people in the metropolitan area, making it considerably smaller than Ottawa.

However, it seems not that Allentown was appealing, but that Ottawa was an unappealing home. Ottawa has consistently finished last in attendance in the International League. It might be the case that there is just very little interest in baseball in Canada as opposed to sports like hockey and football.[17]

In certain cities there are other options for entertainment that might lead to lower interest in professional baseball. The closest substitutes would be other sports options. Contrary to what was suggested in the anecdote about the Ottawa Lynx, the general effect of having a hockey team is that cities with hockey teams are more likely to have baseball teams, not less likely. While this result could be that the variable is accidentally accounting for population in a nonlinear manner, it could also be that it indicates a city's willingness to construct stadiums for sports teams. A city that is willing to build a nice arena for a hockey team might also be willing to build a brand-new ballpark for a baseball team.

Since not all cities are alike, the underlying interest in baseball may also be important to teams locating to a particular city. While we cannot measure variations in interest across cities, low attendance in a particular location given the team's success and market size would be an indication that baseball does not have much appeal in the area. If a number of teams have entered and abandoned the metropolitan area, that would also be an indication that the metropolitan area is not as interested in baseball as other entertainment options, as seems to be the case in Ottawa.

The probability of a team moving into a particular city is dependent upon the willingness of the city to construct a quality stadium for the team. Typically this willingness will be correlated with the interest of the public in having a team move there. However, there can be a disconnect between the interests of the citizens and the administrators of the city. The interests of the city's mayor and councils can often override the interest of the public when it comes to stadium construction.

DISCUSSION

Every city in North America with a population greater than 2.4 million has at least one MLB team (except for Montreal). No team is located in a city with a population below 1.5 million. Cities with populations between these values are the most obvious choices for either future expansion teams or franchises that move.

The population findings discussed above shed light on potential markets for future expansion or franchise moves. In their threats to move, the Florida Marlins' most talked-about destination was San Antonio. San Antonio has a smaller metropolitan area than a number of other cities, including Portland, Sacramento, and Charlotte. However, San Antonio is relatively close to Austin, with a population of approximately 1.4 million and no major-league teams, and Houston with a population of approximately 5.3 million and one major-league team. Those secondary markets might have made San Antonio more attractive than larger cities such as Portland and Sacramento.[18] Another reason was San Antonio's greater likelihood of building a publicly funded stadium for the team, something Portland was reluctant to do.

Thomas Bruggink and Jason Zamparelli developed a Viability Index for Major League Baseball and ranked San Antonio ninth as a site for a future major-league team.[19] Washington (which in their model is separated from Baltimore) was first and has already seen a team move into the city. Based on their Viability Index, the two best locations for a future team would be Salt Lake City and Charlotte.

When it comes to the minor leagues, Table 8.4 suggests which cities should be considered for any future expansion teams or existing teams looking for a new home.

Grand Rapids and Jacksonville seem particularly well suited to a promotion to AAA. Both are on the top 10 list for AAA teams in Table 8.4, and both already have a stadium capable of seating the AAA minimum capacity of 10,000. Birmingham (actually the suburb of Hoover) is also a possibility for a AAA team. It is on the top 10 list and has a stadium with a capacity of 10,000. Also, the stadium was originally designed to be expanded to seat 26,000 and was one of five finalists for a AAA franchise when the AAA leagues expanded in 1993.[20] However, since that time there have been two additional expansion franchises at the AAA level (in 1998) and numerous franchise movements, and yet Birmingham does not have a AAA team. It may be that the new stadium constructed in Hoover, despite being less than twenty years old, is now out of date relative to many other minor-league stadiums.

Grand Rapids has another advantage in that it is also relatively close to two major-league teams that have neither their AAA nor their AA franchise nearby: the Chicago White Sox and the Milwaukee Brewers. None of the three AA leagues operates in the Midwest, so they cannot have a nearby AA franchise. The White Sox AAA affiliate is in Charlotte and Milwaukee's is in Nashville. Having their AAA affiliate in Grand Rapids would give the teams the proximity advantages other teams have enjoyed. With the announcement that a new team in Allentown would be the Phillies' AAA affiliate, there are no other obvious locations that have a proximity advantage for the major-league cities until we get down to pretty small cities.

Once we get beyond the major leagues and AAA, geography becomes a key factor in determining the locations of teams. Four of the top 10 cities on the AA list for future franchises are located quite far from any of the three AA leagues (Eastern, Southern, and Texas).

Table 8.4 cannot be considered to be a comprehensive list of possible sites. In addition to the fact already mentioned that some cities can have unaccounted factors that would be to their advantage for having a team, two additional types of locations are not included in the list. Each city is limited to one team in the model and some cities have multiple teams. Because American and Canadian data cannot be compared directly, Canadian cities are excluded as well.

Over the last ten years there has been a migration of teams from Canada to the United States at all levels of the minor leagues. Pacific Coast League teams moved from Calgary and Edmonton to Albuquerque and Austin (actually the suburb of Round Rock). The International League's only team in Canada, Ottawa, will be moving to Allentown for the 2008 season. Teams in Lethbridge, Alberta, and Medicine Hat, Alberta, moved to Missoula and Helena, Montana, respectively. Part of the reason these teams moved was low attendance. Ottawa has been among the bottom teams in attendance in the International League for years. Medicine Hat was the only team to average below 1,000 fans a game in the Pioneer League in 2002. One Canadian team that drew fairly well was the Edmonton Trappers. However, there is some indication that the other teams did not like traveling all the way to Edmonton. Nashville and Tacoma are not close to each other, but once the Calgary franchise moved to Albuquerque, none of the teams was less than 700 miles from Edmonton.

In 1996 there were two major-league teams, seven affiliated minor-league teams, and seven independent minor-league teams in Canada. Unless they can draw new teams, as of 2008 only one major-league team, one affiliated minor-league team, and four independent league teams will remain in Canada. Given the size of a number of markets in Canada, they would seem obvious choices for future teams, but the recent support that Canadian teams have been shown relative to cities south of the 49th parallel may make future teams reluctant to relocate there.

Northern New Jersey, based on population, income, and corporate support, would seem one of the most obvious choices for an expansion team. Even if the new team was at a severe disadvantage relative to the established teams, the great size of the New York area would make up for that. Ten percent of the New York market (2.19 million) would still exceed the entirety of the Portland market (2.06 million) or the Sacramento market (2.16 million). However, the two New York teams, the Mets and Yankees, currently have rights to the area and could veto a team being given to that market.

The excessive market areas designated by MLB pretty much preclude teams going into metropolitan areas with existing teams. However, the most appealing market for an additional team beyond the New York market does leave open a possibility for an additional major-league team. The Los Angeles territory designated to the Dodgers and Angels only encompasses Orange, Los Angeles, and Ventura counties and excludes Riverside and San Bernardino counties. Those two counties have a combined population of almost 4 million people and are only represented by four High-A California League teams. The cities of Riverside and San Bernardino are more than fifteen miles from the county border, and thus eligible for a team.

There is also the possibility of a minor-league team in the same market as a major-league team. This fact may be surprising given the strict rules that exist for locating new teams in a market with teams, but three reasons may explain this possibility. Historical precedence would explain the presence of such teams as Tacoma in Seattle's metropolitan area. Also, the presence of a spring-training facility increases the likelihood of hosting a minor-league baseball team because of the increased likelihood of a suitable stadium in the location. All of the spring-training facilities are in Arizona and Florida and there are a large number of minor-league teams in Phoenix, Tampa, and Miami.

Finally, teams have tried to go around the rules by locating in the exurbs of some major cities. In 1993 the Kane County Cougars began playing in the far western suburbs of Chicago.[21] More recently the Frisco Roughriders, located on the northern edge of the Dallas area, started playing in the Texas League. Of course, as these invasions take place, the teams institute rules to protect them from further incursions. The rules that are currently in place would not have allowed the Kane County Cougars to play where they currently do without the permission of the two Chicago major-league teams, the White Sox and Cubs.

The large markets with only one major-league team and no affiliated minor-league teams in their area include Houston, Philadelphia, Detroit, and Atlanta. The Philadelphia Phillies and Houston Astros have done an effective job of defining their territory in such a way that no team could enter into the respective metropolitan areas without their permission. A cursory analysis of the Houston metroplex would suggest that the Astros in particular would seem to be quite susceptible to another team's moving into the metropolitan area. In addition to having a large population, it is quite substantial geographically, encompassing twelve counties. However, the Astros' territorial rights include eight of those counties, excluding only a few of the least populated ones and essentially creating a ring around Houston eighty miles wide.

A minor-league team could enter the Detroit metropolitan area by locating in Flint, on the northern side of the city, which would be fifteen miles from the edge of the Tigers' territory. The other possibility would be for a team to locate in Windsor, Canada, right across the Detroit River from Detroit. According to the Major League Constitution, the Detroit territory only mentions American counties. Though Windsor is within fifteen miles of Detroit, a team on the outskirts of Windsor would comply with MLB rules.

CONCLUSIONS

This chapter has identified methods for determining where future major- and minor-league teams will locate. Major-league sites that make sense include Portland, Charlotte, Salt Lake City, and San Bernardino. AAA sites would include Orlando, Jacksonville, Grand Rapids, and Vancouver. AA sites are a little more restricted because none of the leagues operates in the West or Midwest, but possible sites include Charleston, Springfield (Massachusetts), Lafayette (Louisiana), and Baton Rouge if it recovers sufficiently from Hurricane Katrina.

The analysis provided here also points to additional topics for future study. One area that needs additional consideration is the factors that influence teams to move from Canada to the United States and vice versa. The movement of teams from Canada to the United States over the last five years is one of the key issues in determining the locations of baseball franchises, but the reasons behind this trend are not clear.

Additionally, the phenomenon of independent baseball leagues requires additional analysis. The above study focused on the affiliated leagues because of the inherent instability of the independent leagues, but further work on the underlying economics of the independent leagues is needed as well.

ACKNOWLEDGMENT

The author would like to thank Glenn Morrison, Katie Shannon, Daniel Tauritz, Julie Gallaway, and the editors for their helpful suggestions.

NOTES

1. The number of teams and leagues does not include leagues outside of the United States and Canada such as the Venezuelan Summer League or the Mexican League. It also excludes fall leagues, which are mostly developmental leagues and restricted to climates suitable for baseball in the fall (Arizona and Hawaii).

2. The exception to the lack of expansion in the minor leagues is in two of the rookie leagues: the Gulf Coast League and the Arizona League. These two leagues are run directly by the major-league clubs and each major league's team in these leagues is located at their spring training facility. Teams are added and subtracted whenever a change in affiliation takes place in one of the other Rookie or Short-Season A leagues.

3. M. C. Davis, "Called Up to the Big Leagues: An Examination of the Factors Affecting the Location of Minor League Baseball Teams," *International Journal of Sport Finance* 1, no. 4 (2006): 253–264.

4. Throughout this chapter the definition of *metropolitan area* is the one that encompasses the greatest area. For areas that are included in Combined Statistical Areas (CSA), the CSA is used. For other areas, Metropolitan Statistical Area (MSA) is used.

5. The Canadian and American metropolitan areas cannot be directly compared because of differences in definitions and methodologies for determining metropolitan areas.

6. Buffalo's actual market size may be larger since the metropolitan areas do not include neighboring areas in Canada. A similar issue may apply to Detroit and San Diego as well. The numbers for population in New Orleans are from 2003, which is before Hurricane Katrina hit. Obviously the population has fallen even more since then, but New Orleans was a relatively small city regardless.

7. Davis, "Called Up to the Big Leagues."

8. J. J. Siegfried and J. D. Eisenberg, "The Demand for Minor League Baseball," *Atlantic Economic Journal* (1980): 59–69.

9. S. E. Branvold, D. W. Pan, and T. E. Gabert, "Effects of Winning Percentage and Market Size on Attendance in Minor League Baseball," *Sport Marketing Quarterly* 6, no. 4 (1997): 35–42.

10. North Carolina Citizens for Business and Industry, "What's Behind the Major Growth in the Minor Leagues," 2001, www.nccbi.com/NCMagazine/2001/mag-06.01baseball.htm (accessed March 15, 2008).

11. J. A. Winfree, et al., "Location and Attendance in Major League Baseball," *Applied Economics* 36, no. 19 (2004): 2117–2124.

12. R. S. Kraus, *Minor League Baseball Community Building Through Hometown Sports* (New York: Haworth Press, 2003).

13. Davis, "Called up to the Big Leagues."

14. Winfree et al., "Location and Attendance in Major League Baseball."

15. G. Knowles, K. Sherony, and M. Haupert, "The Demand for Major League Baseball: A Test of the Uncertainty of Outcome Hypothesis," *The American Economist*, 36, no. 2 (1992): 72–80; D. Rascher, "A Test of the Optimal Positive Production Network Externality in Major League Baseball," in *Sports Economics: Current Research,* ed. J. Fizel, E. Gustafson, and L. Hadley (Westport, CT: Greenwood, 1999), 27–45; M. B. Schmidt and D. J. Berri, "What Takes Them Out to the Ball Game?" *Journal of Sports Economics* 7, no. 2 (2006): 222–233.

16. Branvold, Pan, and Gabert, "Effects of Winning Percentage and Market Size on Attendance."

17. W. Scanlan, "Glory Days: Remembering When the Lynx Mattered," *Ottawa Citizen*, August 27, 2006, http://www.canada.com/ottawacitizen/columnists/story.html?id=4f241464-044a-4d0f-a922-9bc3e131a72b (accessed March 15, 2008).

18. Miami (the current home of the Marlins) is substantially larger than any of the other talked-about markets, so any move on their part would not be consistent with a hypothesis about team locations based on population. San Antonio might just represent the most logical outside option to use as a threat in order to get a new publicly funded stadium.

19. T. H. Bruggink and J. M. Zamparelli, "Emerging Markets in Baseball: An Econometric Model for Predicting the Expansion Teams' New Cities," in *Sports Economics Current Research,* ed. Fizel, Gustafson, and Hadley, 45–59.

20. A. T. Johnson, *Minor League Baseball and Local Economic Development* (Urbana: University of Illinois Press, 1993).

21. R. A. Baade and A. R. Sanderson, "Minor League Teams and Communities," in *Sports, Jobs & Taxes,* ed. R. G. Noll and A. S. Zimbalist (Washington, D.C.: Brookings Institution Press, 1997), 452–493.

Nine

The College Football Postseason Mess: Economic Perspectives

Michael Mondello

Despite ongoing controversy connected with determining the National Collegiate Athletic Association's (NCAA) Division I-A college football (DIACF) champion, DIACF remains the only NCAA sport without a legitimate playoff system to decide its national champion. Therefore, the purpose of this chapter is to examine the history of the NCAA, DIACF's postseason, controversies associated with the Bowl Championship Series (BCS), previous playoff proposals, and economics associated with the postseason.

THE NATIONAL COLLEGIATE ATHLETIC ASSOCIATION

Historically, football's brutal nature, typified by mass formations and gang tackling, frequently resulted in serious injuries and occasionally death. Consequently, while several institutions recommended the sport undergo reform, others stopped playing altogether. To advocate change and preserve football, President Theodore Roosevelt summoned college athletic leaders to several White House conferences to discuss potential changes related to player safety. In early December 1905 New York University Chancellor Henry M. MacCracken convened a meeting of thirteen institutions to initiate changes in the rules governing football. At a subsequent meeting on December 28, 1905, in New York City, the Intercollegiate Athletic Association of the United States (IAAUS) was founded by sixty-two members. The IAAUS officially was constituted March 31, 1906, and took its present name—the National Collegiate Athletic Association (NCAA)—in 1910.[1]

The NCAA, consisting of approximately 1,000 institutions, administers eighty-eight championships in twenty-three sports for its member institutions allowing more than 40,000 male and female student-athletes the opportunity to annually compete for national titles in various sports. These championships began with a tennis tournament in 1883 and have been conducted under NCAA auspices since 1921, when the national collegiate track and field championships were instituted. Reorganization of the NCAA membership structure in 1973 led to the establishment of division championships in each of the NCAA's three new membership classifications—divisions I, II, and III. A Division I-AA football championship was added in 1978, and women's championships became part of the NCAA program in 1981–82.[2]

Currently, there are 10 national collegiate championships for which all divisions are eligible—three for men, four for women, and three men's/women's events. There are 26 Division I championships (13 men, 13 women), 25 Division II championships (12 men, 13 women) and 27 Division III championships (13 men, 14 women). Championships for men are offered in one or more divisions in baseball, basketball, cross country, football (except in Division I-A), golf, gymnastics, ice hockey, lacrosse, soccer, swimming and diving, tennis, indoor track, outdoor track, volleyball, water polo, and wrestling. Similarly, women's championships are sponsored in basketball, bowling, cross country, field hockey, golf, gymnastics, ice hockey, lacrosse, rowing, soccer, softball, swimming and diving, tennis, indoor track, outdoor track, volleyball, and water polo.[3]

Despite the fact that all other NCAA team and individual champions are determined by structured playoffs, the NCAA's most visible sport, football, remains without a true playoff arrangement. Specifically, DIACF is categorically unique because the eventual national champion is not solely determined by on-field performance but rather by combining on-field performance with coaches lobbying for the most votes in two national polls.[4]

SIGNIFICANT DEVELOPMENTS IN COLLEGE FOOTBALL

To understand how the controversy surrounding DIACF developed, a historical overview of major college football is warranted. In 1894, prior to the official formation of the NCAA, the first bowl game reportedly occurred when the University of Chicago's Alonzo Stagg invited the University of Notre Dame to play a game to help generate civic support. Furthermore, in an effort to attract fans to warmer climates, the modern bowl era began in 1935 with the inception of the Orange and Sugar Bowls.[5]

Since 1976, several proposals to establish a DIACF championship have been introduced, calling for the NCAA to provide a playoff system similar to other NCAA sports. Inevitably, when playoff discussions materialized, two issues continued to bring these conversations to an impasse: impact of postseason championships on the current bowl format and the welfare of student-athletes. Paradoxically, these concerns illustrate the dichotomy of the NCAA's interest in protecting a primary moneymaking phenomenon like the bowl games, while simultaneously keeping a watchful eye on the interests of college athletes.[6]

Unlike other college and professional sports, where champions are determined by a structured playoff system, the DIACF season culminates with a series of bowl games. While bowl games such as the Rose Bowl have storied traditions, most bowl participants were selected based on an institution's conference affiliation. Although the NCAA instituted a playoff system for other college football divisions, the bowl system has remained intact for Division I-A schools.[7]

In an attempt to address the persistent controversy over selecting a national champion, a new format was developed in 1992 to objectively identify a single champion—the Bowl Coalition. The stated purpose of the Bowl Coalition was to ensure the national champion was determined each season by matching the first- and second-ranked teams in a postseason bowl game. Although this decision was generally well received, the monopolistic practices and exclusivity raised additional concerns. In particular, since the Bowl Coalition excluded both conferences (Big Ten and Pacific 10) and teams, allegations surfaced alleging this constituted a violation of the antitrust laws as stipulated in the Sherman Act.[8]

Prior to establishing the Bowl Coalition, a college football team was invited to participate in a postseason bowl game for one of two reasons. First, a school was awarded the opportunity to participate in a bowl game based upon a team's standing in its respective conference. For example, by virtue of winning the Big Ten conference championship, an institution automatically qualified to play in the Rose Bowl. Similarly, the Pacific 10 (Pac-10) champion was awarded the other slot in the Rose Bowl as the conference champion. The second method used to select postseason bowl participants was based on a bidding process where a number of bowl representatives would independently invite institutions to participate in their bowl game.[9]

Although the newly formed Bowl Coalition successfully paired the top two teams in two of the three years it existed, one noteworthy disadvantage remained. Namely, this system's exclusion of specific conferences failed to produce a national championship game. For example, between 1945 and 1991, the two top-ranked teams played only eight times.[10]

In 1995 the Bowl Coalition underwent a major revision with the advent of the Bowl Alliance. The Bowl Alliance combined five key conference champions and four major bowls. Collectively, the conferences consisted of the Southeastern (SEC), Southwestern (SWC), Big Eight, Atlantic Coast (ACC), Big East, and one independent institution, the University of Notre Dame. These five conferences and Notre Dame teamed with the Federal Express Orange, USF&G Sugar, IBM Fiesta, and Mobile Cotton Bowls to change the methods used to select postseason bowl participants.[11]

Under the new guidelines delineated in the Bowl Alliance agreement, conference champions were selected to play in the Orange, Sugar, and Cotton Bowls, while the Fiesta Bowl reserved two slots. Based on these newly adopted standards, the Bowl Alliance attempted to increase the likelihood of a national championship game. This was strengthened by controlling the pairings in bowl games and including two additional at-large spots open to all Division I-A teams winning at least eight games or being ranked in the top twelve. Although the Big Ten and Pac-10 conferences agreed to participate in the Bowl Alliance, these institutions chose not to participate in the bowls due to their contractual agreements with the Rose Bowl. Therefore, despite the improvement compared to the Bowl Coalition, the exclusionary practices of the Bowl Alliance continued to jeopardize the opportunity to stage a legitimate national championship game.

Although the creation of the Bowl Coalition and Bowl Alliance increased the number of national championship games played from previous arrangements, one prominent issue remained—the possible suppression of competition with anticompetitive practices. Congress passed the Sherman Act in 1890 in order to protect the competitive process and limit monopolistic practices.[12] According to the Sherman Act, one defining feature of a monopolistic market is the existence of barriers to entry. Critics alleged the Bowl Alliance violated the Sherman Act because it excluded certain bowls and conferences.[13]

As noted in this chapter, the Bowl Alliance possessed this monopolistic practice by preventing certain institutions the opportunity to compete in the designated championship game. Specifically, the Bowl Alliance's selection protocol resulted in the exclusion of fifty Division I-A universities; consequently these institutions were denied the opportunity to compete in the national championship game. College football advocates posited the Bowl Alliance ultimately forced non-Alliance schools into second-tier status.

The financial difference between those institutions affiliated with the Bowl Alliance and those excluded continued to widen and subsequently created further division among DIACF teams. While the formation of the Bowl Alliance significantly enhanced the financial payouts for the participants, these benefits failed to reach a number of Division I-A universities. For example, following the 1996–97 bowl season, universities playing in the Bowl Alliance bowls collected a total of $95.9 million, while non-Alliance bowl participants received only $5.4 million. The disparity between these figures clearly suggests inequity. In fact, the Bowl Alliance included just over half (53%) of the Division I-A schools and yet these very schools collected over 94 percent of the total bowl allocations for the 1996–97 season.[14]

With regard to the Bowl Alliance, several strong arguments suggest the complex agreements among member conferences and bowls resulted in excessively restrictive and exclusive practices to achieve the simple goal of a single national championship game each season. Thus, a good deal of discussion has centered on a Division I-A playoff similar to those conducted by the NCAA in other college football divisions. This system possessed both strengths and weaknesses. That is, a playoff would not restrict certain teams or conferences from competing for the national championship as the Bowl Alliance did. Furthermore, a playoff conducted like the NCAA men's basketball tournament would allow more teams to benefit from the postseason revenue. The profit-sharing would not be restricted to certain conferences, but rather spread among all the Division I-A teams in varying shares.[15]

In response to the Bowl Alliance's exclusion of the Big Ten and Pac-10 conferences, league commissioners and university presidents initiated discussions focusing on strategies to modify DIACF's postseason. Specifically, these negotiations focused on integrating these two conferences into a bowl arrangement matching up the top two teams. The Big Ten and Pac-10 conferences agreed in 1997 to include their champions in the national championship game based on the policies outlined in a modified arrangement called the Bowl Championship Series (BCS).[16]

THE BOWL CHAMPIONSHIP SERIES

In response to controversial postseason events, the Bowl Championship Series (BCS) emerged. The primary goal of the BCS was to establish a five-game arrangement as part of the postseason bowl schedule. This system was designed to have the two top-ranked teams play in a national championship game and create competitive games between eight other teams in four additional bowl games.

The BCS, consisting of the Rose, Sugar, Orange, Fiesta, and National Championship game, runs through the 2010 bowl season. Although the BCS system is still open to many of the same criticisms mentioned previously, the opportunity for participation in one of the BCS games is now open to every Division I-A team. One significant change in the BCS governance occurred in 2004 when Conference USA, along with the Mid-American, Mountain West, Sun Belt, and Western Athletic conferences respectively, were guaranteed 9 percent of the annual BCS net revenue for the 2006–2009 regular season. In addition, if one of these conferences played in one of the BCS games, an extra 9 percent would be paid to the conference.[17]

Participation in the BCS is based on a standings formula. Currently, the BCS standings formula combines six computer-generated rankings (Anderson and Hester, Richard Billingsley, Colley Matrix, Kenneth Massey, Jeff Sagarin, and Peter Wolfe) with two voter polls (*USA Today* Coaches' Poll and the Harris Interactive College Football Poll) to determine the two participating teams in the BCS championship game. The accuracy of these computer rankings have yet to be empirically examined and consequently is open to criticism. Historically, voter polls determined the so-called mythical national champion in Division I-A. A review of college football history reveals numerous seasons when one group of voters (sportswriters) selected a different national champion than another group of voters (coaches) and consequently, an intense controversy ensued.[18]

Since the inception of major college football, attempts to objectively evaluate and select an eventual national champion have been associated with disorganization and disagreement resulting in controversial heated arguments. Until a more valid and reliable system for determining the national champion is developed, such discord will continue to dominate; thereby tainting the process and possibly calling into question the credibility of the BCS. Several recent regular seasons have illustrated the lack of reliability associated with the BCS.

For example, at the conclusion of the 2001 regular season, a significant BCS controversy surfaced in the national media involving the Nebraska Cornhuskers. In the final regular season BCS standings, the Cornhuskers finished second behind the University of Miami, subsequently earning a berth in the National Championship game played at the Rose Bowl in Pasadena, California, on January 3, 2002. This announcement came fifteen days after the Cornhuskers were defeated 62–36 by the eventual Big XII champion, the University of Colorado. Despite the embarrassing loss and the fact Nebraska failed to win their conference championship, the BCS awarded one of the championship slots to the Cornhuskers.

In February 2004, the BCS announced a proposal to add a fifth game to their rotation to improve access for mid-major teams ordinarily denied access to these lucrative postseason games.[19] This decision was a result of Southern California (USC) being omitted from the BCS championship game in 2003 despite being ranked number 1 in both polls. Circumstances like this further raised the question, "Does the BCS selection process place more weight on a team's performance over the entire season or its end-of-season performance?"

Perhaps no regular season created as much debate as in 2006. In an unprecedented move, Ohio State's football coach Jim Tressel declined to vote in the final regular season *USA Today* Coaches Poll. This was a result of the potential influence his vote could have on the team. Ohio State would eventually play in the designated National Championship game. Jim Tressel's decision to abstain from voting represented the first time in the sixteen-season history of the *USA Today* Coaches' Poll a coach elected not to vote.[20]

Following Tressel's action, two football games hosted 3,000 miles apart on December 2, 2006, played significant roles in determining the match-up for the BCS National Championship game. In their final regular-season game, second-ranked Southern California lost to cross-town rival UCLA, 13-9, eliminating the Trojans from an opportunity to compete in their third consecutive National Championship game.

Concurrently, the SEC championship was played in Atlanta between the University of Florida and the University of Arkansas. Florida defeated Arkansas 38–28 to capture the SEC championship and, more important, earned the right to participate in the BCS National Championship game opposite Ohio State. After Ohio State and Florida's 1–2 finish in the final BCS rankings, arguments intensified. Despite completing their regular season two weeks earlier, the University of Michigan's demotion in both the *USA Today* Coaches Poll and the Harris Interactive poll stimulated additional debate regarding the legitimacy of the BCS, the coaches' poll, and politicking among coaches.

On January 8, 2007, the University of Florida dominated Ohio State, 41–14, to claim the school's second national championship, proving they had deserved to play in the BCS title game. Over the past decade, this divisive and contentious method for selecting a national champion has appeared to generate passionate discussions among college football enthusiasts. This is evidenced by a significant increase in chat rooms and Internet Web sites devoted to discussing this very phenomenon in college football's current postseason.

Despite the flaws associated with the BCS, legitimate arguments against a playoff exist. For instance, a playoff might not achieve the ultimate goal of matching the top teams in the nation, since upsets commonly occur, therefore allowing a lower ranked team an opportunity to advance in the playoff instead of a higher ranked team. Given the above-mentioned issues, many of today's controversies (computer rankings, strength of schedules, voter bias) surrounding the national rankings would remain confounding factors.

PLAYOFF PROPOSALS

Although the NCAA commissioned a study addressing the feasibility of a football playoff in 1994, the organization adamantly refused to grant additional dollars to investigate a playoff postseason format in 1998.[21] Even though there have been several discussions about the inadequacies of the BCS since the 1994 study, minimal information about the financial incentives associated with a Division I-A playoff system has been forwarded.

Any discussion of a Division I-A playoff should consider the possible ramifications a playoff might have on student-athletes' class attendance and thus, academic performance. Virtually all Division I-A football players are required to complete final exams in early December. Some argue the timing of a playoff may negatively impact the student-athletes' academic performance and therefore, in an effort to uphold academic integrity, a football playoff should be held following the final exam schedule rather than before. Advocates of academic integrity have argued against a playoff on the premise that college football players miss significant class time due to football-related activities. However, compared to many NCAA-sponsored sports, especially basketball, this argument has yet to be substantiated.

Generally, football players only miss classes on the Friday preceding a road game. Comparatively, college basketball players may miss multiple class sessions during the course of a week due to travel commitments, and for teams advancing into the later rounds of the NCAA basketball tournament class attendance can be minimal. Thus, arguments against a playoff system based on the stipulation of missed classes appear to have several weaknesses that need further empirical examination.

Although no formal playoff system currently exists for DIACF, several proposals have been put forward in the past. Following the 1998 season, *Inside Sports* conducted dozens of interviews with coaches, players, athletic directors, and other influential administrators to share their perspectives on a national playoff for Division I-A football. Five years earlier, then University of California at Los Angeles (UCLA) chancellor Charles Young, headed a twenty-four-member committee to study the feasibility of a playoff. Initially, the group opposed a playoff by a vote of 18–6. However, after further deliberations involving the logistics of a playoff, opinions changed. By the fall of 1994, when Young had requested additional time to make a recommendation, the committee vote swung dramatically in the other direction, with nineteen members favoring a playoff system.[22]

Although there would be several key issues (location of games, payouts per team) involved with establishing a national playoff for DIACF, arguably the most important consideration would be determining the appropriate number of participants. Therefore, once a feasible number of participants are established, issues such as scheduling considerations, game locations, role of the current bowls, and financial implications would need to be addressed.

The 1994 NCAA playoff committee was repeatedly asked about the number of teams that would be appropriate for a playoff. Almost unanimously, the answer was eight. While a number of playoff format have been forwarded both formally and informally, the *Inside Sports* playoff proposal included eight teams. Support for eight teams was strengthened because the inclusion of sixteen teams would dilute the meaning of the regular season whereas including only four teams involved too many arbitrary decisions.[23]

Although the BCS recently extended their contract through the 2010 season, Olympic and World Cup sponsor International Sport and Leisure (ISL) floated an eight-year, $3-billion postseason proposal to athletic directors and college conference officials in 1999. This was part of a proposition guaranteeing every I-A institution a minimum of $1.5 million whether or not they even qualified for a postseason playoff. Under this format, ISL proposed a sixteen-team playoff including the champions of the ACC, Big East, Big Ten, Big 12, Pac-10, and the SEC. Additionally, two more teams would be selected from the other four I-A conferences. The remaining eight openings would be awarded to at-large teams, allowing conference runner-ups and independent institutions the chance to participate. This format had the first-round games played before New Year's Day, the second and third rounds in January, and the national championship played on the weekend prior to the National Football League's (NFL) Super Bowl.[24] Ultimately, the proposal never materialized.

In their 2001 college football preview, *Street & Smith's* recommended a playoff format titled the "Great Eight" which included the champions of the six power conferences (ACC, Big Ten, Big 12, Pac-10, Big East, and SEC) and the BCS's next two highest-ranked teams. Participants hypothetically would be seeded according to the BCS standings utilizing the typical seeded format pairings—1 versus 8, 2 versus 7, 3 versus 6, and 4 versus 5. Under this system, first-round games were to be scheduled on the third weekend in December at the higher-seeded team's home stadium. Following the first round, all teams would play again in four of the five BCS bowls. First-round winners would compete in the championship bracket, while the first-round losers would participate in their usual bowl game. Finally, the championship game would follow a week later at the designated fifth BCS bowl.[25] While several proposals have been considered for a Division I-A football championship, I would propose an eight-team/seven-game playoff structured like one of the models presented in above. This format would include:

- Four quarterfinal games to be played on New Year's Day;
- Two semi-final games to be played on the second Saturday after January 1; and,
- One championship game to be played on the following weekend.

This proposal will be discussed more fully below. Any discussion of a Division I-A playoff should also include alternatives to preserve the majority of bowl games. Currently, thirty-two bowl games are played and under my proposal, a majority of these games would still be played. With a playoff format, a few of the major bowls could host games determining the eventual national championship. Moreover, by staging the playoff games in January, these games would not overshadow the other bowls typically played between Christmas and New Year's Day. As the financial implications associated with DIACF including payouts to respective conferences have escalated, so has the number of bowl games played after January 1. As shown in Table 9.1, the total number of bowl games has doubled since 1980.

A common argument supporting the BCS centers on the idea of the importance of every regular-season game. While this line of reasoning has valid arguments, there is a glaring omission. Specifically, regular-season games are significantly more important when one or both of the participants are undefeated. Consider the following scenario: The University of Florida defeats the University of Miami in the second game of the 2007 regular season, but loses to the University of Tennessee two weeks later. Under the current BCS system, both Miami and Florida would be in positions compromising each team's chance to play in the designated national championship game.

Moreover, teams losing during the course of the regular season generally require extraordinary circumstances in order to be considered for

TABLE 9.1
Growth in Bowl Games, 1977–2006

Period	Number of Years	Number of Bowl Games on/after Jan. 1	Total Number of Bowls
1977–1981	5	4	15
1982–1986	5	5	17
1987–1988	2	6	18
1989–1990	2	7	17–18
1991–1994	4	8	18–19
2000–2001	2	8	25
2002	1	8	28
2003	1	10	28
2004–2005	2	8	28
2006	1	11	32

participation in the national championship game. While there have been recent examples of teams overcoming regular season losses and still playing in the national championship game, a majority of teams with one or more regular-season loss are systematically eliminated from competing for the national championship. Besides overcoming the obstacle of an early season loss, teams continue to rely on polls to determine the national championship match-up.

Scheduling also plays an integral part of the process of selecting teams to play for a national championship. While conference schedules are generally established by conference policy, nonconference schedules are under the control of university athletic departments. For many universities, nonconference games serve multiple purposes. First, the home team's nonconference schedule is typically weak due to the disparity in skill level between the home team and the visiting team. In other words, the visiting team is generally considered the underdog and therefore a long shot to defeat the home team. Thus, home-team alumni are generally content with a weak opponent and more important, a lofty national ranking will be preserved. Although the outcomes of these games are heavily tilted in favor of the home team, visiting teams also benefit. Oftentimes, visiting teams are compensated with participant guarantee payments representing a substantial portion of their overall football revenue. For example, in 2006 Troy University earned almost $2 million by playing consecutive road games at Florida State, Georgia Tech, and Nebraska. While Troy University failed to win any of the three games, their athletic budget was significantly enhanced. Similarly, Florida Atlantic of the Sun Belt Conference made more than $1.8 million in 2006 by opening the schedule with games at Clemson, Kansas State, Oklahoma State, and South Carolina. This is nearly twice what Florida Atlantic made for playing its four nonconference games in 2005.[26]

In addition to the aforementioned issues with the BCS and scheduling concerns associated with trying to alleviate financial concerns, the current system reduces the potential number of high-profile nonconference regular-season games. While some high-profile nonconference games exist (Florida–Florida State, Southern California–Nebraska), many universities avoid scheduling demanding nonconference games in an effort to preserve an unblemished schedule and increase their chances to play in the BCS National Championship game.

These problematic scheduling issues would drastically diminish with the implementation of a playoff. Moreover, with an understanding that a single regular-season defeat would no longer significantly reduce or, in other instances, completely eliminate a team's opportunity to compete for the national championship, universities would be more inclined to play games of national interest as part of their nonconference schedules. For example, potential regular-season match-ups between Nebraska/Michigan, Tennessee/Miami, and Southern California/Florida would undoubtedly create national interest from two perspectives. First, there would be a tremendous response from stakeholders including television networks, alumni, students, and the student-athletes themselves. Second, these additional high-profile games would have the potential to generate significant dollars from television revenues and ticket sales.

ECONOMIC ISSUES ASSOCIATED WITH DIVISION I-A ATHLETICS

According to the NCAA, the number of Division I-A athletic programs operating with a deficit increased from fifty-six programs in 1999 to seventy-four programs in 2001. Consequently, financially challenged athletic departments must explore additional methods to create supplementary income. Clearly, Division I-A football programs are responsible for generating significant dollars within the overall financial structure of Division I-A athletic programs.[27]

Conference Revenue-Sharing Agreements

While the NCAA men's basketball tournament has a systematic payment allocation to participating institutions, bowl revenues are shared according to individual conference policy, although it is possible with recent changes that teams playing in the same bowl game will receive different financial payouts. Champions from the six major conferences generated $17 million each for their leagues in the 2006 BCS games. Interestingly, two other BCS participants—Boise State and Notre Dame—will earn vastly different totals: The $9 million awarded to Boise will be shared with five other I-A leagues while $4.5 million will go to independent Notre Dame.[28]

The BCS receives revenues from two primary sources—television and host bowls. The expected total revenue for the 2006 BCS games is projected to be $89.92 million. Once these payments are made to non-BCS conferences, the remaining monies will be initially split into six equal shares worth $13,866,666 for the participants of the FedEx Orange Bowl, the Nokia Sugar Bowl, and Tostitos Fiesta Bowl. Incidentally, while the Rose Bowl pays its participants directly through a separate contractual agreement, if a conference has more than one team participating in the BCS games (including the Rose Bowl), then the second participant does not receive a full share, but instead a reduced payment of $4.5 million. The difference between the full-share payment, $13,886,666, and the second-share payment of $4.5 million ($9,386,666) would then be divided among the six BCS conferences. However, if no team outside the BCS conferences would be selected, the two BCS conferences with two representatives would receive $21,515,555 and the other four BCS conferences would receive $17,015,555.[29]

The BCS estimates college bowls collectively distributed $187 million in 2006 with 67 percent of those dollars going to the eight teams (and their conferences) selected to participate in the BCS games. The remaining 33 percent consisting of $61 million will then be divided among the forty-eight participants in the non-BCS bowl games.[30] This distribution is illustrated in Table 9.2.

Undoubtedly, institutions competing in major conferences are able to financially benefit. For example, here's how revenues were shared in the SEC for the 2005/06 season:

> The Southeastern Conference will distribute approximately $116.1 million to the 12 league institutions in the revenue sharing plan for the 2005–2006 fiscal year, which ends Aug. 31, 2006, according to league commissioner Mike Slive. The $116.1 million is the highest total ever distributed in SEC history and represents a 4.4 percent increase from the $110.7 million distributed to the schools in 2004–2005. The revenue sharing plans include money generated by football television, bowls, the SEC Football Championship, basketball television, the SEC Men's Basketball Tournament and NCAA Championships. Broken down by categories and rounded off, the $116.1 million was derived from $47.4 million from football television, $20.7 million from bowls, $13.2 million from the SEC Football Championship, $12.1 million from basketball television, $4.4 million from the SEC Men's Basketball Tournament and $18.3 million from NCAA Championships. The average amount distributed to each school which participated in all revenue sharing was $9.68 million. Not included in the $116.1 million was $7.3 million retained by the institutions participating in bowls and $696,000 divided among all 12 institutions by the NCAA for academic enhancement.[31]

The growth in revenues is represented in Figure 9.1.

In contrast, the ACC disperses bowl revenues by implementing a conference-based revenue-sharing formula. Case in point, for participating in the 2001 Orange Bowl, Florida State University was awarded $1.6 million. In addition to receiving an allotted expense allowance, each conference member collects one-ninth of the remaining bowl monies once ticket obligations are adequately met. Collectively, following the conclusion of the 2000/01 bowl season, each school earned money for being a bowl participant as well as

TABLE 9.2
Four-Year Summary of Revenue Distribution for Bowl Championship Series, 2003–2006

	2002/03	2003/04	2004/05	2005/06
Television and title sponsorships	$72,000,000	$75,000,000	$78,000,000	$81,000,000
Revenue from:				
Fiesta Bowl	4,420,000	4,420,000	4,420,000	4,420,000
Sugar Bowl	4,400,000	4,600,000	4,400,000	4,400,000
Orange Bowl	4,600,000	4,400,000	4,700,000	4,600,000
Rose Bowl	1,380,000	1,500,000	1,367,500	1,740,000
Subtotal	14,800,000	14,920,000	14,887,500	15,160,000
Rose Bowl payout	27,924,842	28,799,782	29,234,392	29,733,334
Total BCS revenue	$114,724,842	$118,719,782	$122,121,892	$125,893,334
Distributions:				
Pacific 10	21,477,977	17,528,780	16,247,847	16,594,445
Big 10	21,062,222	22,028,780	16,295,461	21,094,444
Southeastern	16,562,222	17,015,556	16,247,847	16,594,444
Atlantic Coast	16,562,222	17,015,556	16,247,847	16,594,444
Big East	16,562,222	17,015,556	16,247,847	16,594,444
Big 12	16,977,977	21,515,556	20,795,460	16,594,445
Notre Dame	0	0	0	14,866,667
Mountain West	960,000	1,000,000	14,569,583	1,050,000
Western Athletic	960,000	1,000,000	1,050,000	1,050,000
Conference USA	960,000	1,000,000	1,050,000	1,050,000
Mid-American	960,000	1,000,000	1,050,000	1,050,000
Big Sky	180,000	190,000	200,000	225,000
Atlantic 10	180,000	190,000	200,000	225,000
Mid-Eastern	180,000	190,000	200,000	225,000
Gateway	180,000	190,000	200,000	225,000
Ohio Valley	180,000	190,000	200,000	225,000
Southwestern Athletic	180,000	190,000	200,000	225,000
Southland	180,000	190,000	200,000	225,000
Southern	180,000	190,000	200,000	225,000
Sunbelt	240,000	480,000	720,000	960,000
BCS Distribution	$114,724,842	$118,119,782	$122,121,892	$125,893,333
Administrative Expenses	0	$600,000	0	0
Total BCS Distribution & Expenses	$114,724,842	$118,719,782	$122,121,892	$125,893,333

Source: NCAA. Used with permission.

receiving $1,166,666.00 from the conference allotment.[32] Virtually all conferences distribute their bowl revenues after a number of discretionary expenses are paid. While these expenses vary based on conference policy,

FIGURE 9.1
SEC Revenue Distribution Since 1995

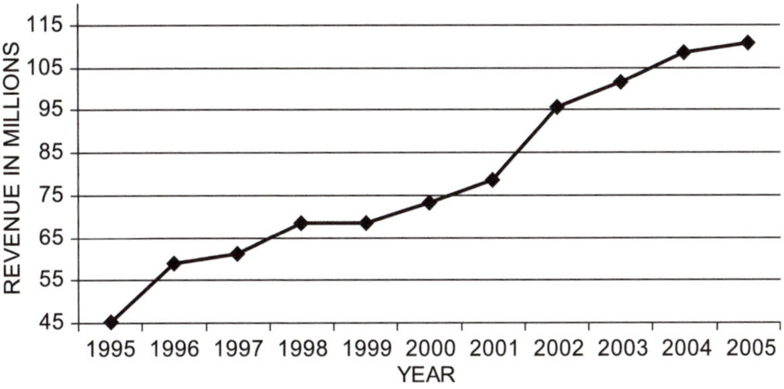

Source: Adapted from SEC data.

they generally include ticket subsidies, travel, and money paid to the conference office. These expenses are specifically outlined in Table 9.3.

Although their payouts are significantly less than BCS bowls, non-BCS bowl games allocated over $64 million to their participants in 2005/06 as depicted in Table 9.4.

NCAA BASKETBALL TOURNAMENT REVENUES

In terms of implementing a DIACF playoff, I would advocate the NCAA follow the format similar to the current NCAA men's basketball tournament. This recommendation is predicated on the following rationale. The NCAA basketball tournament involves collegiate athletics. Since this proposal also includes college athletics, it would be the most logical choice. Attempts to project revenues based on previously reported earnings from professional sporting events such as the NFL playoffs, the World Series, or the World Cup would not seem as logical. Moreover, the NCAA basketball tournament and my playoff proposal would have comparable timeframes as both events would last approximately three weeks and a revenue-sharing plan similar to the one utilized by the NCAA men's basketball tournament could be implemented.

Currently, NCAA basketball tournament revenues are distributed to Division I conferences over a six-year period based on their performance in the actual championship. For example, teams advancing into later rounds earn additional "units." The NCAA policy provides for money to be distributed to

TABLE 9.3
Five-Year Summary of Institutional Expenses for 2005/06 Postseason Bowls

	2005/06 BCS	2005/06 Non-BCS	2005/06 Total	2004/05 Total	2003/04 Total	2002/03 Total	2001/02 Total
Bowl Payout[a]	$125,893,334	$64,358,215	$190,251,549	$186,373,416	$181,044,784	$181,721,956	$154,951,519
Transportation:							
Team and staff	$2,134,428	$8,160,478	$10,294,906	$8,529,472	$7,499,042	$8,702,989	$6,689,427
Band and cheerleaders	$940,894	$2,885,940	$3,826,834	$4,457,282	$3,461,592	$3,811,381	$3,538,067
Official Party	$360,711	$1,093,990	$1,454,701	$1,706,343	$1,765,527	$1,281,878	$1,449,026
Total Transportation Expense	$3,436,033	$12,140,408	$15,576,441	$14,693,097	$12,726,161	$13,796,248	$11,676,520
Meals/Lodging/Per Diem:							
Team and staff	$3,941,574	$9,126,849	$13,068,423	$12,246,030	$12,126,109	$12,587,655	$10,998,518
Band and cheerleaders	$1,155,984	$2,159,818	$3,315,802	$3,339,261	$2,763,320	$2,894,657	$2,883,470
Official Party	$575,474	$990,684	$1,566,158	$1,680,240	$1,601,650	$1,711,537	$1,948,772
Total Meals/Lodging/Per Diem Expense	$5,673,032	$12,277,351	$17,950,383	$17,265,531	$16,491,079	$17,193,849	$15,830,760
Total Travel Expense	$9,109,065	$24,417,759	$33,526,824	$31,958,628	$29,217,240	$30,990,097	$27,507,280
Entertainment	$647,710	$675,049	$1,322,759	$931,240	$761,421	$775,371	$1,073,005
Promotion	$95,010	$677,052	$772,062	$575,305	$708,631	$703,069	$540,116
Awards	$588,221	$3,056,605	$3,644,826	$3,569,593	$3,090,506	$3,456,364	$3,136,878
Equipment and Supplies	$391,959	$1,281,247	$1,673,206	$1,675,274	$1,517,155	$1,520,237	$1,595,264

Tickets Absorbed by Conference and Participating Schools	$1,276,780	$9,522,269	$10,799,049	$9,199,515	$8,576,633	$14,138,915	$10,870,811
Administrative	$891,548	$2,743,166	$3,634,714	$4,939,771	$4,831,638	$4,146,742	$5,435,108
Other	$1,458,963	$4,768,501	$6,227,464	$5,280,656	$4,172,911	$3,832,824	$3,581,044
Conference Sponsorship Fee	$—	$—	$—	$150,000	$—	$—	$1,825,000
Total Game Expense	$5,350,191	$22,723,889	$28,074,080	$26,321,354	$23,658,895	$28,573,522	$28,057,226
Total Expenses	$14,459,256	$47,141,648	$61,600,904	$58,279,982	$52,876,135	$59,563,619	$55,564,506
Excess Revenues over Expenses	$111,434,078	$17,216,567	$128,650,645	$128,093,434	$128,168,649	$122,158,337	$99,387,013

[a] Bowl Championship Series Payout includes Rose Bowl Distribution.
Source: www1.ncaa.org. Used with permission.

TABLE 9.4
2005/06 Postseason Football Non-BCS Revenue Distribution

Bowl	2002/03	2003/04	2004/05	2005/06
Alamo	2,408,248	2,861,189	3,300,392	3,300,000
Capital One	10,003,380	10,254,570	10,513,152	10,762,602
Champs Sports Bowl	1,625,980	1,637,474	1,500,000	1,764,194
Cotton	5,400,000	5,400,000	5,400,000	5,400,000
Emerald	1,500,000	1,500,000	1,500,000	1,500,000
Ft. Worth[a]	0	1,513,148	1,500,000	1,500,000
Gator	3,644,960	3,200,000	3,200,000	3,200,000
GMAC	1,590,760	1,626,000	1,500,000	1,500,000
Hawaii[b]	1,736,000	1,156,276	1,400,000	850,000
Holiday	4,071,576	4,027,232	4,173,630	4,261,910
Houston	2,000,000	2,000,000	2,200,000	1,185,000
Independence	2,521,940	2,504,112	2,000,000	2,400,000
Insight	1,757,888	1,706,084	1,722,880	1,753,868
Las Vegas	1,600,000	1,150,000	1,150,000	1,150,000
Liberty	2,748,628	2,713,094	3,002,924	3,108,219
Meineke Car Care[b]	2,640,772	1,500,000	1,500,000	1,500,000
Motor City	1,686,982	1,500,000	1,500,000	1,500,000
MPC Computers	1,500,000	500,000	500,000	500,000
Music City	1,560,000	1,825,824	2,220,250	1,560,000
New Orleans	1,500,000	650,000	650,000	650,000
Outback	5,100,000	5,300,000	5,500,000	5,700,000
Peach	4,200,000	4,400,000	4,658,046	4,662,422
Poinsettia				1,500,000
Seattle	2,000,000			
Silicon Valley	1,500,000	1,150,000	660,250	
Sun	2,700,000	2,850,000	3,000,000	3,150,000
Total Non-BCS Distribution	$66,997,114	$62,925,003	$64,251,524	$64,358,215

[a]2003/04 was the inaugural year for the Ft. Worth Bowl.
[b]2002/03 was the inaugural year for the Meineke Car Care Bowl, Hawaii Bowl, and the Emerald Bowl.
Source: www1.ncaa.org. Used with permission.

Division I conferences based on their performance in the Division I Men's Basketball Championship over a six-year rolling period (the period 2001–2006 for the 2006/07 distribution, for example). Independent institutions receive a full unit share based on their tournament participation over the same rolling six-year period. The basketball fund payments are dispersed to conferences and independent institutions annually in mid-April. One unit is awarded to each institution participating in each game, except the championship game.

In 2005/06, each basketball unit was worth approximately $164,000 for a total distribution of $122.8 million. In 2006/07, each basketball unit was

$177,000 for a total distribution of $132.6 million.[33] Interestingly, while the NCAA recommends equitable distribution of monies among conferences, this is not a requirement. Similar to the revenue distribution associated with bowl games, institutions competing in the major conferences accrued a majority of basketball revenues. The basketball revenues distributed to the six BCS conferences as well as their share of the funds allocated by the NCAA are included in Table 9.5. Collectively, these six conferences received over 61 percent ($81,357,440) of the total monies allocated, with the ACC, Big 12, and Big East conferences each receiving over $14 million.

TABLE 9.5
Distribution of Basketball-Related Funds According to Number of Units by Conference, 2001–2006

Conference	2001	2002	2003	2004	2005	2006	Total Units	Projected Distribution
America East Conference	1	1	1	1	2	1	7	$1,238,048
Atlantic 10 Conference	7	2	4	10	1	3	27	$4,775,328
Atlantic Coast Conference	15	12	9	19	15	10	80	$14,149,120
Atlantic Sun	2	1	1	1	1	1	7	$1,238,048
Big 12 Conference	9	19	19	14	12	8	81	$14,325,984
Big East Conference	10	12	14	16	13	19	84	$14,856,576
Big Sky Conference	1	1	1	1	1	2	7	$1,238,048
Big South Conference	1	1	1	1	1	1	6	$1,061,184
Big Ten Conference	17	13	13	6	16	9	74	$13,087,936
Big West Conference	2	1	1	2	3	1	10	$1,768,640
Colonial Athletic Association	1	2	1	1	1	6	12	$2,122,368
Conference USA	5	4	9	11	10	5	44	$7,782,016
Horizon League	2	1	4	1	3	2	13	$2,299,232
Ivy Group	1	1	1	1	1	1	6	$1,061,184
Metro Atlantic Athletic Conf.	1	1	1	2	1	1	7	$1,238,048
Mid-American Conference	2	4	2	1	1	1	11	$1,945,504

(continued)

TABLE 9.5 (*continued*)

Conference	2001	2002	2003	2004	2005	2006	Total Units	Projected Distribution
Mid-Continent Conference	1	1	1	1	1	1	6	$1,061,184
Mid-Eastern Athletic	2	1	1	1	1	1	7	$1,238,048
Missouri Valley Conference	3	5	2	2	4	8	24	$4,244,736
Mountain West	1	4	4	3	4	2	18	$3,183,552
Northeast Conference	1	1	1	1	1	1	6	$1,061,184
Ohio Valley Conference	1	1	1	1	1	1	6	$1,061,184
Pacific-10 Conference	17	15	11	4	9	11	67	$11,849,888
Southeastern Conference	11	11	12	13	10	17	74	$13,087,936
Southern Conference	1	1	1	1	1	1	6	$1,061,184
Southland Conference	1	1	1	1	1	2	7	$1,238,048
Southwestern Athletic Conf.	1	1	1	1	1	1	6	$1,061,184
Sun Belt Conference	1	1	1	1	1	1	6	$1,061,184
The Patriot League	1	1	1	1	2	2	8	$1,414,912
West Coast Conference	3	2	3	2	3	3	16	$2,829,824
Western Athletic Conference	3	3	2	4	3	2	17	$3,006,688
Grand Totals:	125	125	125	125	125	125	750	$132,648,000
Amount per unit:								$176,864

Source: www1.ncaa.org. Used with permission.

ECONOMICS OF A FOOTBALL PLAYOFF

A playoff involving eight teams would be comprised of seven games. These eight teams would be seeded based on a ranking system similar to the one employed by the BCS. However, I would endorse one important change to the existing BCS policies, specifically, eliminating the current policy stipulating a conference can only have two of its member institutions included in BCS games. This recommendation is in response to the idea this policy not only penalizes schools having excellent seasons but also rewards less-deserving teams playing in substantially weaker conferences. The 2006 regular season provided support for this change. Three Big Ten schools (Ohio State, Michigan, and Wisconsin) were ranked in the top eight of the final BCS standings. However, despite an impressive 11–1 regular season record and a seventh-place BCS ranking, the University of Wisconsin played in the non-BCS Capital One Bowl. Despite being ranked fourteenth in the final BCS regular-season standings, ACC Champion Wake Forest played in the more prestigious BCS Orange Bowl.

Conference champions not ranked in the top eight would be left out of the playoff. Does a conference champion deserve the opportunity to compete for the National Championship with a relatively weak record and a low national ranking? Perhaps eliminating the policy of only allowing two teams from the same conference into the BCS would eliminate any controversy of automatically including conference champions into the BCS. Another consideration with the current BCS system is conference championship games. While three conferences have championship games (ACC, Big 12, and SEC), three others (Big East, Big Ten, and Pac-10) do not. Consequently, teams playing in conferences without a championship game generally have a competitive advantage in reaching the National Championship game. While it may be argued a team winning a conference championship game could potentially ascend in the final BCS poll, a more common scenario has seen teams losing in the conference championship game and endangering an opportunity to play for the National Championship. Even with these inconsistencies, there have also been occasions where teams have lost their respective conference championship game and still played in the BCS championship game.

Accordingly, the top-ranked team would theoretically have the best chance to reach the championship game although as with any sporting event, upsets are bound to occur. As a reward for earning one of the top four seeds, teams ranked 1–4 would be rewarded with hosting first-round games. Subsequent rounds would be played at neutral sites and include existing bowl games with the final game to be played in the designated National Championship game. Arguments related to how DIACF's postseason should be determined will undeniably continue. Even if changes are forthcoming at the conclusion of the current BCS contract in 2010, any substantial modification to the current postseason format will be subject to many of the same criticisms previously discussed. Furthermore, BCS commissioners will instinctively be challenged to protect their respective institutions to ensure they remain financially competitive. As shown in Table 9.6, the six BCS conferences receive significantly more dollars than non-BCS conferences.

TABLE 9.6
Summary of Bowl Revenues and Expenses by Conference, 2005/06 Postseason Bowls

Conference	Institution's Bowl Revenue	Participating Institution's Expenses	Excess of Revenue over Expenses	Excess Revenue/ Expenses per Conference (%)
ACC totals	23,937,752	8,106,026	15,831,726	12.31%
Big East totals	19,821,378	4,813,095	15,008,283	11.67%
Big Ten totals	33,329,796	9,592,496	23,737,300	18.45%
Big Twelve totals	26,477,497	10,615,178	15,862,319	12.33%
Conf. USA totals	5,658,219	6,236,713	(578,494)	−0.45%
Mid-American totals	2,550,000	1,562,545	987,455	0.77%
Mountain West totals	3,740,000	2,686,734	1,053,266	0.82%
Independent totals	15,616,667	4,020,685	11,595,982	9.01%
PAC-10 totals	21,752,334	5,037,373	16,714,961	12.99%
SEC totals	31,057,905	6,695,626	24,362,279	18.94%
Sun Belt totals	1,285,000	494,894	790,106	0.61%
WAC totals	3,225,000	1,739,539	1,485,461	1.15%
Other distribution	1,800,000	—	1,800,000	1.40%
2005/06 totals	190,251,548	61,600,904	128,650,644	100%
2004/05 totals	186,373,416	58,279,982	128,093,434	
2003/04 totals	181,044,784	52,876,135	128,168,649	
2002/03 totals	181,721,956	59,563,619	122,158,337	

Source: www1.ncaa.org. Used with permission.

Perhaps future regular seasons marked by similar controversies discussed in this chapter will generate significant changes within BCS guidelines. However, even with extensive modifications, whichever system eventually emerges to govern DIACF's postseason, many of the issues raised here will generate passionate debates. The economic and financial ramifications of any change will unquestionably be among the most important to college football's powerbrokers. Nevertheless, while acknowledging the current BCS system has imperfections, maybe accepting the BCS at face value is the best resolution to a complicated question. That is, would DIACF be improved with a playoff or is the BCS functioning effectively?

NOTES

1. Retrieved from www.ncaa.org.
2. Ibid.
3. Ibid.

4. T. Wallace, "Elite Domination of College Football: An Analysis of the Antitrust Implications of the Bowl Alliance," *Sports Lawyers Journal* 6 (1999): 59.

5. Ibid., 63.

6. Ibid.

7. L. Darling, "The College Bowl Alliance and the Sherman Act," *Hastings Communication and Entertainment Law Journal* 23 (1999): 436.

8. Ibid.

9. Ibid., 438.

10. Ibid.

11. Retrieved from www.bcsfootball.org.

12. Wallace, "Elite Domination of College Football," 62.

13. Darling. "The College Bowl Alliance and the Sherman Act," 440.

14. Ibid., 441.

15. Ibid., 441, 443.

16. Retrieved from www.bcsfootball.org.

17. Ibid.

18. Ibid.; R. Wilson, "Validating a Division I-A College Football Season Simulation System," Proceedings of the 2005 Winter Simulation Conference, Orlando, Fla., 2005.

19. T. Callaghan, P. Mucha, and M. Porter, "The Bowl Championship Series: A Mathematical Review," *Notices of the American Mathematical Society* 51 (2004): 888.

20. R. Russo, "Florida Sneaks Past Michigan to Land Spot in Title Game against Ohio State," www.usatoday.com/sports/college/football/2006-12-03-bcs-title-game (accessed March 15, 2008).

21. W. Suggs, "Can $3 Billion Persuade Colleges to Create a Playoff for Football?" *Chronicle of Higher Education* 45 (1999): A53.

22. M. MacCambridge, "End the Tug of War," *Inside Sports* 17 (1998): 38–43.

23. Ibid.

24. Suggs, "Can $3 Billion Persuade Colleges to Create a Playoff for Football?"

25. B. Spear, "Deciding It on the Field," *Street & Smith's College Football* 65 (2001): 55–59.

26. P. Thamel, "In College Football, Big Paydays for Humiliation," *New York Times*, August 23, 2006, A1.

27. D. Fulks, *Revenues and Expenses of Divisions I and II Intercollegiate Athletic Programs: Financial Trends and Relationships—2001* (Indianapolis: NCAA Publishing, 2002).

28. M. O'Toole, "$17M BCS payouts great, but ..." *USA Today*, December 12, 2006, www.usatoday.com/sports/college/football/2006-12-06-bowl-payouts_x.htm?POE=SPOISVA (accessed March 15, 2008).

29. Retrieved from www.bcsfootball.org.

30. Ibid.

31. Retrieved from www.secsports.com.

32. B. Morrison, "ACC Bowl Notes," Atlantic Coast Conference (2001), retrieved from www.theacc.com.

33. Retrieved from www.ncaa.org.

Ten

Player Drafts in the Major North American Sports Leagues

Kevin G. Quinn

The primary determinant of a sport team's competitive success is the quality of the athletes that it carries on its roster. Given the relatively short careers of athletes in North American sports leagues (NASLs), roster restocking is a matter of considerable importance and interest to leagues, teams, and their fans.

There are three avenues by which a team in an NASL may go about the annual business of roster assembly. The first is by signing "free agents." Free agents are players who are considered under league rules to own the rights to their own services—to a greater or lesser degree—and therefore are permitted to form contracts with teams for those services. A second method teams use to assemble rosters is via trades and purchases of players whose rights are owned by other teams in the league. The third way in which teams may acquire players is via player drafts.

Player drafts assign the rights to a drafted player to a single team; no other team in the league is permitted to contract with the player for his or her athletic services. Such market restrictions would typically run afoul of antitrust law, but U.S. labor law allows players to gain the benefits of collective bargaining at the expense of giving up antitrust protections. Therefore, the collective bargaining agreements (CBAs) between leagues and their players' unions specify which players are considered true free agents, which have limited free agency, which may veto trades or sales, which are eligible for player drafts, and the rules under which such drafts occur.

There are three types of player drafts: Entry drafts, expansion drafts, and dispersal drafts. Entry drafts, by far the most regular and significant of the three types, allow teams to claim exclusive rights to players entering the league. Expansion drafts take place when a league increases its number of teams. The new teams are allowed (usually with significant restrictions) to claim players from incumbent team rosters. Dispersal drafts are held when a league decreases its number of teams or when a rival league collapses and players from the defunct teams or leagues are individually claimed by the remaining clubs.

ORIGINS OF PLAYER ENTRY DRAFTS

The primary distinguishing feature of NASLs' player labor markets in the first half of the twentieth century was the "reserve system." The reserve system allegedly was proposed in secret at an owners' meeting of the National League (NL) in 1879 by Arthur Soden, the proprietor of the Boston Braves. Soden suggested that each team be allowed to "reserve" up to five players who then would be off-limits to all other clubs. The system apparently proved to be effective immediately, as the lessened degree of competition over players led to lower salaries by 1880.[1] The NL increased the number of reserved players so that by 1890 teams' entire rosters were reserved.[2]

During the twentieth century, the *Federal Baseball* decision strictly legally permitted only Major League Baseball (MLB) to engage in a practice so blatantly at odds with American antitrust law, but *de facto* reserve systems were adopted by all NASLs in some form or another. These were unilaterally maintained by the leagues until the last quarter or so of the twentieth century, at which time players' unions began to win free agency for some of their members through the courts and through the collective bargaining process.[3]

While MLB's reserve clause eliminated competition for existing league players, it had no such effect for entering players who had not yet signed professional contracts. The system treated amateur player scouting and signing as a form of venture capitalism, encouraging teams to scour the country for prospects, signing them as early as possible so as to get them reserved for their teams. Teams owned these players in perpetuity—or at least until they did not want to pay them anymore—and it was expected that a low percentage of signings yielded a star. In both MLB and the National Hockey League (NHL), uncommitted amateur players typically were signed upon finishing high school, or even earlier, and parked in player development farm systems. Very few players in MLB or the NHL systems were ready for the big league immediately upon signing. However, this was not the case in the National Football League (NFL), giving amateur footballers considerably more bargaining power than baseball or hockey players.

The NFL's realization of entering players' market power and economic rents came in its sixth year of operation. Immediately upon completion of the University of Illinois's 1925 college football schedule, Red Grange left school to play two regular-season games and nineteen exhibition games with the Chicago Bears for a reported $100,000.[4] The next year, the prospect of a looming arms race for new talent led Bears' owner George Halas—rather shamelessly—to propose a rule that would prohibit teams from acquiring players whose classes had not yet graduated. Even more brazenly, Halas himself broke this rule in 1930, but he was not alone in doing so. In 1931, NFL president Joe Carr fined several teams $1,000 each for such offenses.[5]

Following the 1934 season, University of Minnesota star fullback and linebacker Stan Kostka found himself the subject of a bidding war between the Philadelphia Eagles and the Brooklyn Dodgers. Brooklyn "won" Kostka with a then-princely salary offer of $5,000. Kostka played for only one season, appearing in nine games, with 63 rushing attempts for 249 yards, and six pass attempts, all incomplete.[6]

NFL owners, determined not to further endure such folly during a very difficult Depression-era business environment, inaugurated the first NASL "reverse-order-of-finish" player entry draft, held at the Philadelphia Ritz-Carlton Hotel on February 8, 1936.[7] A total of eighty-one college players were selected in nine rounds by the nine NFL teams. With its first pick, Philadelphia chose Jay Berwanger, who coincidentally also was the winner of the first Heisman trophy.[8] His rights were traded to the Chicago Bears, but Halas was unwilling to meet Berwanger's demand for a $25,000 two-year contract, and Berwanger never did play in the NFL. Today, the NFL draft runs for seven rounds, and approximately 250 players are drafted each April.[9] A total of 22,358 entry players have been drafted by NFL teams during the league's 1936–2006 player entry drafts.[10]

The National Basketball Association (NBA) was the first NASL after the NFL to institute a player entry draft, doing soon after the league was organized in 1947, but other leagues eventually followed suit.[11] Leagues that now hold annual player entry drafts include the NHL, MLB, the Arena Football League, the WNBA, Major League Soccer, and the Australian Football League. Even World Wide Entertainment (WWE) holds an annual draft lottery to redistribute talent among its various wrestling leagues, although the competitive legitimacy of the WWE draft is not entirely clear.

In the early years of the NBA draft, there were no limits on the number of rounds and surviving records are a little sketchy, but the NBA draft became for all intents and purposes a ten-round affair in the late 1970s and early 1980s. The league had little following at first, so its early drafts included opportunities for "geographic picks." In advance of the draft each year, a team could opt to forego its first-round reverse-order-of-finish pick in favor of selecting any college player from its exclusive territory (as defined by the league). This system, in place until 1965, eventually allowed the New York Knicks (.388 record in 1964/65) instead of the San Francisco Warriors (.213 in 1964/65) to get Princeton's Bill Bradley, that year's most promising entering player. The territorial system then was abolished, and from 1966 until 1984, the NBA flipped a coin to determine which of the last-place teams in its two conferences would have the first overall pick. In 1985 the league went to a lottery system to determine the picking order for nonplayoff teams, and the draft was reduced to seven rounds. In 1989, it was further limited to its present two rounds.[12]

The NHL held its first reverse-order-of-finish Amateur Draft on June 5, 1963, at the Queen Elizabeth Hotel in Montreal. Draft picks were limited to amateur players seventeen and older who were not already "sponsored," or claimed, by an NHL club on a "finders-keepers" basis, so the draft was not particularly significant at first.[13] This changed when the league ended its recognition of sponsorship lists and the drafting of seventeen-to-nineteen-year-olds beginning with the 1969 Universal Draft. A total of eighty-four players were drafted that year, more than four times the average of the previous six drafts. Beginning with the 1995 draft, the NHL has assigned the first pick according to a weighted lottery.[14] From 1963 through 2006, 8,827 players have been taken in the NHL player entry drafts. The NHL draft is truly an international affair—of the 290 players chosen in 2002, 110 were from Europe, 101 from Canadian Major Junior leagues, 41 from the NCAA, 6 from U.S. high schools, and 32 from other North American leagues. The most recent NHL collective bargaining agreement, signed in 2005, reduced the NHL draft from nine to seven rounds.[15]

The last of the four major NASLs to sponsor a player entry draft was MLB, which began doing so in 1965. This was done over the strenuous objections of the larger-market teams, which had the resources to root out more than their share of good young players, and to later buy those that their scouts had missed. No team was more satisfied with this status quo than the New York Yankees, who between 1920 and 1964 had mastered the system to the tune of an average winning percentage of 0.619. On the other hand, the smaller-market teams strongly supported the idea of an entry draft, not least because they could improve their profitability by spending less to obtain the rights to young talent via the draft.[16]

From 1965 through 1986, the MLB draft was a complicated affair, consisting of a set of rounds in June and another in January. Both the June and January drafts featured two "phases": a regular phase for previously undrafted players, and a secondary phase for players drafted earlier who had decided to go to college instead of entering professional baseball. The January draft allowed teams to pick college dropouts and junior college players who had not been picked the prior June. As a growing number of players in the 1980s opted for college over the minor leagues, the myriad drafts essentially were collapsed into a single June Regular Phase First-Year Player Draft beginning with 1987.[17] Held via conference call over two days, the draft is conducted in a reverse-order-of-finish manner, but draft picks alternated between the AL and the NL through 2004. In 2006, MLB teams selected a total of 1502 players in the fifty rounds of this June draft, and between 1965 and 2006, a total of 58,645 players were selected in all the MLB First-Year Player drafts (50,164 in regular phases and 8,481 in supplemental phases).[18]

Unlike the NFL, NHL, and NBA drafts, the MLB draft does not include international amateur or professional players; they remain free agents until signed by a MLB team. As a result, most MLB teams maintain "training academies" in Latin America, particularly in the Dominican Republic, where teams negotiate with local *buscones* or agents who procure and control promising teenaged prospects. The sometimes-shady business practices of the *buscones* have led to increasing calls for better regulation and oversight by both MLB and Latin American governments.[19]

An exception to the international free-for-all for baseball talent is found in the relationship between MLB and Japanese baseball. The two leagues have a "working agreement" that calls for each league to respect the player contracts of the other. This pact, which came in the wake of a 1964–1965 dispute between the Nankai Hawks and San Francisco Giants over the services of pitcher Masanori Murkami, is believed to be largely responsible for why no Japanese player jumped to MLB until Hideo Nomo signed with the Los Angeles Dodgers in 1995.[20]

PLAYER ENTRY DRAFTS AND COMPETITIVE BALANCE

There are two primary economic arguments supporting player entry drafts. The first, offered most frequently by leagues, is that such drafts promote competitive balance vis-à-vis the finders-keepers/scouting arms race approach. From a league's perspective, lack of competitive balance is a public "bad" because it reduces the appeal of the sport. The Cleveland Browns' dominance of the All-American Football Conference (1946–1949) is believed to have contributed to its eventual demise. It should be noted, however, that Berri, Schmidt, and Brook and Szymanski have criticized the blanket claim that significant competitive balance is necessary for a sports league's economic success. In any event, sports economists tend to cast a distinctly jaundiced eye on the claim that entry drafts promote competitive balance.[21]

The main source for economists' skepticism is the Rottenberg Invariance Principle/Coase Theorem.[22] The invariance principle claims that changes in the initial allocation of the labor rights of young players will not change their eventual affiliation if player transfers have sufficiently low transactions costs.

This argument can be illustrated as follows: Consider a star player on a small revenue-market team. If a larger revenue-market team is able to earn more profit for a given winning percentage, then the star player has more value in the larger market. If player transactions markets are efficient, then selling the star from the smaller- to the larger-market team would constitute a mutually beneficial exchange. Thus, as long as these markets function well, competitive balance should not be affected by the introduction of the draft—a player will end up in the same place, regardless of which team originally owns his rights. However, it is true that assigning the star's original rights to the smaller- versus the larger-market team will result in more profit for the smaller team, and less for the larger team.

There is substantial evidence in favor of fairly robust draft-pick and player-trading markets. Massey and Thaler identified 334 draft-day trades in the NFL between 1987 and 2004—about 8 percent of all picks, or an average of nearly twenty per year. Similarly, the 2005 NBA draft saw trades that involved twenty-four of the total of sixty picks made, and there were eleven trades involving 2005 NHL draft picks.[23] Although MLB forbids the trading of draft picks or of drafted players for at least one year, North American professional baseball features many minor- and major-league player trades, some of which include cash. These transactions, along with the player trades and sales that occur in the other NASLs, speak to the general vibrancy of player and draft-pick markets.

The Rottenberg/Coase perspective with respect to player entry drafts is supported by an analysis of within-season competitive balance for the AL, NL, and the NFL both before and after the imposition of the MLB and NFL drafts.[24] The analysis finds that these drafts did not result in increased competitive balance, and that players end up distributed throughout the league in similar fashion with or without the draft.

Other investigators, however, suggest a somewhat less perfect realization of Rottenberg/Coase in practice. For example, Surdam's general examination of talent transfer in MLB's American League (AL) during 1946–1984 finds some substantiation for claims that transactions costs were low enough during the period to permit the reallocation of some talent from smaller- to larger-market teams. However, he does find evidence of some "sand in the gears" of player markets.[25] Indeed, leagues have been known to chill player transactions purposefully on some occasions in the name of better competitive balance. Former MLB Commissioner Bowie Kuhn's series of vetoes of player sales between the Oakland A's and the New York Yankees and Boston Red Sox in 1971 is the classic case of such intervention; Kuhn cited "the best interests of baseball" as the reason for his decision. Another example is the NFL's "Rozelle Rule," named after then-commissioner Pete Rozelle, which required punitive compensation from teams signing free agents to teams losing them. The compensation was determined by the commissioner on a case-by-case basis, the apparent purpose of which was to suppress player transactions markets, thereby increasing incumbent teams' monopsony power over players. In 1975, the Rozelle Rule was found to be a *per se* violation of the Sherman Antitrust Act (*Mackey vs. NFL*).[26]

WAGE EFFECTS OF PLAYER ENTRY DRAFTS

The second major claim made about the economic consequences of player entry drafts is *not* often made in public by sports leagues, although it is nearly universally held by sports economists.[27] Specifically, it is that such drafts bestow monopsony power on drafting teams at the expense of players.[28] This power manifests itself in restrictions on players' free agency for their first few years in the league. Table 10.1 shows the extent to which these restrictions now exist in the four major NASLs.

While the most intuitive evidence of the consequences of player market restrictions is the rapid growth of NASL players' average salaries in the wake of greater free agency, there also have been many careful economic studies of the degree of such monopsony exploitation.[29] The most noteworthy of these have concerned MLB, wherein player productivity is most easily measured independently of other players. Before free agency arrived for MLB players, Scully estimated that they earned on average only about 20 percent of their true values; even after free agency, he later found that players still only were paid 29–45 percent of their values. Zimbalist similarly estimated that the most highly monopsonized players (those with less than three years of service) in 1989 earned only a fifth of what would have been earned as free agents.[30]

It should be noted that these estimates of exploitation do not take into account the significant training costs incurred MLB teams before a player is ready for the big league.[31] While other NASL teams make significant human capital investments in their newest players, this is more the case in the NHL than in the NBA or NFL. NBA and NFL players are generally expected to make contributions in the season immediately following their being drafted.[32]

TABLE 10.1
Restrictions on Free Agency for Entry Draftees for Major North American Sports Leagues

League	Years to Free Agency for Entry Draftees
MLB	• After six years on an MLB roster or disabled list • Eligible for final-offer arbitration after three years on an MLB roster or disabled list
NBA	Restricted: • First-round picks: after four years if team extends qualifying offer • All other veteran players with three or fewer season Unrestricted: • First-round picks: four years if team does not extend qualifying offer, *or* two years if team does not pick up third-year option per rookie salary scale, *or* • Three years if fourth-year option not picked up • All other players: after four or more seasons (Significant additional detailed provisions in NBA CBA apply).
NFL	Restricted: • Three years (if contract expired) Restricted FA incumbent team has right of first refusal; if qualifying offer is denied, incumbent team receives compensatory draft pick Unrestricted: • Four years (if contract expired)
NHL	Restricted: • After contract expiration for non-"entry-level" players who do not yet qualify for unrestricted free agency Unrestricted: • North American players not drafted by age 20 • 2006: 29 years old or with eight or more years of NHL service • 2007: 28 years old or seven years of service • 2008–2010: 27 years old with seven years of service

Sources: Various Web sites.

Such contributions, evidenced by Figures 10.1 and 10.2, suggest that not all of the market power created by an entry draft accrues to the drafting team. If so, entering players likely would make quite a bit less than they do. Because professional careers are so short in the NASLs, players' unions tend to represent the interests of current players at the expense of future entering players. Owners, who generally consider longer time horizons and perhaps have smaller discount rates, are content to take their benefits in collective bargaining in the form of restrictions of future players.

Figure 10.3 compares the compensation of first-round draft choices in recent drafts in the NFL, NBA, and MLB, indicating that the top entering players indeed are quite well compensated.[33] Even if they are not paid

FIGURE 10.1
Average Number of Games Started in Each of Player's First Four Seasons among NFL Draftees, 1999–2004

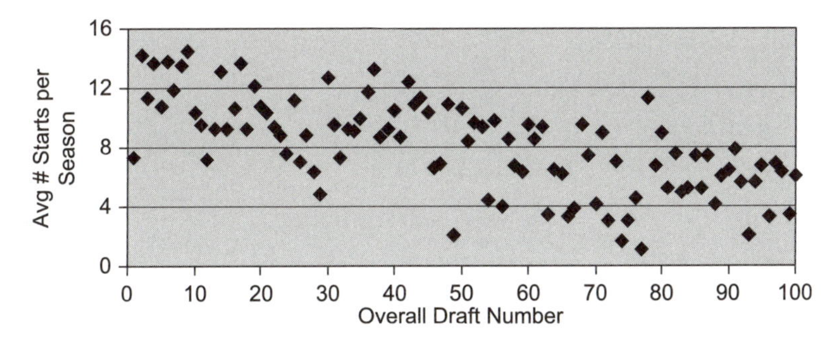

Source: K. G. Quinn, "Who Should Be Drafted? Predicting Future Professional Productivity of Amateur Players Seeking to Enter the National Football League," presented at 2006 meetings of the Western Economic Association, San Diego, 2006.

according to their full value to their teams, they clearly earn more than their next-best employment opportunity would pay. This result would be hard to explain if all the market power was held by teams instead of entering players. Rookie pay is so high in part because each draft pick is a valuable resource to a team—it represents its claim on the very best of the available entering talent.

Failure to arrive at a labor contract, particularly for the top picks, has competitive and economic consequences for the drafting team. According to

FIGURE 10.2
Minutes Played by First-Round NBA Picks, 2005/06 Season

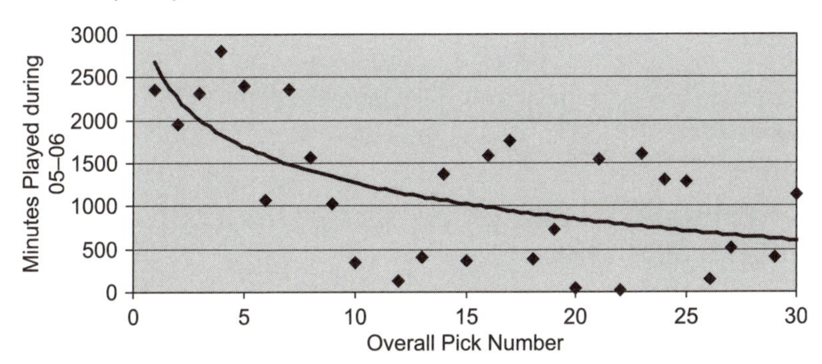

Source: Adapted from data obtained at Basketball-Reference.com.
Note: Logarithmic trend line added (MinPlyd = -611 ln(Pick) + 2680; $R^2 = 0.41$).

FIGURE 10.3
Comparison of First-Year Player Compensation by League

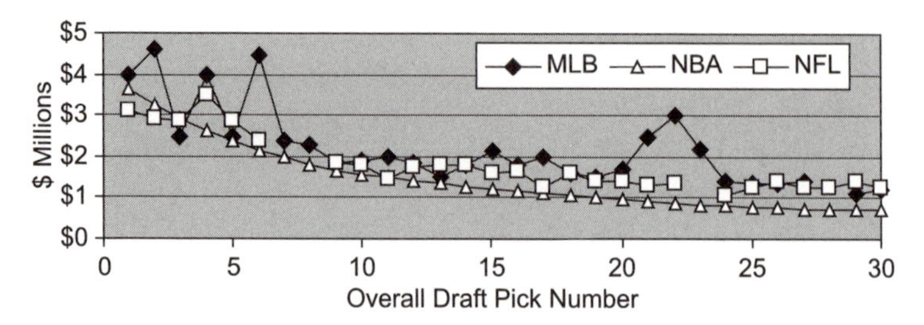

Source: Adapted from data obtained at Basketball-Reference.com.
Notes: MLB data are from 2002 and include signing bonus only. NBA data represent the 2005/06 league rookie salary scale. NFL data are from 2003, and represent the average annual compensation if player's contract is not voided (contract lengths run between five and seven years).

the Nash Bargaining Solution model the outcome of a two-party "divide-the-pie" bargaining situation depends on each party's outcome in the event of no deal.[34] For drafted players, the no-deal outcome is their next-best employment opportunity, which will almost certainly be less pleasing and for a fraction of the pay that top big-league rookies earn. On the other hand, the no-deal outcome for the team is to forgo the opportunity to land one of the few blue-chip players available to it.

Further evidence in support of the Nash model is found in the rapid increase in rookie salaries when a NASL finds itself in rivalry with an upstart league.[35] In these cases, a draftee's pay becomes significantly greater as his no-deal option gets sweeter. In the past, this has led to teams taking extreme measures to keep their draftees away from the other league, such as the assignment of "babysitters" to players during the NFL's rivalry with the American Football League (AFL) during the 1960s.[36] Bidding wars for entering players provide part of the powerful economic impetus for rival leagues to merge, as happened eventually between the AFL and NFL, between the American Basketball Association and the NBA, and between the World Hockey Association and the NHL.

THE RESPONSE TO THE ENTRY DRAFT INFORMATION PROBLEM: SCOUTING

Figures 10.1 through 10.3 suggest that that top picks typically are valuable contributors, and are well paid, but every sport's lore includes legendary draft busts, steals, and undrafted gems far too numerous to detail here. Prior to every draft, there is a great deal of uncertainty associated with prospects' eventual quality; the true value of a player may not be realized until many years later. Football great Brett Favre still was considered to be a bit of a bust several seasons after being chosen by the Atlanta Falcons in the second round of the 1991 NFL draft. MLB drafts are notoriously inaccurate—only about two-thirds of the players picked in the first round ever even appear in a big-league game.

Despite the inherent uncertainty, rookie compensation levels belie the high stakes associated with entry drafts. This problem has spawned sophisticated player scouting regimes in the NASLs. Teams maintain significant in-house scouting operations, hire multitudes of independent firms and individuals, and form multiteam scouting syndicates in their efforts to generate more reliable predictions about prospective draftees. In addition, the leagues themselves provide additional centralized scouting services to teams. The economics of the situation dictate that teams will continue to spend ever more on scouting entering players as long as the return to doing so continues to increase. But notwithstanding the hundreds of millions of dollars devoted to the evaluation of entering players, the process remains more black art than science.

By the 1930s, MLB already had rather large scouting systems, but the early NFL drafts were more akin to those of a friendly fantasy league than to the modern televised spectacle. While a few teams, such as the Los Angeles Rams, had begun to assemble rudimentary scouting networks by the end of World War II, many team executives still prepared for upcoming drafts by reading through copies of *Street & Smith's Football Yearbook* and other such publications.[37]

Eventually, more "scientific" methods were called into service. Soon after his coaching career began with the Los Angeles Rams in 1946, the legendary Paul Brown began to use forty-yard-dash times and cognitive tests in his evaluation of players. The Rams were successful on the field, and other teams began to copy their approach. Among these was Tex Schramm's Dallas Cowboys.

Schramm, who had worked for the Rams during the 1950s, did a stint with CBS Sports during their coverage of the 1960 Olympics at Squaw Valley, where he was impressed by the IBM computers used in the calculation of statistics and times. He managed to convince the Rams and the San Francisco 49ers to go in with the Cowboys on the cost of development of a computerized player evaluation model. The model, which took four years to develop, was first employed in the 1965 draft. Other teams soon formed similar scouting syndicates. Among the modern day successors of these syndicates are the BLESTO and National scouting services.[38]

An important source of entering NFL player information comes from college football programs which are only too happy to "help" the NFL and its teams with their evaluations—having their players drafted is mightily helpful in their own recruiting. Among the forms of this assistance are the college-hosted "Pro Days" in which pro scouts are invited to campus to check out the wares. The current centerpiece of the NFL's predraft analysis, however, is the annual Scouting Combine, held in Indianapolis each February. Approximately 300 prospects are invited to take part in a series of tests, measurements, and workouts for the benefit of personnel decisionmakers for all thirty-two teams. The NHL now also has a scouting combine held in late May and early June, and the NBA's annual Pre-Draft Camp is beginning to evolve into an event similar to the NFL's Combine, complete with player measurements.

Players invited to the combines do not always choose to participate. Moving up or down even a few picks can have sizable economic ramifications for players, and some are advised by their agents not to go. This can be a difficult situation for players and teams as it introduces a greater degree of uncertainty into the mix—exactly what the combines are designed to reduce, and a classic example of an unintended consequence.

A most interesting recent trend—to economists, at least—is occurring in MLB. Baseball scouting has long been the subjective province of grizzled "baseball men" who nomadically wander the countryside in search promising youngsters. This paradigm is now being challenged by egg-headed statisticians hunched over computers seeking to make scouting less art than science. The efforts of the best-known practitioner of this approach, Oakland Athletics' general manager Billy Beane, have been chronicled in the best-selling book *Moneyball*.[39] Like his predecessor Sandy Alderson, Beane is a devoted follower of Bill James, the godfather of modern baseball statistical gurus. Beane has been successful in stretching the A's relatively small payroll into remarkable competitive success, but his approach remains controversial among the baseball *cognoscenti*.

ELIGIBILITY ISSUES IN PLAYER ENTRY DRAFTS

As evidenced by George Halas's early poaching of ungraduated college players and the subsequent NFL rules against the practice, the matter of which players are eligible for player entry drafts is as old as the drafts themselves. In the NFL and NBA, the long-time benchmark was that a player's high school class was to have graduated at least four years earlier in order for him to be eligible for the entry draft, but this has been eroded significantly, much to the chagrin of college coaches.

Moses Malone is recognized as the first modern player to jump from high school directly to professional basketball when he joined the ABA's Utah Stars in 1974. The following year, Darrell Dawkins was selected fifth overall by the Philadelphia 76ers, making him the first player to be drafted by the NBA right out of high school. In the twenty subsequent NBA drafts (1976–1995), a total of twenty high school seniors and college freshmen declared themselves eligible for the NBA draft. From 1996 through 2003, however, sixty-one such players declared themselves draft-eligible and fifty-four were drafted, about half of them in the first round. While this group includes megastars such as Kevin Garnett and Kobe Bryant, a significant fraction of those not drafted in the first round played only a handful of NBA games or not at all.[40]

Slightly older players have fared only a little better. Of the 129 underclassmen that declared themselves eligible for the NBA draft from 1997 to 2000, only 40 found themselves on an NBA roster as of June of 2001.[41] NBA Commissioner David Stern has long been a critic of younger players playing in the league, and the NBA's latest collective bargaining agreement, signed in 2005, created a nineteen-year-old age floor for NBA rookies. The league claims the moral high ground in its distaste for high school entrants, but there is economic advantage in doing so. It is much less expensive for NBA teams to scout the top 100 or so NCAA men's basketball programs than it is to keep track of the nation's thousands of high school teams. Furthermore, older rookies mean more polished and productive rookies who will be unrestricted free agents for smaller fractions of their playing careers.

In 1990 third-year college students became eligible for the NFL draft in the wake of Oklahoma State running back Barry Sanders's 1989 challenge to the prevailing four-year rule.[42] Underclassmen eligibility was further tested by Ohio State running back Maurice Clarett, who unsuccessfully petitioned the NFL, and then the courts under antitrust law, to declare him eligible for the draft after only one year of college. The NFL cites a variety of reasons for their rule, including risk of injury due to the lack of physical maturity of younger players, but their teams also can benefit economically from later career-starts as players spend a greater number of their most productive years under monopsony.

In contrast to the NFL and NBA, the NHL and MLB have long had a tradition of the pursuit of younger players, typically those seventeen years old or older. In the case of MLB, any resident high school senior in the United States, Canada, or Puerto Rico graduating from high school is eligible for the draft, as are all junior college players. Players from four-year colleges must have completed at least their junior year and be at least twenty-one years old in order to be eligible.[43]

In the NHL, early control of young players going back to the "Original Six" days was accomplished via the "A," "B," and "C" Forms, which sought to bind players to teams as early as their sixteenth birthdays. The A Form gave teams negotiation rights in the wake of a tryout, but the B and C Forms gave clubs exclusive amateur and professional options rights.[44] There was a procedure to reserve even younger players, but such reservations and options were eliminated with the 1969 draft. From 1987 through 1991 eighteen- and nineteen-year-old players could only be chosen in the first three rounds, but this stipulation was dropped beginning with the 1992 draft. The 2005 NHL CBA specifies that players must be eighteen years old to be eligible for the draft, and that all such players are automatically eligible without having to declare themselves so.

REVERSE-ORDER-OF-FINISH VERSUS LOTTERY ENTRY DRAFTS

The lottery system was meant to reduce the primary moral hazard associated with reverse-order-of-finish drafts: the incentive for teams to lose more games at the end of disappointing seasons so as to move up in the draft.[45] Currently such lotteries are practiced in the NBA and NHL, wherein nonplayoff teams in each league are eligible.

In the NHL, there is only one winner of the Draft Drawing lottery, and the outcome does not affect the draft order for the remainder of the first round or for subsequent rounds. The winning team is allowed to move up a maximum of four places relative to the reverse-order-of-finish in the first round, and no team will move down more than one place in the first round relative to the reverse-order-of-finish. Table 10.2 depicts the chances of winning the NHL Draft Drawing lottery, and getting the first pick (for teams finishing thirtieth through twenty-sixth in terms of points) or moving up four spots (teams ranked twenty-fifth through fifteenth).[46]

In the NBA, fourteen ping-pong balls (numbered 1 through 14) are mixed in a drum, and four balls are drawn three times (with replacement) to assign the first three picks of the upcoming draft. Each of the fourteen nonplayoff teams is assigned a subset of the 1001 possible combinations, with the number of combinations awarded to each team determined by the teams' reverse-order-of-finish during the prior regular season.[47] Table 10.3 shows the probabilities for the 2006 lottery teams (includes the effect of ties in the standings during the 2005/06 season).

TABLE 10.2
Probabilities of Winning NHL Draft Drawing Lottery by Final Standings Points Rank

Points Rank	Probability of Winning (%)
30th	25.0
29th	18.8
28th	14.2
27th	10.7
26th	8.1
25th	6.2
24th	4.7
23rd	3.6
22nd	2.7
21st	2.1
20th	1.5
19th	1.1
18th	0.8
17th	0.5

Source: Adapted from Pittsburghpenguins.com (2006).

FAN INTEREST IN ENTRY DRAFTS

The prospect of a good draft pick can to some degree retain fan interest for teams late in disappointing seasons. In addition to electronic media coverage, a growing variety of publications and Web sites are primarily dedicated to the prospect of informing fans about prospects in advance of league entry drafts. In recent years, the NASLs have become more cognizant of this interest and have begun to treat their drafts as an additional opportunity to market their sports. Media coverage of the NFL and NBA drafts is particularly intense.

The cable sports behemoth ESPN was only a year old and available in a mere seven million homes when it first broadcast the NFL draft in 1980. Because there then was little thought by the NFL that the event would be interesting, the draft was held on a Tuesday and Wednesday afternoon until it moved to the weekend in 1985.[48] In 1988, about 1.7 million watched the draft on ESPN, and five years later the number only had grown to 2.5 million. By 2004, however, 31 million viewers decided to tune away at some point from the first month of the MLB season to check out the NFL draft.[49]

The NBA draft also enjoys substantial attention, but not as much as the NFL draft. Whereas the June 2006 ESPN-televised NBA event drew 2.2 percent of all American cable viewers, the first five hours of the NFL draft two months earlier drew 5.2 percent.[50] Both the NBA and NFL drafts,

TABLE 10.3
Probabilities Associated with the 2006 NBA Draft Lottery

			Probabilities (%)			
Team	2005/06 Record	Number of Combi-nations Assigned	1st Pick	2nd Pick	3rd Pick	1st, 2nd, or 3rd Pick
Portland Trailblazers	21–61	250	25.00	21.60	17.80	64.40
New York Knicks	23–59	199	19.90	18.80	17.00	55.70
Charlotte Bobcats	26–56	138	13.80	14.30	14.50	42.60
Atlanta Hawks	26–56	137	13.70	14.10	14.20	42.00
Toronto Raptors	27–55	88	8.80	9.70	10.60	29.10
Minnesota T-Wolves	33–49	53	5.30	6.40	7.10	18.80
Boston Celtics	33–49	53	5.30	6.40	7.10	18.80
Houston Rockets	34–48	23	2.30	2.70	3.40	8.40
Golden State Warriors	34–48	22	2.20	2.40	3.00	7.60
Seattle Supersonics	35–47	11	1.10	1.30	1.60	4.00
Orlando Magic	36–46	8	0.80	0.90	1.00	2.90
New Orleans Hornets	38–44	7	0.70	0.80	1.00	2.60
Philadelphia 76ers	38–44	6	0.60	0.70	0.90	2.20
Utah Jazz	41–41	5	0.50	0.60	0.70	1.80

Source: "Throwing Games and the NBA Draft Lottery," Sports-law.blogspot.com, 2006, http://sports-law.blogspot.com/2006/04/throwing-games-and-nba-draft-lottery.html (accessed October 30, 2006).

however, are much more closely watched by the public than the either of NHL or MLB offerings. While NBA and NFL draftees generally are expected to play right away in their respective leagues, all but only the very top NHL and MLB picks spend significant time—as long as several years—in the minor leagues. Still, there is growing interest in these drafts, particularly for the NHL. While the NHL first opened up its draft to a live audience of 2,500 fans in 1980, 2006 saw live coverage of the seven-round affair on ESPN2 in the United States and on TSN in Canada.[51] By contrast, MLB's draft is held during its regular season, so its draft is eclipsed by actual competition, and live coverage generally was limited to MLB.com and MLB radio until 2007, when ESPN began to televise portions of it.

LEAGUE EXPANSION DRAFTS AND PLAYER DISPERSAL DRAFTS

When a NASL expands, the new teams must somehow assemble a roster from scratch.[52] It is in the best interest of the league to create expansion teams that are at least somewhat competitive—failure to do so would diminish the franchise fees that the league collects from new owners and result in too many unattractive contests with incumbent teams. Therefore, in addition to entering the expansion teams at the top of their first entry drafts, the usual custom for expanding NASLs is to hold "expansion" drafts.

Typically, incumbent teams are allowed to protect a significant portion of their rosters; that is, declare those players ineligible for the expansion draft. Furthermore, there is typically a limit to the number of players that the expansion team(s) may select from any one incumbent team. Tables 10.4–10.7 provide information regarding expansion drafts held in MLB, the NFL, NBA, and the NHL, respectively. The list below summarizes the detailed rules governing one specific recent expansion draft (for the NBA's Charlotte Bobcats in 2004).

TABLE 10.4
MLB Expansion Draft Information

Year and League	City	Draft Procedures
1961 AL	Los Angeles; Washington	• 15 of the 40 man rosters of existing teams made available, including 7 from the 25-man roster from 9/1/60 • Had to draft 28 players from this pool @ $75,000 each: 10 pitchers, 2 catchers, 6 infielders, 4 outfielders, 4 unrestricted • Could also draft one player from each farm system for $25,000 each
1962 NL	Houston; New York	• 15 of the 40 man rosters of existing teams made available, including 7 from the 25-man roster from 8/31/61 • Had to draft 2 players from each team @ $75,000 each and could pick a third from this pool for $50,000 each • After the preceding picks, existing teams made two more players available with one player drafted from each team (8 existing teams, so 4 per expansion team) @ $125,000 each
1969 AL	Kansas City; Seattle	• Existing teams could protect 15 players (not limited to 40-man rosters), then 3 more players with each player selected from the team • Each expansion team drafts 30 players, 3 from each team @ $175,000 each
1969 NL	Montreal; San Diego	• Existing teams could protect 15 players (not limited to 40-man rosters), then 3 more players with each player selected from the team

(*Continued*)

TABLE 10.4 (*continued*)

Year and League	City	Draft Procedures
		• Each expansion team drafts 30 players, 3 from each team @ $200,000 each
1977 AL	Seattle; Toronto	• Existing teams could protect 15 players (not limited to 40-man rosters), then 3 more players after the third round, then 2 more after the forth round • Each expansion team drafts 30 players, 3 from each team @ $175,000 each
1993 NL	Colorado; Florida	• Existing teams could protect 15 players from the 40-man roster, then 3 more players (NL) or 4 more players (AL) after the first two rounds; in the third round, only 8 of the 14 AL teams can lose players
1998 MLB	Arizona; Tampa Bay	• Existing teams could protect 15 eligible players in the first round, then 3 more after each of the first two rounds; only 7 teams from each league lose players in the third round • Eligible players include the entire 40-man roster, plus all players draft in 1994 or earlier and those 19 or older when drafted in 1995

Source: K. G. Quinn and P. M. Bursik, "Growing and Moving the Game: The Effects of MLB Expansion and Team Relocation, 1950–2004," presented at the NINE Annual Spring Training Conference, Tuscon, 2006; D. Pappas, "Chronology of Expansion and Relocation," 1997, http://roadsidephotos.com/baseball/expansion.htm (accessed March 13, 2005).

Selection Rules

- The Bobcats will select a minimum of fourteen players who are under contract or restricted free agents for the 2004/05 season.
- The Bobcats may select no more than one player from each team.
- The Bobcats can only select players that are left unprotected by an NBA team.
- Each of the twenty-nine NBA teams may protect a maximum of eight players on its roster who are under contract or are restricted free agents at the conclusion of the 2003/04 season.
- Each of the twenty-nine NBA teams will designate the players on its roster who are eligible for selection by the Bobcats.
- Each of the twenty-nine NBA teams must designate at least one player on its roster to be eligible for selection by the Bobcats, even if the team does not have eight players under contract or as restricted free agents for the 2004/05 season.
- Any eligible restricted free agent selected by the Bobcats shall immediately become an unrestricted free agent.
- Unrestricted free agents are not eligible to be protected nor are they eligible to be selected by the Bobcats.

TABLE 10.5
NFL Expansion Draft Information

Year	Team(s)	Franchise Fee	Number of Nonentry Players Selected	Comments
1960	Dallas Cowboys	$600K or $1 million	36 @ $15K each (included in franchise fee)	Hall of Fame value from newspaper accounts; Dallas did not participate in 1960 NFL player entry draft
1961	Minnesota Vikings	$600K or $1 million	36 @ $15K each (included in franchise fee)	Hall of Fame value from newspaper accounts
1966	Atlanta Falcons	$8.5 million		
1967	New Orleans Saints; Cincinnati Bengals (AFL); Miami Dolphins (AFL)	$8.5 million (NO); $7.5 million (Cin and Mia)	40 (Cin) 31 (Mia)	Vrooman indicates that the 1966 and 1967 franchise fees each include 42 expansion draftees @ $200K each
1976	Seattle Seahawks; Tampa Bay Buccaneers	$16 million each	39 each	
1995	Carolina Panthers; Jacksonville Jaguars	$140 million each (each received only half-share of league television revenues 1995–99)	35 (Car) 31 (Jax)	Pool = 168 players (6 from each incumbent team); each incumbent team could lose a max of 3 players; Car and Jax each required to pick between 30 and 42 players
1999	Cleveland Browns	Approx. $300 million	37	Pool = 180 players (6 from each incumbent team); each incumbent team could lose a max of 3 players; Cle required to select between 30 and 42 players and is required to use 38 percent of their projected sal cap in the draft.
2002	Houston Texans	$700 million	19	Pool = 155 players (5 from each incumbent team); each incumbent team could lose a max of 2 players

Sources: J. Quirk and R. D. Fort, *Pay Dirt: The Business of Professional Team Sports* (Princeton, N.J.: Princeton University Press, 1997); J. Vrooman, "Franchise Free Agency in Professional Sports Leagues," *Southern Economic Journal* 64, no. 1 (1997): 191–219.
Note: Some franchise fees were paid over time.

TABLE 10.6
NBA Expansion Draft Information

Year	Team(s)	Expansion Fee	Number of Nonentry Players Selected
1966	Chicago Bulls	$1.25 million	18
1967	San Diego Rockets; Seattle SuperSonics	$1.75 million each	10 (SD); 15 (Sea)
1968	Milwaukee Bucks; Phoenix Suns	$2 million each	18 each
1970	Buffalo Braves; Cleveland Cavaliers; Portland Trailblazers	$3.7 million each	11 each
1974	New Orleans Jazz	$6.15 million	14
1980	Dallas Mavericks	$12 million	22
1988	Charlotte Hornets; Miami Heat	$32.5 million each	11 (Cha); 12 (Mia)
1989	Minnesota Timberwolves; Orlando Magic	$32.5 million each	11 (Min); 12 (Orl)
1995	Toronto Raptors; Vancouver Grizzlies	$125 million each	14 (Tor); 13 (Van)
2004	Charlotte Bobcats	$400 million	19

Sources: J. Quirk and R. D. Fort, *Pay Dirt: The Business of Professional Team Sports* (Princeton, N.J.: Princeton University Press, 1997); "NBA Expansion Drafts," NBAhoopsonline.com, 2006, http://nbahoopsonline.com/History/Expansiondrafts.html (accessed October 30, 2006).

TABLE 10.7
NHL Expansion and Dispersal Draft Information

Year	Team(s)	Franchise Fee	Number of Nonentry Players Selected	Comments
1967	Cleveland Barons; Los Angeles Kings; Minnesota North Stars; Philadelphia Flyers; Pittsburgh Penguins; St. Louis Blues	$2 million each	120 (20 players per team)	
1970	Buffalo Sabres; Vancouver Canucks	$2 million each	25 (Buffalo) 20 (Canucks)	
1972	Atlanta Flames; New York Islanders	$6 million each	21 each	
1974	Kansas City Scouts; Washington Capitols	$6 million each	24 each	

(*Continued*)

TABLE 10.7 (*continued*)

Year	Team(s)	Franchise Fee	Number of Nonentry Players Selected	Comments
1979	Edmunton Oilers; Hartford Whalers; Quebec Nordiques; Winnepeg Jets	None (result of WHA-NHL merger)	16 (Edm) 16 (Har) 17 (Que) 17 (Win)	Incoming teams allowed to protect 4 players; NHL teams allowed to reclaim other former WHA player rights; then incoming teams could draft
1991	Minnesota North Stars; San Jose Sharks	$45 million (SJ only)	24 from Min to SJ 10 each (1 for Min and SJ each from each of the other teams in league)	Represented the undoing of the 1978 merger of the North Stars and the Barons; Min could protect 16 players from SJ
1992	Ottawa Senators; Tampa Bay Lightning	$45 million each	21 each	Incumbent teams allowed to protect 14 skaters and 2 goalies
1993	Florida Panthers	$45 million	24 each	Incumbent teams could protect 15 players, and only lose 1 goalie or defenseman
1998	Nashville Predators	$80 million	26	One player from each incumbent team; incumbents could protect 12-15 players
1999	Atlanta Thrashers	$80 million	26	One player from each incumbent team; incumbents could protect 12–15 players; Nash could protect all players
2000	Columbus Blue Jackets; Minnesota Wild	$80 million each	26	Newest incumbent teams could protect all players; others could protect 12–15 players

Sources: Various Web sites.

Salary Cap Rules

- Charlotte will have a salary cap in its first season equal to 66 percent of the salary cap applicable to the rest of the league and a salary cap in its second season equal to 75 percent of the salary cap applicable to the rest of the league.
- Charlotte will be permitted to sign any restricted free agent it selects in the expansion draft using the same "Bird," "Early Bird," or "Non-Bird" exception that the player's prior team would have had.[53]

Before the advent of salary caps, the list of expansion draft–eligible veterans was hardly an all-star team; it usually was comprised of the worst players on incumbent teams. Consequently, expansion teams generally have struggled competitively, although they typically win at least some contests (the 0–11–1 1960 Dallas Cowboys and 0–16 1976 Tampa Bay Buccaneers notwithstanding). In recent years, teams have sometimes decided not to protect good players with high salary cap values, which partially can explain the playoff wins of the Carolina Panthers and Jacksonville Jaguars during their second seasons. For tax-advantage purposes, a substantial amount of expansion teams' franchise fees sometimes have been attributed to player acquisition costs via the expansion drafts.

In the event that a team folds or a rival league collapses, a league will hold a player dispersal draft in an effort to avert an expensive scramble for newly free agents. The first of these in recent times occurred in 1976 in the wake of the merger of the ABA with the NBA. The Spirits of St. Louis and Kentucky Colonels were not invited to enter the NBA with the other ABA franchises, and twelve players from these two teams were selected by NBA teams. The 1979 WHA-NHL merger resulted in a complicated talent dispersal process in which NHL teams were generally allowed to reassert their entry rights to former WHA players. The four WHA-cum-NHL franchises then could restock via an expansion draft. However, unlike the demises of the ABA and WHA, the collapse of the United States Football League (USFL) did not result in a merger with the NFL. Shrewdly anticipating the USFL's end, which came following the 1985 season, the NFL used the June 1984 Supplemental Draft to assign the rights of USFL and Canadian football league players. Eighty-four players were selected in that draft, including future Hall of Famers Steve Young and Reggie White.

CONCLUDING REMARKS

Player drafts have become part of the DNA of North American sports leagues and a source of considerable fan interest. While players' unions have worked to earn free agency for veteran players, they have not been as keen to win those rights for entering players. North American sports leagues' player entry drafts are typically conducted in reverse-order-of-finish wherein teams with the worst records the prior seasons have first choice of entering amateur players. However, this approach can tempt teams into losing games at the end of poor seasons in order to improve the quality of their next draft, so some leagues have introduced lottery assignment of top picks.

League claims—contrary to economic theory—that player entry drafts are necessary to maintain competitive balance are supported by very shaky evidence, if at all. On the other hand, there is clear empirical support for the claim that such drafts afford drafting teams substantial monopsony power, allowing them to exploit players by paying them less than they would earn in a free market. By making draft choices significant but scarce resources, entry drafts also bestow some market power on drafted players. Consequently, a highly drafted entering player has some bargaining power with his new team. The large first-year salaries of the top entering players attest to this bargaining power.

While amateur player entry drafts are annual affairs, leagues also make use of draft systems on other occasions as well. Expanding leagues hold expansion drafts to quickly stock new teams' rosters with veteran players, although these players are generally of below-average quality. Leagues also use drafts in the event of league contraction or the failure of a rival league to disperse talent without creating expensive auctions for newly free players.

NOTES

1. R. D. Fort, *Sports Economics* (Upper Saddle River, N.J.: Prentice-Hall, 2006).

2. "The Collective Bargaining Agreement for Fans, the 1800s," CBAforfans.com, http://www.cbaforfans.com/1800s.html (accessed October 31, 2005). According to another source, teams' entire rosters were reserved by 1883; Feldman, "A Baseball's Transition to Professionalism," http://www.sabr.org/cmsFiles/Files/feldman%20J-KA%202002.pdf (accessed October 31, 2005).

3. Fort, *Sports Economics,* indicates that while the reserve clause began dropping from player contract boilerplates during the 1950s, real competition for player services did not begin in MLB until 1976, in the NBA until 1981, in 1993 in the NHL, and in 1994 in the NFL.

4. Grange subsequently quit the team when the Bears rejected his demand for one-third of the team's 1926 gate. Grange and his agent, C. C. Pyle, then sought their own NFL franchise in New York, an idea that was promptly vetoed by the owner of the Giants, Tim Meara. Grange and Pyle then formed a rival league, which disbanded after only one season. Grange sat out the 1928 season, returning to play for the Bears from 1929 to 1934.

5. P. Williams, *The Draft* (New York: St. Martin's Press, 2006).

6. M. Leeds and P. von Allmen, *The Economics of Sports* (Boston: Addison-Wesley, 2005); Stan Kostka's past stats, history, and awards, Database.football.com, http://www.databasefootball.com/players/playerpage.htm?ilkid=KOSTKSTA01 (accessed October 6, 2006).

7. Fort, *Sports Economics.* A reverse-order-of-finish draft is one in which the least competitively successful team in the league during the prior season has the first pick; the second-worst has the second pick, and so on. Following the first pick of the best team during the prior season, a second round begins with the worst team again picking first, and so on. Fort indicates that there may have been a geographic draft in the NFL prior to 1935.

8. The award was known in 1935 as the Downtown Athletic Club Award, but was renamed after John Heisman in 1936.

9. "Biography—Jay Berwanger," Hickok.sports.com, http://www.hickoksports.com/biograph/berwangr.shtml (accessed October 6, 2006). In addition to the seven rounds, teams are awarded "compensatory picks" for the loss of restricted free agents to other teams.

10. "NFL Draft," NFL.com, http://www.nfl.com/draft (accessed October 6, 2006). The NFL also holds a June supplemental draft for players who were not eligible for the April draft, but that has become obsolete (e.g., academic, NCAA rulings). According to the NFL History Network (the http://nflhistory.net/shared/draft.asp), except for 1984, records of these drafts remain spotty.

11. J. Quirk and R. D. Fort, *Pay Dirt: The Business of Professional Team Sports* (Princeton, N.J.: Princeton University Press, 1997).

12. "NBA Draft." ArmchairGM.com, http://armchairgm.com/mwiki/index.php?title=NBA_Draft (accessed October 6, 2006). See below for details regarding the NBA draft lottery.

13. The NHL once allowed the reservation of players who were not yet under contract. Leeds and von Allmen (*Economics of Sports*) recount the story of Chicago Blackhawks great Bobby Hull, who was reserved at the age of eleven years.

14. See below for details regarding the NHL draft lottery.

15. "Futures—NHL Entry Draft—Draft History," NHL.com, http://www.nhl.com/futures/drafthistory.html (accessed October 6, 2006); "NHL Entry Draft," Wikipedia.com, http://en.wikipedia.org/wiki/NHL_Entry_Draft (accessed October 5, 2006); "NHL Entry Draft Primer," About.com, 2006, http://proicehockey.about.com/cs/prospects/a/nhl_draft_basic.htm (accessed October 30, 2006); "Collective Bargaining Agreement," NHL.com, 2005, http://www.nhl.com/nhlhq/cba/index.html (accessed October 31, 2006).

16. See S. Rottenberg, "The Baseball Player's Labor Market," *Journal of Political Economy* 64, no. 3 [1956]: 643–676, about the competitive balance issues associated with player entry drafts.

17. "MLB Draft," Wikipedia.com, http://en.wikipedia.org/wiki/MLB_Draft (accessed October 31, 2006). MLB still runs the "Rule 5 Draft" each January at the end of the winter meetings; this draft each year allows a few players mired in the minor-league system of one team to have a shot at another major-league roster. For more details see R. Neyer,

"Transactions Primer," ESPN.go.com, 2005, http://espn.go.com/mlb/s/transanctionsprimer.html (accessed October 31, 2006).

18. "Amateur Baseball Draft, 1965–2005," TheBaseballCube.com, http://www.thebaseballcube.com/draft/index.shtml (accessed October 6, 2006); and "History—2006 First-Year Player Draft—June Regular Phase," MLB.com, http://mlb.mlb.com/NASApp/mlb/mlb/history/draft/draft.jsp?year=2006&type=junreg (accessed October 6, 2006).

19. A. M. Klein, *Growing the Game: The Globalization of Major League Baseball* (New Haven, Conn.: Yale University Press, 2006).

20. Ibid.

21. D. J. Berri, M. B. Schmidt, and S. L. Brook, *The Wages of Wins* (Palo Alto, Calif.: Stanford University Press, 2006); S. Szymanski, "Tilting the Playing Field: Why a Sports League Planner Would Choose Less, Not More, Competitive Balance," Imperial College, Tanaka Business School, London, South Kensington Campus, 2004.

22. Rottenberg, "Baseball Player's Labor Market"; R. Coase, "The Problem of Social Cost," *Journal of Law and Economics* 3 (1960): 1–44. Sports economists are fond of pointing out that Rottenberg's thesis predates the highly similar, but better-known Coase's by five years.

23. C. Massey and R. H. Thaler, "The Loser's Curse: Overconfidence vs. Market Efficiency in the National Football League Draft," 2005, mimeo accessed at http://faculty.fuqua.duke.edu/%7Ecadem/bio/massey%20&%20thaler%20-%20loser%27s%20curse.pdf (accessed March 15, 2008); "2005 Draft Pick Transactions, 2006," N-C-Systems.com, http://www.n-c-systems.com/hoops/DraftTrades/2005.html (accessed October 31, 2006); "2005 Draft Trade Tracker," ESPN.com, 2006, http://sports.espn.go.com/nhl/draft2005/news/story?page=05drafttradetracker (accessed October 31, 2006).

24. R. D. Fort, *Sports Economics,* 2nd ed. (Upper Saddle River, N.J.: Pearson/Prentice-Hall, 2005).

25. D. Surdam, "The Coase Theorem and Movement in Major League Baseball," *Journal of Sports Economics* 7, no. 2 (May 2006): 201–221.

26. *John Mackey, et al., v. NFL, et al.,* 407 F Supp. 1000 (D. Minn., 1975), Rev'd on per se issue F. 2d 606 (Eighth Cir. 1976); E. R. Garvey, "From Chattel to Employee: The Athlete's Quest for Freedom and Dignity," *Annals of the American Academy of Political and Social Science, Contemporary Issues in Sport* 445 (September 1979): 91–101.

27. J. J. Seigfried, "Sports Player Drafts and Reserve Systems," *Cato Journal* 14, no. 3 (Winter 1995); L. M. Kahn, "The Sports Business as a Labor Market Laboratory," *Journal of Economic Perspectives* 14, no. 3 (Summer 2000): 75–94.

28. A monopsony is defined as a market with a single buyer. Monopsonized labor markets are characterized by lower wages than an otherwise competitive labor market.

29. Fort, *Sports Economics,* 2nd. ed.

30. G. Scully, "Pay and Performance in Major League Baseball," *American Economic Review* 64, no. 5 (1974): 915–930; G. Scully, *The Business of Major League Baseball* (Chicago: University of Chicago Press, 1989); A. Zimbalist, *Baseball and Billions* (New York: Basic Books, 1992).

31. A. Krautmann, E. Gustafson, and L. Hadley, "Who Pays for Minor League Training Costs?" *Contemporary Economic Policy* 18, no. 1 (2000): 37–47.

32. There is some discussion that in the wake of the NBA Collective Bargaining Agreement signed in 2005 the league sought to strengthen the National Basketball Developmental League, and encourage teams to make more use of it for younger players.

33. MLB data represent 2002 signing bonuses only, and were taken from rodneyfort.com. NBA data represent 2005/06 rookie salary scale data according to NBA from NBA Rookie Salary Scale, http://www.nba.com/news/cba_rookiesalary_050804.html. NFL data represent average annual contract value to player if not voided for 2003 draft choices, and were taken from rodneyfort.com (note—player contract length ranged between five and seven years).

34. J. F. Nash, "The Bargaining Problem," *Econometrica* 18 (1950): 155–162.

35. Quirk and Fort, *Pay Dirt*.

36. P. Williams, *The Draft: A Year Inside the NFL's Search for Talent* (New York: St. Martin's Press, 2006).

37. Ibid.

38. Ibid.

39. M. Lewis, *Moneyball: The Art of Winning an Unfair Game* (New York: W. W. Norton, 2003).

40. D. T. Rosenbaum, "How the NBA Turned a Trickle of Underclassmen Leaving School Early into a Flood," 2003, mimeo, http://www.uncg.edu/bae/people/rosenbaum/leavingearly1.pdf (accessed October 31, 2006). The article attributes the increase in younger players to the 1995 NBA CBA, which increased the financial penalty for college players to stay in school.

41. W. Drehs, "Lure of Stardom Can Glitter like Fake Gold," June 20, 2001, ESPN.go.com, http://espn.go.com/nba/draft2001/s/2001/0618/1215705.html (accessed October 31, 2006).

42. Williams, *The Draft*.

43. "Events: First-Year Player Draft Rules," MLB.com, 2006, http://mlb.mlb.com/NASApp/mlb/mlb/draftday/rules.jsp (accessed October 31, 2006).

44. J. C. H. Jones, "The Economics of the National Hockey League," *Canadian Journal of Economics* 2, no. 1 (February 1969): 1–20.

45. B. A. Taylor, and J. G. Trogdon, "Losing to Win: Tournament Incentives in the National Basketball Association," *Journal of Labor Economics* 20, no. 1 (January 2002): 23–41.

46. "NHL Draft Drawing to Be Conducted April 20," Pittsburghpengiuns.com, 2006, http://www.pittsburghpenguins.com/team/press/arts/1823.0.php (accessed October 30, 2006).

47. Note that only 1000 of the 1001 combinations are assigned to teams. In the unlikely event that the one unassigned combination is drawn, the drawing is redone. "Evolution of the Lottery," NBA.com, 2006, http://www.nba.com/news/lottery02_evolution.html (accessed October 30, 2006).

48. The move to the weekend even then was not precipitated by television coverage. Rather, the Marriott Marquis hotel in New York, where it was held, wanted to charge more during the week. The NFL, still the lean operation, chose to move the days rather than pay more for the space. (Williams, *The Draft*).

49. Ibid.

50. M. Heistand, "Quick Pics, 'Fly Cam' Make NBA Draft More Appealing to TV Audience," USAToday.com, June 28, 2006, http://www.usatoday.com/sports/columnist/hiestand-tv/2006-06-27-hiestand_x.htm (accessed October 25, 2006).

51. "Futures—NHL Entry Draft," NHL.com, 2006, http://www.nhl.com/futures/drafthistory.html (accessed October 25, 2006).

52. Vrooman includes a treatment of league expansion based on the theory of clubs; see J. Vrooman, "Franchise Free Agency in Professional Sports Leagues," *Southern Economic Journal* 64, no. 1 (1997): 191–219.

53. "Expansion Selection and NBA Draft Story," NBA.com, 2005, http://www.nba.com/bobcats/inside_tracks_expansion_selection.html (accessed October 30, 2006).

Eleven

Globalisation and the Evolving Player-Agent Relationship in Professional Sport

Daniel S. Mason and Gregory H. Duquette

INTRODUCTION

In recent years, professional athletes such as Tiger Woods, Yao Ming, and David Beckham have become global celebrities whose names and images reach beyond that of their respective sports. This has been facilitated both by their athletic successes, and also by their media presence established through endorsements, sponsorships, and advertising. Due to sports' global appeal, many transnational corporations such as McDonald's and Nike have sought to capitalise by sponsoring sporting events and paying athletes to promote their products and services. These relationships have become so lucrative for athletes that many can earn more from endorsements than they can from their playing salaries. For example in 2003, European soccer star David Beckham earned £5.5 million playing for Manchester United, yet he earned an estimated £15 million a year from his sponsorship deals with such companies as Pepsi and Adidas (Walsh *et al.*, 2004). These high salaries and sponsorship fees are not limited to team sport. Athletes in individual sports such as tennis and golf can earn similar amounts, as evidenced by tennis star Venus Williams' US$40 million/five-year deal with Reebok (McCarthy, 2000) or Tiger Woods' US$100 million/five-year deal with Nike (Craig, 2002).

Most athletes are very involved in maintaining and improving their playing talents. For this reason, athletes acquire the services of agents who seek out endorsement opportunities with prospective firms. The agent's role is critical since a professional athlete can continue to endorse products long after his/her playing career has ended. The agent must establish a good rapport with companies because a strong relationship with said companies could mean a long-standing contractual relationship and may also provide endorsements for other athletes being represented by said agent. This is in addition to the traditional role that agents used to play for professional athletes, which was to assist them in negotiating their playing contracts. The purpose of this paper is to examine player representation in professional sports within the context of broader changes in the global market. Following an overview of agency theory and the traditional role fulfilled by agents on behalf of players, we review how changes have impacted players and agents in professional sport. We then discuss the implications these changes have for the player-agent relationship in terms of the traditional principal-agent relationship proposed by agency theorists.

AGENCY THEORY AND PLAYER AGENTS

Agency theory examines the dynamics of principal-agent relationships, whereby the agent contracts with the principal to perform a duty or service on behalf of the principal (Alchian and Demsetz, 1972; Eisenhardt, 1989; Jensen and Meckling, 1976). The relationship between an athlete and an agent is consistent with the single-principal, single-agent dyad proposed in agency theory (Mason and Slack, 2001).[1] As principal, the player hires the agent to perform a specific duty (such as seeking out endorsement opportunities on the player's behalf or, in the case of team sport, negotiating the terms of the contract between player and team) because the principal lacks either the time or the skill to perform the duty as competently as the agent (Macdonald, 1984). As agency theorists contend, a contract (which can be either implicit or explicit) exists between the two parties that sets out the duties to be performed by the agent on behalf of the principal, and the means through which the agent will be compensated. The contract itself can be in the form of an explicit, written contract between the two parties, but also consists of an implicit bond between principal and agent. In the case of players and agents in professional sports, the athlete delegates authority to the agent to negotiate contracts with prospective firms that seek to align their products and services with the player, a negotiation in which it is assumed that the agent has specific knowledge and skills that the player lacks, and that the agent has better knowledge of (caused by information asymmetry). However, since the agent has specific knowledge of his/her own abilities and effort, the agent also has the opportunity to act self interestedly without detection by the principal (Nilakant and Rao, 1994), particularly in instances where the principal cannot evaluate agent behaviour (Jones and Butler, 1992). In the case of agents seeking endorsement opportunities on behalf of players, players may not be aware of the relationship that develops and is maintained by both the agents and the firms seeking to contract with the players.

Self-interested behaviour can be divided into several categories. According to Eisenhardt (1989), *adverse selection* occurs when agents misrepresent their abilities in order to contract with principals; these are agent claims that the principal cannot verify. Similarly, principals may have difficulty determining the amount of effort that agents put forth in performing for the principal. This problem is called *moral hazard*, or shirking on the part of the agent (Eisenhardt, 1989). Another problem, as suggested by Lewis and Sappington (1993), is *agent ignorance*. This occurs when agents cannot fulfil their duties because of incompetence. These types of agent behaviours incur *agency costs*. The first are *monitoring costs* that are created by efforts to detect any unwanted agent behaviour. The second, *bonding costs*, are assumed by agents in order to show prospective principals that the agent has a desired level of competence. The final type of agency cost is *residual loss*, which is the decrease in welfare to the principal as a result of self-interested agent behaviour (Jensen and Meckling, 1976).

THE ORIGINS OF THE AGENT PROFESSION IN PROFESSIONAL SPORT

Compared to other industries, the business of athlete representation is a relatively new form of principal-agent relationship.[2] Athletes in professional sports leagues have organised collectively and formed players' associations, who negotiate as a single unit with leagues over basic working conditions. However, unlike unions in other industries, players' associations do not negotiate individual player salaries (Shropshire, 1989), which was traditionally the responsibility of the athlete.[3] As salaries climbed in the 1960s, players required additional financial planning and management, an area where most athletes lacked the knowledge or time to carry out themselves (Baker, 1990). In addition, team managers were able to keep salaries low by negotiating with inexperienced players over playing contracts. This was because managers had much more extensive experience in contract negotiations with a number of players, and had knowledge of what athletes were earning. To overcome the bargaining imbalance, other parties emerged to negotiate on behalf of the players, to overcome the athletes' lack of bargaining ability and business acumen, and fill the void created by players' associations not negotiating salaries on behalf of their members (Crandall, 1981). For this reason, the widespread use of agents emerged in professional sports during the mid to late 1960s (Barnes, 1985; Fraley and Harwell, 1989), as pioneers such as

Bob Woolf and Marty Blackman began counselling football and baseball players with regard to their contract negotiations (Sobel, 1987).

As several individuals began representing players, other industry changes were occurring that facilitated the arrival of player agents in professional sports. As explained by Powers (1994, p. 255), "no single incident can be pointed to as the sole catalyst for the dramatic increase in the number of sports agents in this new industry," although a number of key changes during this time affected the arrival of agents. Ruxin (1982) attributed the rise of player agents to the presence of rival leagues and increased player mobility in sport. Both gave athletes greater freedom and therefore more bargaining leverage (which astute agents could exploit) with management. For example, Roberts (1992) claimed that rival leagues forced teams into negotiating multi-year contracts to avoid losing players; athletes signing larger, longer, and more complex terms would benefit from the help of an experienced negotiator. Miller *et al.* (1992) and Fraley and Harwell (1989) also credited increased media coverage, which led to larger television contracts and product exposure, in the creation of the need for agents. The subsequent increase in demand for sport and athletes meant that new opportunities for endorsement income became available. All of these changes occurred at a time when league revenues were increasing dramatically. Schubert *et al.* (1986) reported that agents arrived only after professional sports became a highly profitable industry and players began to seek increased compensation for their contributions to league revenues.

According to Fraley and Harwell (1989) the arrival of the agent in the professional sports industry was facilitated by the abolition of the reserve clause and option clauses, which increased a player's mobility and bargaining power by allowing players to seek offers from competing teams rather than staying bound to one club. Similarly, the emergence of rival leagues presented athletes with alternative employment opportunities. Finally, increased television coverage resulted in greater league revenues which could be spent on player salaries and television exposure for athletes, and could allow athletes to seek endorsement opportunities to supplement their playing wages. While some players had used the services of agents as early as 1925 (Gould, 1992), it was not until the mid-1960s that player agents became commonplace (Gallner, 1974).

Agents provide a number of services to players (Champion, 1990). Ultimately, the agent's role is to maximise a player's earnings during a very short career span, and establish a means through which the athlete can maintain lifelong financial stability (Ehrhart and Rodgers, 1988). As contracts have become more lucrative and complex, agents must be aware of many issues, such as state and local taxation laws (Baker, 1990), and non-resident taxes affecting athletes in host communities and in competing cities (Ekmekjian, 1994). Thus, an agent requires specific knowledge that the player lacks. This provides the need for the agent's services. In addition, the agent also serves other purposes in negotiating on the player's behalf. Ehrhart and Rodgers (1988) noted that sports contract negotiations could lead to bitter relations with team management, which can last for prolonged periods of time. Agents then act as a buffer between player and team when the relationship is strained by hostile negotiations (Barnes, 1996). This can also occur in situations where athlete-firm relations are strained, such as when one party seeks to renegotiate or even terminate the terms of an existing endorsement agreement. Perhaps most importantly, athletes using agents can concentrate on improving their on-the-field performance without distraction.

Agents in professional sport are compensated in any of four ways:

1. an hourly wage
2. a flat rate
3. a percentage of the athlete's salary (performance-contingent)
4. any combination of the first three methods (Schubert *et al.*, 1986).

Since athlete representation began, the majority of agents have relied on a performance-contingent compensation system, although agents' remuneration as a percentage of the salary paid to players has decreased somewhat with a more competitive agent market, and increases in athletes' earnings (Mason and Slack, 2003). The number of sports agents in North America has been estimated to be anywhere between 2000 (Bulkeley, 1985) and 10,000 (Stevenson, 1991). As of 2002, the National Basketball Association (NBA) had 350 registered agents and 350 players on its league rosters, the National Hockey League (NHL) 186 agents and 750 players, the National Football League (NFL) 1,112 agents and 1900 players, and Major League Baseball (MLB) 328 agents and 1200 players (Shropshire and Davis, 2003). According to FIFA, there are over 1,300 licensed player agents in world football, with over 200 registered in England alone. However, the actual number of practising agents is even greater when one considers that some of these leagues will only register agents that already represent a player who is on a major-league roster, so these figures do not include aspiring agents. As agent pioneer Bob Woolf (1989) has claimed, the player agent business "went from zero competition to an industry in which everyone with a telephone could find a niche" (p. 100).

PROFESSIONAL ATHLETES AND THE CHANGING GLOBAL MARKET

Agents entering the profession today are faced with different challenges and opportunities than those faced by agents 15 years ago. The emergence of transnational corporations within an increasingly integrated global market has had a profound impact on the business of professional sports. For transnational corporations such as Coca-Cola and Visa, globalisation has been characterised by shifts in the roles of the nation-state and local communities and a reduction of barriers to the mobility of labour (Robins, 1997). Thus, many transnational corporations have expanded their operations internationally and become increasingly more global in scope. In other words, these transnational corporations have expanded into different fields, often creating new synergies in the process. Within the parameters of globalisation, sport has emerged as a strategic focus for many transnational corporations. The lines between media, entertainment, and sport have become blurred as new entities have emerged with far-reaching influences. For example, the four major US television networks are each owned by transnational corporations: CBS (Viacom Inc.), Fox (News Corporation), ABC (Walt Disney Company), and NBC (General Electric Company). Under the direction of Fox News Corporation, CEO Rupert Murdoch has established ownership interests in English Premiership teams and Major League Baseball's Los Angeles Dodgers. Disney has also become involved in sport franchise ownership, having owned both the Anaheim Angels (MLB) and Anaheim Mighty Ducks (NHL). Already holding the US rights to five Olympics from 2000 to 2008, NBC recently paid a record $2.201 billion for the right to televise the 2010 and 2012 games (Shipley and Ahrens, 2003). These examples suggest that corporate interests in media, entertainment, and sport are becoming increasingly intertwined. Within this context sport produces particular styles, images, and meanings that appeal to consumers of products and services provided by transnational corporations with global strategic interests (Maguire, 1999).

Thus, the potential appeal for transnational corporations of associating with global athletes has intensified, as they attempt to market their products to broader bases of consumers. In this instance the role of the agent is to explore and obtain endorsement opportunities for players, opportunities that are directly related to the appeal of the athlete. Conversely, the primary goal of the corporation in associating with athletes is the increased revenue generated through this relationship. Thus, global corporations are primarily interested in associating with athletes with a broad level of appeal.

The Increasing Importance of Endorsements

The scope of endorsements has become an important issue for both athletes and agents. With the exception of a few elite athletes whose appeal virtually guarantees them opportunities, obtaining endorsements is the product of the hard work, contacts, and acumen of agents. In contrast, player salaries are determined more by playing ability and market forces, or by restrictions imposed by collective bargaining agreements. Thus, it could be argued that the amount of endorsements earned by a player would be highly dependent upon the abilities of the agent, and the marketability of the athlete. In addition, agents receive a much higher percentage of a contract's value in compensation for their endorsement services—while agents typically receive commissions of 2–5% for negotiating salaries for players, agents may receive up to 25% for obtaining endorsement deals (Soshnick, 2002). For players with high marketability, agents will often reduce their fees for negotiating player contracts, opting instead for a larger share of endorsement revenues.

The money that can be generated through endorsement opportunities has led some agencies to focus more on this area of representation rather than traditional playing contract negotiations. Some agencies have dropped negotiating player contracts completely to focus on what are considered the more profitable areas of promotional events and endorsements. One company, the Boston-based agency Woolf and Associates, now focuses exclusively on these areas or, as one former agent states, "where the growth is" (Opdyke and Hechinger, 2001). In fact, many present-day agencies such as IMG have segmented their operations with specialised agents in charge of specific areas of representation.

Another reason why agents may be less concerned with contract negotiations relates to the evolution of collective bargaining in professional team sport, where salary caps reduce the influence that agents can have on increasing player salaries. This has further diminished the role of the agent in contract negotiations. For example, National Basketball Association (NBA) all-star player, Ray Allen, negotiated his US$70.9 million/six-year contract without an agent, saving US$2.8 million in fees (Spears, 2001); this is an example of where an athlete is virtually guaranteed to make the maximum allowed by the collective bargaining agreement, and does not need to pay an agent a percentage of the contract to gain a salary that the player already knows he/she will receive.

In other instances, there are cases of players terminating their relationship with agents due to players perceiving that their agents have failed to secure endorsement deals (Broussard, 2000). Most professional athletes are increasingly aware of their value in negotiating playing contracts. They are also becoming more aware of the need to have someone to help them be "marketed." As one agent in England stated, "football players are the pop stars of the new age, so they have to be managed like pop stars" (O'Connor, 2002).

Thus, while initially serving to negotiate playing contracts, today's agents are more concerned with getting athletes "plugged in" to the broader entertainment firmament. Compared to other celebrities in the entertainment industry who typically hire the services of business managers, career managers, agents, and marketing experts, professional athletes have historically worked with one or a few advisors. In contrast, present-day sports agencies often fill these multiple roles working for their clients (Greenberg, 2002) which, as will be discussed later in this paper, has implications for the player-agent relationship.

The Emergence of Transnational Agencies

Just as transnational corporations like Nike, McDonald's, and Coca-Cola have emerged as global enterprises in the past decades, so have large-scale, multinational, multisport agencies that represent professional athletes. These all-inclusive agencies can respond to a variety of needs and provide varying services to players, and typically represent a broad spectrum of athletes from a variety of sports. An example includes the SFX Sports Group, which bought 14 private sports agencies for US$1.5 billion in 1999 (Farhi and Behr, 1999). As a global sport agency, SFX currently represents over 500 of the world's elite professional athletes in baseball, basketball, football, golf, tennis, and soccer. Similarly, Canadian-based Assante Sport Management Group purchased San-Francisco-based Steinberg, Moorad and Dunn for US$120 million and assumed administration of over US$20 billion in client assets (Farhi and Behr, 1999). Another powerful agency is Octagon, the sports and event marketing division of The Interpublic Group of Companies, the world's largest advertising and marketing communications group. Created in 1997 and expanding globally in 1999, Octagon has become one of the leading agencies in the international sports marketing sector with over 1,500 employees in offices throughout the world (Octagon.com, 2004). These "super agencies" are adapting to meet the needs of today's athletes while simultaneously changing the nature of the sports agency business.

No sports agency demonstrates this trend more than the International Management Group (IMG). IMG is considered to be the largest sport management agency in the world, generating US$1.4 billion in revenues in 2001 alone and employing over 3500 employees worldwide. Founded in 1966 by American Mark McCormack, the company now represents over

1000 athletes, many of whom are considered superstars in their respective sports (Thompson, 2002). One of IMG's strengths is identifying young talent, a crucial element of the sport management business. A forerunner in the scouting of young athletes, IMG has numerous star athletes as clients. For example, the agency began targeting professional golfer Sergio Garcia at age 14; he signed with IMG four years later. Yugoslav tennis player Monica Seles was one of the first athletes to go through an IMG sports academy and develop into a celebrity athlete. IMG identifies athletes at a young age and covers the cost for them to attend one of their academies under the assumption that the company will get to represent the athlete in his/her future career.

"Athletes of the Corporation"

Today's global celebrity athletes are often associated as much with the products that they endorse as with their own home teams or countries. Given the amount of money involved in sport sponsorship, professional athletes (and their agents) are becoming increasingly beholden to the corporate interests with which they associate. The interests of a transnational corporation are global in scope and synergistic in strategy. Accordingly, as representatives of these corporate interests, many elite professional athletes have been placed in compromising situations during the course of their careers when acting as representatives of their team or their country. Thus, athletes have been forced to make decisions that affect their ability to represent their countries on a global stage, or even compromise other sponsorship agreements made by their parent leagues or other governing bodies. Perhaps the most notable example occurred during the 1992 Barcelona Olympic Games when, during the gold medal presentation for basketball, Michael Jordan and other players who were Nike clients draped US flags over the rival Reebok logo (the official Olympic sponsor) on their uniforms to avoid controversy with their own sponsor.

More recently Kim Clijsters, the second-ranking player in women's tennis in 2003, pulled out of the 2004 Athens Olympics because she was not allowed to wear apparel from her own sponsor. When asked, Clijsters said she would not take part in the games because the Belgian Olympic Committee prohibits its athletes from wearing apparel not made by team sponsor Adidas. Clijsters has a deal with the manufacturer Fila which stipulates she can only play in that company's clothing (Rovell, 2003). Apparently Clisters's [*sic*] willingness to comply with her sponsor's restrictions has taken precedence over her desire to represent her country in international competitions.

Borderless Athletes

As athletes become more widely known and associated with the products and services they endorse, they become less associated with their countries of origin. This reduction in barriers to labour migration in sport has resulted in a rise in "borderless athletes" (Chiba *et al.*, 2001). A group of athletes in different sports from different countries has emerged that represent a wide array of products and services with a global reach. One such athlete is professional golfer Tiger Woods, a client of IMG. It is projected that Woods will earn US$1 billion by 2011, when he is 35 years old. In 1996, Woods signed a five-year deal with Nike for US$40 million. In 2001, Nike paid US$100 million for another five-year relationship with Woods. The reason for this level of compensation is that Woods delivers a broad mix of viewers to advertisers in golf telecasts, one that is worth a 40–60% increase in viewership when he is in contention during a tournament (Craig, 2002). Thus, Woods' immense worldwide appeal translates into tremendous leverage in his pursuit of endorsement opportunities.

(Market) Ability

At one time, the demand for an athlete's services was solely related to his/her ability to perform in a given sport. However, athletes today have additional value based on their popularity and ability to associate with other products and services. For this reason, endorsement potential is highly dependent on the athlete's appearance and appeal to the consumer demography being targeted. While this would seem to make elite athletes with highly marketable performances and personalities a highly coveted resource for agents, the marketability of athletes is not limited to accomplished and/or star players. Because of her appearance and corresponding marketability, Anna Kournikova has earned endorsement income that far exceeds her more talented (and less marketable) counterparts in women's tennis. Having never won a tournament on the WTA tour, Kournikova earned over US$12 million from endorsements in 2001 alone. Conversely, Lindsay Davenport, a US Open and Wimbledon champion, earned less than half that amount (Valenti, 2001).

Agents and transnational corporations have also targeted athletes that offer excellent endorsement opportunities within markets of different ethnicities. Athletes such as the NBA's Eduardo Najera (Mexico) and professional tennis' Paradorn Srichaphan (Thailand) are seen as attractive clients for endorsements because they appeal to a broad and growing audience of consumers in Latin America and Asia, respectively (Soshnick, 2002;

Hruby, 2002). Najera has been the focal point of a US$8.5 million advertising campaign by America Movil S.A., owner of Mexico's largest mobile phone provider. Combined with his role as a spokesperson for Nike and Anheuser Busch, Najera already earns more from his endorsements than from playing professional basketball (Ridgell, 2002). Similarly, Srichaphan has a multimillion dollar shoe and clothing endorsement contract with Adidas, and is so popular in his native country that Thai Airways (another sponsor) has a video channel on its flights devoted solely to coverage of his matches. According to Colin Smeeton, Director of Tennis for agency SFX, Srichaphan was able to obtain a "premium" due to his status as a "cultural icon" in Southeast Asia (Mullen, 2003).

Similarly, transnational corporations also seek to use athletes to penetrate new markets. Perhaps the most coveted untapped market is China. According to Octagon's director of strategic marketing and media, "multinational companies are looking to mine China" (Isidore, 2003). To do so, corporations and teams are targeting Chinese athletes popular in their homeland. Even before basketball player Yao Ming was drafted to play in the NBA, he had been contracted by Nike, and now also has endorsement agreements with Apple computers and Visa (Isidore, 2003). Further, recognising the importance of the Chinese market, English Premiership teams are seeking out Chinese players for their rosters. Since the signing of Fan Zhiyi and Sun Jihai in 1998, the English team Crystal Palace is said to have the most supporters in the world (Mitchell, 2004). Similarly, when Manchester City played Everton late in 2003 (both teams having Chinese players on their rosters), it was estimated that the viewing audience in China alone was 360 million (Ducker, 2003). The growth potential within the Chinese market has transnational implications for today's sport agencies. Thus, it would appear that in today's professional sport climate, athletes and agents must take into account a number of new factors when considering endorsement opportunities. The next section identifies the implications of these changes for the player-agent relationship.

IMPLICATIONS FOR THE PLAYER-AGENT RELATIONSHIP

As noted above, representing professional athletes is a potentially lucrative profession that has many opportunities for qualified agents, and has been dramatically affected by changes to the global market. While agents initially negotiated playing contracts, today's agents, athletes, and firms have become increasingly intertwined within the broader umbrella of the global entertainment industry. The following discusses the implications that these changes have for the player-agent relationship in professional sport.

Endorsement Contracts Superseding Playing Contracts

Agents receive a considerably higher fee for obtaining endorsement contracts (usually between 15 and 25%) than they do for negotiating an athlete's playing contract (2–5%). There are two primary reasons for the discrepancy in fees. First, obtaining an endorsement deal typically requires more work on the part of the agent, whereas agents usually simply have to facilitate between player and team with player contracts; and second, agent certification programmes established by professional sports leagues' players' associations have set caps on fees that can be charged by agents for contract negotiations.[4] For example in the NBA, the players' union sets 4% as the maximum that agents can charge a player for negotiating a contract. Yet player agent David Falk has also worked to secure endorsements and other off-the-court deals for players like Michael Jordan and Alonzo Mourning. An agent like Falk would typically receive 20% of Jordan's negotiated deals with such companies as Nike and Gatorade, as well as the "Michael Jordan" cologne and the movie *Space Jam*.

These considerations, combined with the fact that players can still earn endorsements after their playing days are over, may cause agents to be more inclined to spend time seeking out endorsement opportunities for players, than on contract negotiations. This may result in agents seeking to represent only those athletes with the greatest potential for ancillary earnings to supplement their playing salaries. It may also reduce the ability of less marketable players to get adequate representation.

Conflicts of Interest for Agencies

The rise of large-scale agencies may create conflicts of interest for their clients. As many sports agencies become more vertically integrated, the potential for conflicts of interest to occur increases. This phenomenon arises when agencies that represent athletes also help negotiate stadium construction projects, and when owners of league franchises are also involved as part-owners of agencies, and when agents represent both owners and players (*e.g.*, the NBA's Michael Jordan and NHL's Mario Lemieux). Likewise, IMG also sells advertising in different arenas and stadiums and runs a number of cultural events involving athletes (Thompson, 2002). Further, some larger agencies represent a substantial number of clients, where certain athletes may get privileges to the detriment of others. A conflict of interest arises here when an agent, in order to serve the interests of one client, may do so to the detriment of another. For example, two players represented by the same agent may be vying for one endorsement contract with a corporation. In this instance the interests of one athlete may be compromised in order to serve the interests of the other.

Within its billion-dollar industry, IMG has weathered its share of critics who charge the company with multiple examples of conflicts of interest. One competing agency labelled the company "a benevolent dictator." These allegations centre around the company's perceived monopoly or "hand-in-every-pot" approach to sport management (Vinella and Thomas, 2001). For example, in addition to representing a number of top athletes, IMG is involved in sports programming on television and the internet, event management, operating sport academies, and golf course design. Consequently, IMG's wide-ranging economic interests potentially influence sport and/or breed conflicts among the many athletes it represents. A hypothetical example would be where IMG steers one of its athletes to compete in an event that it owns. IMG does not dispute its attempts to vertically integrate its operations; however, it dismisses criticisms as the scheme of envious competitors attempting to discredit the leader in the field.

IS THE AGENT'S BOND WITH THE CORPORATION ERODING THE BOND WITH THE ATHLETE?

The changes described above have substantially altered the nature of the relationship between athletes and their agents. While both agents and athletes find themselves in a more lucrative environment, several issues have arisen that may compromise the traditional *principal-agent*, *player-agent* relationship in professional sport. Several potential problems may arise that affect the athlete-agent relationship. Specifically, these involve the manner by which agents establish a rapport with firms seeking to enter into endorsement agreements with athletes, the number of athletes being represented by agents, and the variety of services provided by agencies.

The changing nature of the industry, whereby athletes and sports have become increasingly commodified and part of the broader entertainment industry, has resulted in a tendency for agents to become more closely aligned with the interests of the transnational corporations that agents seek to contract with on behalf of athletes, rather than any one particular athlete. With the exception of several unique athletes, it has become in the better interests of agents to cultivate long-term, mutually beneficial relationships with firms, rather than athletes. Some arguments for this transition follow.

Athletes and endorsers have had relationships that have soured due to the behaviour of the athlete. Poor behaviour exhibited by some athletes may result in consumers developing negative product associations. As a result, some companies are abandoning their deals with athletes altogether due to recent increases in athlete scandals. In many cases, it is the nature of the athlete's transgression that affects how the sponsor acts. As the president of one sports marketing firm has stated, "there are certain levels of controversy that advertisers tolerate, but never dishonesty or lack of integrity" (Blevins, 2002). Players endorsing companies producing family-oriented products are subject to even higher moral standards (Krouse, 2002). If the athlete's transgression does little to affect the consumer's feeling toward the brand, it is not considered relevant (Krouse, 2002). However, if a company's brand is negatively affected due to their sponsored athlete's image, agents must often serve as a peace-broker in these times of crisis, especially if significant endorsement dollars are on the line.

Yet more and more corporate sponsors are demanding morals clauses within an athlete's contract and many agents have a moral turpitude clause negotiated into a player's contract (Lidz, 2002). In situations where the athlete has engaged in a behaviour that might compromise his/her endorsement agreement with a firm, it would be incumbent upon the agent to attempt to make sure that the athlete would not lose the endorsement. In other words, the agent must try to maximise the athlete's income despite the actions of the athlete. However, it would not necessarily be in the best interests of an agent, particularly one who has multiple clients that each have endorsement contracts with a single corporation, to alienate that sponsoring firm by siding with an athlete who has violated the terms of a morals clause. Alienating the firm would make it difficult for the agent to arrange future endorsement deals with his/her other clients. Thus, the agent has a dilemma, whether to act in the best interests of the principal (the athlete), or to make sure that future contracting relationships are not jeopardised, by smoothing over the situation between athlete and firm. In such a case, the agent may seek a solution to the problem between athlete and sponsor that is not in the best interests of the offending athlete, in order to ease future transactions with the corporation that is attempting to sever the relationship with the client.

Finally, and perhaps most importantly, the agent has a strong interest in developing and maintaining a strong bond with the endorsing firm rather than any one player. Representing athletes with an endorsement profile offers the sports agent an opportunity to gain a stronger foothold in the corporate world. As one agent stated, "You want to have your tentacles in a lot of areas and you recognise that if you want to have access to the Chairman of Coke or McDonald's or whatever company . . . it helps to have top athletes who can open these doors" (Fainaru-Wada and Kroichick, 2001). Thus, the agent views the athlete not only as a principal to whom a duty of service is owed, but also as a means to forge a potentially lucrative relationship with a corporation.

The discussion above suggests that due to the increasingly personal manner in which they interact with firms in order to obtain endorsement opportunities for athletes, agents are developing strong ties with endorsing firms as well as with their own athletes. Quite simply in many instances, it may be in the agent's better interests to maintain strong ties with firms more than they do with players. We discuss the implications of this in terms of agency theory below.

DISCUSSION AND CONCLUSION

The scenarios described above are classic examples of moral hazards, where the agent does not act in the best interests of the principal (in this case, the athlete). Athletes who contract the services of agents have the problem of monitoring agent behaviour due to information asymmetry that exists between the two parties. Typically, information asymmetry favours the agent, who has a greater knowledge of his/her personal skills and effort. In this case, this would include the extent of the agent's relationship with the corporation seeking an endorsement arrangement with the athlete. Agency theory posits ways in which information asymmetry can be eliminated, thereby reducing traditional agency problems. However, this will not occur when the costs of creating, implementing and enforcing monitoring mechanisms exceed the agency costs that will be reduced by monitoring (Demsetz, 1983; White, 1992). Agent opportunism can be decreased by making agent rewards contingent on outcomes when agent actions are difficult or costly to monitor (Eisenhardt, 1989). A performance-contingent compensation scheme will be effective if both the agent and the principal seek the same reward, but also results in the transfer of risk from principal to agent. Principals are assumed to be risk-neutral, while agents are considered risk-averse (Nilakant and Rao, 1994). For example, an agent working on a commission represents a player who is holding out for a higher contract will not be paid until the player has signed a new agreement, or reports to play again for the team. The agent, to avoid the risk of not getting paid, might then encourage the player to accept a lower salary (which may not be in the best interests of the athlete) in order to ensure that the agent is paid. The solution to agent opportunism is achieved by balancing the costs of monitoring with the level of an agent's aversion to risk (Eisenhardt, 1989; Kren and Kerr, 1993).

Nevertheless, agents representing professional athletes are mostly compensated by commissions (Greenberg, 1993; Mason and Slack, 2001). Thus, one of the suggested solutions to the agency problem of moral hazard is already in place. The problem here is that, although the agent may receive higher compensation when the principal gets paid more in a particular endorsement agreement with a firm, the agent recognises that the long-term payoff of subsequent agreements regarding other athletes lies in retaining a good relationship with the firm. Thus, the agent will not likely attempt any negotiations that would sour the firm's attitude toward the player and/or agent. In doing so, the agent is not likely to maximise the returns for the athlete in any given negotiation. This follows Singh and Sirdeshmukh (2000), who noted that:

> Agents benefit from relational exchanges because these allow them to amortise the bonding investments over multiple exchanges . . . thus, it is in the self-interest of the agents to act in a manner that builds confidence in their reliability and integrity to ensure that current exchanges persist over time. (p. 153)

However, that trust is cultivated with the firm, not the athlete. Because the average career of a professional athlete rarely exceeds five years, and only a select few have the cachet to continue endorsing products and services after their playing careers are over, then the agent is better off developing this mutual trust and relationship with firms that are likely to pursue agreements with other athletes represented by the agent in the future.

A similar problem is faced by principals, agents, and clients in sales positions. According to Dubinsky *et al.* (1980), salespeople are often put in positions where they must reach short-term sales goals (and appease their principals), while trying to ensure long-term success (by developing customer confidence). As Kurland (1995) explained, the agent has two primary responsibilities; one to the principal, and the other to the client. Kurland's (1996) research has examined this phenomenon; however, her work has examined situations where the agent has not acted in the best interests of clients in order to serve the principal. For example an agent who is interested in obtaining a commission (such as from the sale of a product) may not consider the long-term interests of the client (by selling the client an item that is defective, or not needed). Here the agent is interested in maintaining ties with the principal, at times at the expense of the interests of the client. In the case of player agents, the opposite is true—agents, in order to maintain a strong tie with clients (firms who have endorsement agreements with players), may not act in the best interest of their principals (the players). Kurland (1996) argues that the use of straight commissions encourages agents to act in ways detrimental to clients, as they attempt to maximise their compensation from principals. However, as we can see from the professional sports industry, the changing conditions and new techniques developed to bring stakeholders together have, in fact, outweighed the power of performance-contingent compensation systems to align principal and agent interests.

This paper has identified changes to the player-agent relationship in the professional sport/entertainment industry, which suggests that the influence of interests external to the traditional player-agent relationship will continue. As "off-the-court" interests and opportunities are presented to professional athletes, the relationship between principal and agent will be further impacted. Future research should examine how agents develop ties with firms involved in professional sport, and the manner in which athletes are able to monitor the behaviour of their agents. Commissions aside, one solution to agency problems involves monitoring agent behaviour. However, individual players lack the requisite time and resources to do this. Perhaps other stakeholders, such as players' associations could attempt to closely monitor agent behaviour with regard to endorsements on behalf of athletes. The resulting information could help athletes avoid contracting with agents whose conflicts of interest compromise their ability to adequately represent the athlete's best interests.

NOTES

From Volume 1, Issue 1/2 (2005) of the *International Journal of Sport Management and Marketing*, "Globalisation and the evolving player-agent relationship in professional sport," by Daniel S. Mason and Gregory H. Duquette, pp. 93–109. Used with permission.

1. Although many players hire the services of large, multi-employee agencies that provide a variety of services, the player (as principal) contracts only with one agent (in this case the large agency firm). Any additional services provided on the player's behalf that are outsourced by the agency firm are thus subject to their own independent principal-agent relationships. However the player, as agent, still enters into only one contract with the large agency firm.

2. While some agents have operated in professional sport for centuries, the widespread use of agents in sport, particularly professional team sport, has only occurred since the 1960s.

3. Players' associations do negotiate basic salary parameters, such as minimum salaries and caps on team or player amounts, while also negotiating ancillary monies such as licensing fees from trading cards.

4. The duties that agents perform in negotiating playing contracts for athletes are limited in a number of ways. First there are ceilings and minimums that are determined through the collective bargaining process. Second, in most cases, the player's rights are owned by a single team, which allows the agent to focus his/her negotiations with a single party. In contrast, obtaining a successful endorsement for an athlete would be more dependent upon the contacts and work of the agent.

REFERENCES

Alchian, A. A., and Demsetz, H. (1972) "Production, information costs, and economic organization." *American Economic Review*, vol. 62, pp. 777–795.

Baker, W. H. (1990) "The tax significance of place of residence for professional athletes." *Marquette Sports Law Journal*, vol. 1, pp. 1–39.

Barnes, J. (1985) *The Amateur Athlete's Guidebook*. Canadian Interuniversity Athletic Union.

Barnes, J. (1996) *Sport and the Law in Canada*, 3rd ed. Toronto: Butterworths.

Blevins, J. (2002) "Scandal hurts Ohno's image: Advertisers may go elsewhere." *Denver Post*, January 25, p. 1D.

Broussard, C. (2000) "Pro basketball: Marbury and Falk part and hurl accusations." *New York Times*, June 27, p. 5D.

Bulkeley, W. M. (1985) "Sports agents help athletes win—and keep—those super salaries." *Wall Street Journal*, March 25, p. 31.

Champion, Jr., W. T. (1990) *Fundamentals of Sports Law*, Rochester, NY: Lawyers Cooperative Publishing.

Chiba, N., Ebihara, O., and Morino, S. (2001) "Globalization, naturalization, and identity: The case of borderless athletes in Japan." *International Review for the Sociology of Sport*, vol. 36, pp. 203–221.

Craig, M. (2002) "Beyond a shadow of a doubt: Folks who measure these things say Tiger Woods is the most powerful athlete in the world." *Minneapolis-St. Paul Star Tribune*, August 14, p. 3S.

Crandall, J. P. (1981) "The agent-athlete relationship in professional and amateur sports: The inherent potential for abuse and the need for regulation." *Buffalo Law Review*, vol. 30, pp. 815–849.

Demsetz, H. (1983) "The structure of ownership and the theory of the firm." *Journal of Law and Economics*, vol. 26, pp. 375–390.

Dubinsky, A. J., Berkowitz, E. N., and Rudelius, W. (1980) "Ethical problems of field sales personnel." *MSU Business Topics*, Spring, vol. 28, pp. 11–16.

Ducker, J. (2003) "Chinese soccer star draws record TV audience." Manchester Online, January 4, retrieved July 5, 2004, from http://www.manchesteronline.co.uk/news/s/48/48443_chinese_soccer_star_draws_record_tv_audience.html.

Ehrhart, C. W., and Rodgers, J. M. (1988) "Tightening the defense against offensive sports agents." *Florida State University Law Review*, vol. 16, pp. 633–674.

Eisenhardt, K. M. (1989) "Agency theory: An assessment and review." *Academy of Management Review*, vol. 14, pp. 57–74.

Ekmekjian, E. C. (1994) "The jock tax: State and local income taxation of professional athletes." *Seton Hall Journal of Sport Law*, vol. 4, pp. 229–252.

Fainaru-Wada, M., and Kroichick, R. (2001) "Agents of influence: Massive conglomerates now wield tremendous power over the games you see on the field." *San Francisco Chronicle*, March 11, p. 1C.

Farhi, P., and Behr, P. (1999) "Taking his game to the next level: David Falk steps up to a pivotal role at the SFX group of sports agencies." *Washington Post*, December 13, p. 17F.

Fraley, R. E., and Harwell, F. R. (1989) "The sports lawyer's duty to avoid differing interests: A practical guide to responsible representation." *Hastings Commercial and Entertainment Law Journal*, vol. 11, pp. 165–217.

Gallner, S. (1974) *Pro Sports: The Contract Game*. New York: Charles Scribner's Sons.

Gould, M. T. (1992) "Further trials and tribulations of sports agents." *Entertainment and Sports Lawyer*, vol. 10, pp. 9–14.

Greenberg, D. (2002) "Power player: Although he represents Kobe Bryant and other star athletes, sports agent Arn Tellem says business, not glamour of celebrities, keeps him in the game." *Los Angeles Business Journal*, July 1, p. 19.

Greenberg, M. (1993) *Sports Law Practice*. Charlottesville, VA: Michie Company, vol. 1.

Hruby, P. (2002) "Thailand's finest: Agassi-slayer Paradorn Srichaphan is the top Asian player in men's tennis." *Washington Times*, August 14, p. 1C.

Isidore, C. (2003) "Yo! Yao stands alone: Chinese star breaking endorsement ground for foreign-born stars, but relatively few will follow." CNN Money, February 28, retrieved July 8, 2004, from http://money.cnn.com/2003/02/28/commentary/column_sportsbiz/sportsbiz.

Jensen, M. C., and Meckling, W. H. (1976) "Theory of the firm: Managerial behavior and ownership structure." *Journal of Financial Economics*, vol. 3, pp. 305–360.

Jones, G. R., and Butler, E. R. (1992) "Managing internal corporate entrepreneurship: An agency theory perspective." *Journal of Management*, vol. 18, pp. 733–749.

Kren, L., and Kerr, J. L. (1993) "The effect of behavior monitoring and uncertainty on the use of performance-contingent compensation." *Accounting and Business Research*, vol. 23, pp. 159–168.

Krouse, P. (2002) "Endorsement embarrassments: Celebrity foibles can test partnerships." *Cleveland Plain Dealer*, September 7, p. 1C.

Kurland, N. B. (1995) "The unexplored territory linking rewards and ethical behavior." *Business and Society*, vol. 34, pp. 34–50.

Kurland, N. B. (1996) "Trust, accountability, and sales agents' dueling loyalties." *Business Ethics Quarterly*, vol. 6, pp. 289–310.

Lewis, T. R., and Sappington, D. E. M. (1993) "Ignorance in agency problems." *Journal of Economic Theory*, vol. 61, pp. 169–183.

Lidz, F. (2002) "Arn Tellem: The Arn of the deal." *Sports Illustrated*, May 27, p. 72.

Macdonald, G. M. (1984) "New directions in the economic theory of agency." *Canadian Journal of Economics*, vol. 17, pp. 415–440.

Maguire, J. (1999) *Global Sport: Identities, Societies, Civilizations*. Cambridge: Polity.

Mason, D. S., and Slack, T. (2001) "Industry factors and the changing dynamics of the player-agent relationship in professional ice hockey." *Sport Management Review*, vol. 4, pp. 165–192.

Mason, D. S., and Slack, T. (2003) "Understanding principal-agent relationships: Evidence from professional hockey." *Journal of Sport Management*, vol. 17, pp. 38–62.

McCarthy, M. (2000) "Advertisers shift focus to female athletes." *USA Today*, December 12, retrieved from http://www.usatoday.com/money/advertising/ad0051.htm.

Miller, L. K., Fielding, L. W., and Pitts, B. G. (1992) "A uniform code to regulate athlete agents." *Journal of Sport and Social Issues*, vol. 16, pp. 93–102.

Mitchell, K. (2004) "Sport focus: China emerges as a sports powerhouse." Buzzle.com, May 22, retrieved November 16, 2004, from http://www.buzzle.com/editorials/text5-22-2004-54553.asp.

Mullen, L. (2003) "'Cultural icon' Srichaphan to get more that $1 million a year from Adidas." Sports Business Journal, September 29, retrieved July 6, 2004, from http://www.prosportsgroup.com/SportsAgentNews/Sep2003/News/Srichaphan.htm.

Nilakant, V., and Rao, H. (1994) "Agency theory and uncertainty in organizations: An evaluation." *Organization Studies*, vol. 15, pp. 649–672.

O'Connor, A. (2002) "The most cynical game in football." *The Times of London*, September 23, p. 12.

Octagon.com. (2004) Retrieved July 12, 2004, from http://www.octagon.com/who_we_are/background.php.

Opdyke, J. D., and Hechinger, J. (2001) "Don't do what I did: Derek Sanderson wasted the millions he made hockey; now he nets rich young stars for a Wall St. money manager." *Montreal Gazette*, June 7, p. 6B.

Powers, A. (1994) "The need to regulate sports agents." *Seton Hall Journal of Sport Law*, vol. 4, pp. 253–276.

Ridgell, P. (2002) "You can't keep a good man." Latino Leaders, December 1, retrieved July 6, 2004, from http://www.latinoleaders.com/articulos.php?id_sec=1&id_ejemplar.

Roberts, G. R. (1992) "Agents and agency: A sports lawyer's view." *Journal of Sport and Social Issues*, vol. 16, pp. 116–120.

Robins, K. (1997) "What in the world's going on?" In P. du Gay (Ed.), *Production of Culture, Cultures of Production*. London: Sage, pp. 11–66.

Rovell, D. (2003) "Clijsters out of Olympics in sponsor dispute." ESPN.com, December 1, retrieved June 3, 2004, from http://espn.go.com/tennis/news/2003/1201/1675164.html.

Ruxin, R. H. (1982) "Unsportsmanlike conduct: The student-athlete, the NCAA, and agents." *Journal of College and University Law*, vol. 8, pp. 347–367.

Schubert, G. W., Smith, R. K., and Trentadue, J. C. (1986) *Sports Law*. St. Paul, MN: West Publishing.

Shipley, A., and Ahrens, F. (2003) "NBC gets two Olympic games for $2.2 billion." *Washington Post*, June 7, p. A1.

Shropshire, K. L. (1989) "Athlete agent regulation: Proposed legislative revisions and the need for reforms beyond legislation." *Cardozo Arts and Entertainment Law Journal*, vol. 8, pp. 85–112.

Shropshire, K. L., and Davis, T. (2003) *The Business of Sports Agents*. Philadelphia: University of Pennsylvania Press.

Singh, J., and Sirdeshmukh, D. (2000) "Agency and trust mechanisms in consumer satisfaction and loyalty judgments." *Journal of the Academy of Marketing Science*, vol. 28, pp. 150–167.

Sobel, L. S. (1987) "The regulation of sports agents: An analytical primer." *Baylor Law Review*, vol. 39, pp. 702–786.

Soshnick, S. (2002) "Perfect pitchman: Dallas' Eduardo Najera, the only Mexican-born player in the NBA, has struck gold with endorsements." *San Diego Union-Tribune*, May 4, p. 2D.

Spears, M. J. (2001) "NBA stars flying solo: Denver's McDyess, Van Exel part of trend to shed agents." *Denver Post*, November 28, p. 1D.

Stevenson, S. (1991) "As the big day nears, it's the agent who does the signal calling." *New York Times*, April 17, p. B5.

Thompson, R. (2002) "Going for the green: Jerry Maguire they're not, Canada's top sports agents hit the links." *National Post*, June 21, p. 1.

Valenti, C. (2001) "Beauty and the bucks." ABCNews.com, July 13, retrieved June 3, 2004, from http://abcnews.go.com/sections/business/DailyNews/Womenstennis_Marketing_010713.html.

Vinella, S., and Thomas, C. A. (2001) "The grandmaster of the sports deal." *Cleveland Plain Dealer*, April 22, p. 11A.

Walsh, C., Campbell, D., and Barnett, A. (2004) "Offside! England stars blasted for avoiding tax on fortune from TV ads." *The Observer*, June 6, retrieved June 10, 2004, from http://observer.guardian.co.uk/uk_news/story/0,6903,1232465,00.html.

White, W. D. (1992) "Information and the control of agents." *Journal of Economic Behavior and Organization*, vol. 18, pp. 111–117.

Woolf, B. (1989) "Agents on campus." In R. E. Lapchick and J. B. Slaughter (Eds.), *The Rules of the Game: Ethics in College Sport*. New York: Macmillan, pp. 99–109.

Twelve

A Review of the Post–World War II Baseball-Card Industry

Arthur Zillante

If the Upper Deck Company (Upper Deck) successfully purchases the Topps Company, Inc. (Topps), the baseball-card industry will have come full circle in under thirty years. A legal ruling broke Topps' monopoly in the industry in 1981, but Upper Deck's purchase would return the industry to a monopoly. By 2007 the industry had experienced a boom-and-bust cycle that led to the entry and exit of a number of firms, numerous innovations, and changes in competitive practices.[1] The goal of this review is to see how secondary market forces and primary market behavior have interacted in the innovations produced as competition between manufacturers intensified and in how competitive practices changed over time. Traditional economic analysis assumes competition along one dimension, such as quantity or price competition, with little consideration of whether or not the choice of competitive strategy changes.[2]

Baseball cards have undergone changes in the past half-century as the industry and hobby have matured, but the last twenty years have seen the most dramatic changes. Prior to World War II baseball cards were primarily used as premiums or advertising tools for tobacco and candy products.[3] Today, the baseball-card industry is typically defined as the producers of nationally distributed picture cards of major-league baseball players, licensed by Major League Baseball (MLB) and either the Major League Baseball Players Association (MLBPA) or individual major-league baseball players. Since firms must be granted licenses by MLB and the MLBPA to produce cards that appeal to collectors on a national basis, entry into the industry is regulated by those two entities. The MLBPA also has to approve the final product, and will oftentimes make suggestions to the manufacturers about the design and price of the product.[4] Not all manufacturers secure a license from MLB. Michael Schechter Associates has never acquired a national license from MLB but has acquired licenses from the MLBPA, airbrushing any part of the team logos on the players' uniforms that appear in the picture so as not to infringe on any of MLB's trademarks. However, these cards are not fully embraced by consumers, in part because they tend to be regional issues and in part because they lack MLB team logos.

Baseball cards are sold to consumers in retail outlets, such as Wal-Mart or Target, as well as in hobby shops. Card manufacturers are typically prohibited in their licensing agreements from selling directly to final consumers and sell cases of cards to retail outlets, major hobby dealers, and wholesalers. *Cases* are comprised of a fixed number of boxes of cards, although the number of boxes varies depending on the manufacturer and product. *Boxes* of cards may be sold by the wholesalers to smaller hobby stores, or by retail chains and hobby stores to consumers. Boxes of cards are comprised of packs of cards. *Packs* are the smallest packaged individual unit that a consumer can purchase. Packs consist of the individual cards of a particular brand and may contain any number of different types of cards.

Base cards comprise the bulk of the pack and make up the base set of the brand. A *set,* or *brand,* of cards is determined by the brand name given to the cards made available in a pack by the manufacturer. *Insert* or *chase cards* are cards available in packs at a lower rate than base cards. Most insert cards are part of a small insert set, which is theme based and may include baseball All-Stars, rookie prospects, or the favorite players of the owner of the manufacturing company. Other types of insert cards will be discussed as needed.

Manufacturers release brands throughout the course of the year. Many brands are released in a single series, but some are released in multiple series. Typically, the packs from one series do not contain the cards available in another series. Given that manufacturers now produce multiple brands, the "flagship" brand of a manufacturer is the one that bears the manufacturer's name. For instance, Topps produces both *Topps* and *Stadium Club* and *Topps* is considered the flagship brand.[5]

The survival of brands depends on their ability to fill a market niche. As former Topps employee Marty Appel states: "You hear people say there's too much stuff being produced, that it's too confusing, and to a large degree it's true. However, Topps feels that if you have a message behind each product, like we do, you should be successful."[6] A similar statement is made in Topps's annual reports, as one of Topps's goals is "to ensure that each brand of sports card has its own unique positioning in the marketplace." Thus the theme and design of the brand can be viewed as defining the brand.

The actual production of baseball cards consists of photographing the players, developing the brand's theme, designing the cards, obtaining the statistics and text necessary for the card backs, physically producing the cards, and shipping from manufacturer to wholesaler or retailer. Once the technology to produce the cards is in place, the most difficult part of the process is developing the brand's theme. In 2001, the Topps Web site, www.topps.com, reported that the process of producing a set, from inception to shipment, is about six months. Upper Deck provides a slightly longer estimate, stating that the entire process of developing a brand takes about forty weeks with the actual printing of the cards taking about one week.[7] Currently, Topps reports that the entire process takes thirty weeks while Upper Deck reports a six-month time frame.[8]

What follows is a description of the changes that have occurred in the baseball-card industry in the past sixty years. The years are broken into three time periods: the Pre-*Fleer v. Topps Ruling* era (1948–1980), Between MLBPA Strikes (1981–1994), and Product Proliferation and Industry Consolidation (1995–2006). In each of these time periods the major innovations in trading cards are discussed along with changes in competitive practices.

PRE-*FLEER V. TOPPS* RULING, 1948–1980

Early Competition (1948–1955)

Following the lead of earlier industries, Bowman Gum Company (Bowman) issued the first set of postwar baseball cards in attempt to boost sales of chewing gum in 1948. Prior to World War II, the Gum Inc. Co., an earlier company of Jacob Bowman, had issued cards under the name Play Ball. The Leaf Gum Company (Leaf) followed Bowman and produced a set in 1949. While Leaf discontinued production after one year, Bowman produced card sets from 1948 to 1955, at which time the company was purchased by Topps.[9] Topps first produced a card set in 1951, although it was more a game than what would now be considered a traditional set of picture cards. In 1952 Topps produced its first "true" set and competed head-to-head with Bowman for four years. After Topps' purchase of Bowman in 1955, the company held a virtual monopoly in the sale and production of cards depicting current major-league baseball players for twenty-five years.

From 1951 to 1952, Topps and Bowman signed players to individual contracts. The specifics of the contracts varied depending on the player under contract and violations of contracts were debated in court.[10] In 1952 the Topps and Bowman sets had 221 players in common. By 1953 the total was down to 115, in 1954 the total players in common fell to 84, and by

1955 it was down to 44. Part of this may have been due to player selection, but exclusive contracts were beginning to be used by the manufacturers and enforced by the courts. A famous example is the 1954 *Bowman* card of Ted Williams. Given his exclusive contract with Topps, the Williams card in the 1954 *Bowman* set was ultimately replaced with Jimmy Piersall.

Given that the manufacturers were signing some players to exclusive contracts and that some players, such as Stan Musial, did not sign contracts with either manufacturer, neither manufacturer could produce a set of cards that included all major-league players. Topps' largest set during this time was 407 cards in 1952 and the set size decreased each year, with a low of 206 cards in its 1955 set. Bowman's set size had no discernible pattern as its smallest set was 160 cards in 1953 while its largest set was 320 cards in 1955. The 1953 set was issued in two series, one in color and the other in black and white. Hobby lore has it that the black-and-white series was produced due to lack of funds to produce a second color series. In addition to competition for player contracts, competition is evident in pack prices during this time. Bowman had been charging a penny per card in a pack, but Topps packaged six cards for a nickel. Bowman subsequently increased the amount of cards in its nickel packs to seven in 1954 and nine in 1955 while Topps remained at six.

Topps' Monopoly Years (1956–1980)

From 1956 to 1980, Topps had a virtual monopoly on producing baseball cards with active players. Topps' primary competitor was the Fleer Corporation (Fleer); however, since Topps had exclusive licenses with most of the players in major-league baseball, Fleer did not provide much competition. Topps obtained these exclusive licenses by signing prospects while they were in the minor leagues. Topps initially signed only top prospects until a scout declined to offer Maury Wills a contract while he was in the minor leagues. Wills won the 1962 National League Most Valuable Player award but refused to sign a contract with Topps until 1967 due to this perceived slight. Afterwards Topps signed virtually all minor-league players to contracts, with a standard contract being a $5 signing fee plus $125 when they reached the major leagues.[11] Fleer made minor headway by signing Ted Williams to an exclusive contract near the end of Williams' career, but for the most part Fleer was relegated to producing cards of players no longer active in major-league baseball.

The Federal Trade Commission (FTC) filed suit against Topps on February 8, 1962, charging Topps with monopolizing the baseball-card industry. Although the FTC action in 1962 failed, Fleer continued to pursue the possibility of producing baseball cards.[12] Fleer offered $25,000 plus 5 percent of receipts on 5×7 glossy photos, for which Topps did not have exclusive rights.[13] The MLBPA declined and Fleer filed a lawsuit in June 1975 accusing Topps and the MLBPA of illegal restraint of trade. Fleer won this case against Topps, although the MLBPA was cleared of wrongdoing, and was granted licenses by MLB and the MLBPA to produce baseball cards in 1981.[14] At the same time the Donruss Company (Donruss) was also granted licenses to produce cards in 1981.

During this time period a typical set of cards produced by Topps was released in multiple series over the course of the baseball season. Prior to 1957 the card size varied, but in 1957 Topps established what would become the conventional card size of 2.5 inches by 3.5 inches. Topps produced only one conventional brand each year, although Topps did produce some products that differed from the conventional brand either in size or in product type. For instance, in 1960, Topps produced a set of baseball player–themed transfer "tattoos," a set of "Giants" (cards larger than the conventional size) in 1964, and a set of stamps in 1969.[15] Some items were printed for national distribution, while other items were tested in specific markets. This appears to be an early effort by Topps to develop a market for multiple baseball-related collectibles.

In addition, throughout the 1960s Topps routinely inserted "bonus items" into packs of cards, essentially a premium for its premium, as the stated primary purpose of the baseball cards was still to sell more gum. These bonus items were usually stamps, coins, transfer tattoos, or posters of individual players or teams. These insert items are the precursors to the modern inserts, although most modern inserts are cards of the conventional size with a lower print run than the base set.

The number of inserts increased slightly in the late 1960s and early 1970s. This increase may be due to the fact that the MLBPA was able to obtain an increase in the amount that Topps paid players for use of their likeness. Prior to 1969, each player received $125 for the year from Topps. After 1969 the player's fee was increased to $250 and the MLBPA received 8 percent of all revenues up to $4 million dollars and 10 percent on any amount over $4 million.[16] Although little information is known about actual production numbers from this era, it is reported that Topps sold 250 million cards in 1972.[17]

Pricing Policies

From 1956 to 1973 cards were sold primarily through retail outlets in penny, nickel, or dime packs, which reflected the suggested retail price

(SRP) for a pack of cards. The number of cards per pack was typically such that the price per card of a pack averaged a penny per card, although in the 1950s Topps' nickel packs had six cards per pack and one stick of gum. Topps retained the policy of packaging cards at the rate of six cards for a SRP of five cents until 1961, when it began packaging the cards at a SRP rate of a penny per card. From 1961 to 1973 the SRP of a pack of cards remained at a penny per card, although Topps replaced penny packs them with dime packs. In 1974 Topps lowered the amount of cards per pack to eight while keeping the SRP of a pack at ten cents. This marks the first time that the ratio of SRP per pack to cards per pack exceeded one penny. From 1975 to 1977 Topps sold packs of ten cards for fifteen cents. In 1978 Topps sold fourteen cards for twenty cents, in 1979 twelve cards for twenty cents, and in 1980 fourteen cards for twenty-five cents.

Topps also sold cards via cello and rack packs. The term *cello pack* is derived from the cellophane wrapping that Topps used for these packs. Cello packs contained more cards than wax packs and the price/card ratio was slightly better for the consumer than in a standard wax pack. A *rack pack* is essentially three wax packs packaged together in one bundle. Although originally sold flat, the term *rack pack* likely originated when the packs were attached to a strip of plastic material with a hole in it so that they could hang on a rack at a retail outlet. Again, consumers typically received a slight discount when purchasing a rack pack when compared to three single packs.

Release Policy

Topps typically released one brand of cards in a few series throughout the year. Some of these series of cards were printed in different quantities than the others (although in most cases the cards included in a series were printed at the same rate), with the latest series typically produced in the lowest amounts due to the time of its release near the end of the baseball season. Topps' standard was to have seven series, as it did from 1959 to 1970. Prior to 1959, Topps increased the number of series each year, although this was likely due to the fact that the size of the base set was increasing each year (from 210 in 1955 to 572 in 1959).

In 1974 Topps changed its release strategy. No longer were cards released in series but all at once. From 1974 until 1992 Topps released brands in this fashion, with two small exceptions in 1974 and 1976, when Topps issued its first traded sets. A *traded* (or *update*) set features players who made a significant contribution during the season and were not included in the regular set of Topps or players who were traded during the season shown wearing in their new uniforms. In 1974 and 1976 traded cards were only available in packs that could be purchased later in the year, while the regular cards were available in packs that could be purchased any time throughout the year. Topps' rationale for changing from multiple series to a single series is visible on an advertisement on a Topps wax box in 1974, which explains that making all cards from the set available in a pack will "Keeps Topps baseball exciting and selling all season long."

Secondary Market (1948–1980)

During the 1970s, the increase in values of baseball cards was seen as a market explosion. A Honus Wagner T206 card sold for $1,500 and some cards from the 1950s sold for as much as $15 each.[18] The 1952 *Topps* Mickey Mantle was selling for $100 and the 1974 Topps San Diego/Washington variations were selling for $2 apiece.[19] A 1952 *Topps* high series of 96 cards had an offer of $1,600 but the seller refused, wanting $1,800.[20] Putting this in perspective, in the 1940s legendary collector Jefferson Burdick created a price guide with suggested prices for cards. Burdick suggested vintage (tobacco cards prior to World War I) cards in good condition sell for two cents and more recent (gum and candy) cards sell for one cent.[21]

As prices of baseball cards increased, the hobby was noticed by the popular press. Large conventions were held as early as 1969 in Southern California, and "The National" has been an annual sports-card show since 1971.[22] There were dozens of publications dedicated to the hobby, but most were discussions of the hobby in general and not geared toward reporting prices. In 1979 Dr. James Beckett published *The Sport Americana Baseball Card Price Guide*. This book became the standard for pricing throughout the hobby, and ultimately led to the creation of the monthly magazines published by Beckett Publishing. As there is during every time period, collectors had two major complaints: rising retail prices and too much product.

BETWEEN MLBPA STRIKES (1981–1994)

In 1981 Donruss and Fleer began production of baseball cards featuring active players, which marked the first time in twenty-five years that more than one manufacturer produced a significant set of cards of active players. In 1981 Donruss and Fleer included a piece of bubblegum in their packs, but an appeals court ruled that Topps did have the monopoly right to the production of baseball cards with confectionery products as well as the monopoly right to sell baseball cards without tying them to another product.[23] After the appellate ruling, Fleer packaged its baseball cards with stickers while Donruss packaged its cards with puzzle pieces. If baseball cards were previously viewed as promotional tools to sell bubblegum, this decision by Donruss and Fleer to continue production without tying the cards to a confectionery product marks the beginning of baseball cards as a stand-alone product.

The three manufacturers produced card sets from 1981 to 1987 with little competition. The only other manufacturer granted a license by MLB and the MLBPA was Optigraphics, Inc., which produced *Sportflics* in 1986, but *Sportflics* was actually quite different from traditional baseball cards. *Sportflics* cards had three pictures that appeared on the card front depending on how the card was tilted when held. Some of the cards, if moved quickly enough, showed a player "in action," either swinging the bat, pitching, or fielding a ball. Since they were so different from traditional brands, *Sportflics* were viewed more as a novelty than a conventional brand, and their inclusion as a competitor to *Topps*, *Fleer*, and *Donruss* is borderline. In the "Owner's Box" column in the February 1989 issue of *Beckett Baseball Card Monthly* (BBCM), which was becoming the hobby's standard for pricing, the decision to exclude *Sportflics* from monthly pricing was announced, citing lack of collector interest in the product. In 1988 Optigraphics produced a conventional set, *Score*, in addition to *Sportflics*. In 1989 MLB and the MLBPA granted licenses to a fifth manufacturer, Upper Deck. Upper Deck was the first company created solely to produce sports cards. From 1989 until 1995, the baseball-card industry consisted of these five manufacturers—Topps, Fleer, Donruss, Optigraphics, and Upper Deck.[24] An additional license was granted to Pacific Trading Cards, Inc. (Pacific) in 1993, but it was not a full license. Pacific could only produce cards that were bilingual (English/Spanish), and Pacific released at most two brands a year from 1993 to 1997. Not all applicants were granted licenses. Companies such as Classic, Frontline, and Action Packed applied and were denied licenses to produce picture cards distributed in pack form on a national basis.

Upper Deck's entry into the market ushered in a new era for baseball cards as their packs and cards differed from the traditional brands in three important ways. First, Upper Deck packs were foil packs rather than the traditional wax pack. A problem throughout the hobby was that wax packs could be opened, the valuable cards removed and replaced with less valuable cards, and then resealed to look like they had not been opened. Upper Deck's foil packs needed to be torn open, and repairing them in a manner to be consistent with the pack being unopened was extremely difficult, if not impossible.[25] Upper Deck also included a tamper-proof hologram on its cards. With rising secondary market prices came counterfeit cards. The hologram made it costly to counterfeit the cards. Finally, the quality of the

Upper Deck cards was much higher than the quality of the other brands. Previously, high-quality cards were released on a limited basis and were only available in factory set form (1980s *Topps Tiffany* and *Fleer Glossy* cards), although Topps' Sy Berger states, "Our [Topps'] people had done all the research and we had the capability to make an upscale product back in the '70s. We just didn't know how our longtime collectors would react."[26]

Upper Deck had a noticeable impact in the appearance of other manufacturers' cards. Comparing 1952 *Topps* to 1990 *Topps* little difference is seen in the quality of the cards beyond the advances in basic photography and printing. In the later years, the photos were crisper and the cards were cut more evenly, but the overall quality of the cards did not change dramatically. Following the introduction of Upper Deck, cards became glossier and were printed on higher-quality card stock. In effect, the popularity of Upper Deck's initial release forced the other manufacturers to upgrade the quality of their cards. This ultimately led to manufacturers creating multiple product lines of differing quality, catering to different market segments.

Many innovations of the early 1990s have become staples in today's products. In 1990 Upper Deck had Reggie Jackson autograph and hand serial number 2,500 copies of a particular card. These cards were then inserted into *Upper Deck HI* series packs. While Fleer had been providing inserts in its packs since 1986, the serial-numbered certified autograph card of Reggie Jackson was a major change in the type of insert card available. In 1991 Donruss became the first manufacturer to provide serial numbers for a set of insert cards, its Elite series. Rather than hand-numbering, these cards were stamped with an individual serial number (e.g. 00432/10000). In addition to providing the production run of the cards, this also serves as some protection against counterfeiting. In 1992 Topps and Donruss both introduced *parallel* cards, Donruss with *Leaf Black Gold* and Topps with *Topps Gold.* A typical parallel card will have the same photograph as the card from the base set, but the insertion rate for parallel cards is lower and there is usually some distinctive change in the card that allows collectors to determine it is a parallel. For instance, the borders of the base set of 1992 *Leaf* are gray, while the borders of *Leaf Black Gold* are black. Topps used gold foil for the lettering in *Topps Gold.* Both manufacturers inserted their parallel cards at a rate of one per pack in 1992. In 1993 Topps introduced refractors in *Finest. Refractors* are parallel cards that use a special coating that refracts light. In addition, the refractors were in extremely limited supply for that time period with a stated print run of 241.

In 1993 Pinnacle released the production numbers for two products, *Select* and *Select Rookie/Traded,* by serial-numbering the cases of the products. This decision to serial number the cases of these products was made in response to a gaffe in 1990 when 1990 *Score* was believed to be in short supply early in the year. The price for the complete set of 1990 *Score* cards increased rapidly based on this perceived short supply. However, late in the year a large number of unopened cases of 1990 *Score* appeared on the market after additional product was shipped, causing the complete set price to drop quickly and shaking collector confidence in Score products. This loss of collector confidence eventually led to Optigraphics renaming itself Pinnacle.[27] In 1994 Fleer introduced *die-cut* cards to the baseball card market. These cards are the same size as a standard baseball card, but the cards are die-cut to enhance the look of the card. The earliest cards were Fleer's Hot Gloves in 1994 *Flair*, in which each card was die-cut to look like a baseball glove.

Release Policy

When Fleer and Donruss first produced cards in 1981, they followed the same release strategy as Topps. Both companies had one brand and one release, in which all the cards for the brand were available in the packs of that release. Other than the production of Fleer and Donruss cards, the major hobby news that occurred in 1981 was that Topps brought back the traded-set concept that originally debuted in 1974. However, in 1981 Topps released the traded cards through hobby stores in factory-set form, not in packs. This marks the first time in which a manufacturer released a major product without releasing it in retail outlets.

Throughout the 1980s the manufacturers followed a fairly standard release schedule: flagship products were released between November and February. For example, 1989 *Score* was available in late November of 1988. Near the completion of the baseball season the manufacturers released their traded or update products, always in factory-set form. Between the release of their primary product in November–February and the release of their traded set the following October, companies released products for other major sports and entertainment as well as other baseball products. These other baseball products, given the name "oddball" products by collectors, differ from the regular issues in a number of ways. The actual physical size of the card may be different (either larger or smaller), the number of cards in the set is smaller, the quantity of cards produced is typically lower than that of the primary products, and the sets contain only star players or rookies. Oddball products also consist of products that are not cards, such as stickers, coins, and tattoos, that were produced in an attempt to reach a wider audience. All three manufacturers released oddball products in pack form as well as in factory-set form throughout the 1980s, and the production of oddball products may be viewed as another attempt at producing multiple brands by the manufacturers, similar to Topps' oddball releases in the 1960s.

In 1989 Upper Deck released its product in two series. However, this release was unlike when Topps released cards in series during its monopoly years. First, Upper Deck released a standard size set of 700 cards in its first series. Its second series was essentially its traded set and contained only 100 cards. In addition, Upper Deck's second series was available in packs along with the cards from the first series. The release of a product in series proved to be an advantage in issuing rookie cards. Given that Topps signs players to individual contracts, Topps can include any player under contract in its sets.[28] Since the other manufacturers only sign a licensing agreement with the MLBPA, they could only include players currently on a team's forty-man roster. Thus, Topps could include cards of players before they reach the major leagues, giving Topps an advantage in the rookie card market. The release of a product in series allows time for some young players to be added to the forty-man roster during the season and allows the other manufacturers to produce those rookie cards.

In 1989 Topps became the first manufacturer to release two different major brands in pack form on a nationwide basis when it brought back *Bowman*.[29] *Bowman*'s consideration as a major set lagged its release date as *Bowman* was released in June but would not be priced in BBCM until September. This decision is mentioned in the "Owner's Box" column of the September 1989 BBCM. This introduction of a second major brand, coupled with the change in quality brought about by the entrance of Upper Deck, changed manufacturers' release strategies during the 1990s. The manufacturers began by releasing a second product to compete with the Upper Deck flagship brand. The second product was typically higher quality with a lower print run than the flagship brand. Donruss launched *Leaf* in 1990, Fleer released *Ultra* in 1991, Topps released *Stadium Club* in 1991, and Pinnacle released *Pinnacle* in 1992. Upper Deck released a less expensive brand in 1994, *Collector's Choice*, to compete with the lower-priced brands.

By 1994 most manufacturers had at least three different established brands, with the brands aimed at different segments of the market. Figure 12.1 shows the total number of brands by manufacturer from 1989 to 1994; the number of brands slowly increased for each manufacturer. Collectors referred to the brand quality levels as basic, premium, and super-premium.

The standard release pattern for manufacturers was for manufacturers to release their flagship products after the baseball season but before Christmas and then to release their premium and super-premium products during the baseball season. One reason may have been to stimulate interest in the new product lines, as the established product lines had a more established

FIGURE 12.1
Number of Brands by Manufacturer, 1988–1994

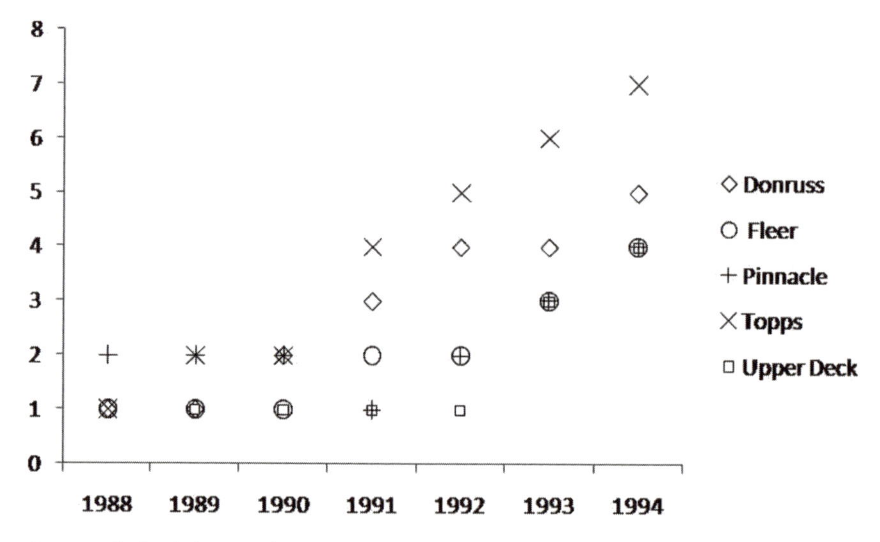

Source: Author's calculations, adapted from *Sports Collectors Digest* (various issues).

collector base, and products released in the summer would be released during the baseball season. *Bowman*, which focused on rookie cards of players still in the minor leagues, was released near the end of the year to allow more time for these potential prospects to mature. While the exact release dates for products from this era are not available, approximate release dates can be determined using the first appearance of a product in the monthly price guides. Table 12.1 lists the appearance in BBCM of each product by month for 1992 and 1993.

Table 12.1 also shows that in addition to the creation of more brands there were more product releases as manufacturers returned to releasing products in series. In addition to allowing manufacturers to produce cards of players who were unknown at the beginning of the season, another benefit to releasing products in series is that if a particular product does sell well, production plans for its later series can be changed or scrapped altogether.[30] Alternatively, if a particular product does well but is not scheduled for multiple series, releasing additional series can capture any excess profits that result from a brand surpassing expectations. One new brand released in 2002 by Topps, *Topps 206*, quickly rose to the top of most consumers' want lists, and Topps released two follow-up series that were not initially scheduled for release.

TABLE 12.1
Month of First Available Pricing in BBCM for 1992 and 1993 Products

Month	1992 Products	1993 Products
January	—	—
February	Donruss I, Score I, Topps	Donruss I, Select, Topps
March	Fleer, Upper Deck	Fleer I, Upper Deck I
April	Donruss II, Score II	Donruss II
May	Stadium Club I	Fleer II, Pinnacle I, Topps II, Ultra I
June	Ultra I	Score I, Stadium Club I
July	Stadium Club II	Leaf I, Score I
August	Leaf I	Pinnacle II, Stadium Club II, Upper Deck II
September	Ultra II	Leaf II, Ultra II
October	Leaf II, Stadium Club III, Pinnacle	Bowman, Stadium Club III, Fun Pack
November	Studio	O-Pee-Chee Premier, Finest, SP, Studio
December	Bowman	Flair

Source: Author's calculations, adapted from James Beckett, Rich Klein, and Grant Sanground, eds., *Beckett Almanac of Baseball Cards and Collectibles,* no. 7 (Dallas: Beckett Publications 2002).

Pricing Policies

In 1981 *Topps* had an SRP of thirty cents per pack of fifteen cards. *Fleer* and *Donruss* also had SRPs of thirty cents per pack in 1981 but *Fleer*'s packs included seventeen cards while *Donruss'* packs included fifteen. From 1982 to 1984, all three manufacturers had fifteen cards per pack with an SRP of thirty cents. In 1985 the SRP of packs began to rise, usually by five cents every one or two years, with *Topps* reaching fifty-five cents in 1992. Cards per pack for the flagship brands remained between fourteen and sixteen cards during this time. In 1993 *Topps'* packs included fifteen cards for sixty-nine cents and in 1994 fourteen cards for seventy-nine cents. Upper Deck did not follow this pricing policy for its flagship brand, which had an SRP of $1 for fifteen-card packs.

For premium and super-premium brands the pricing was quite different. Unlike their flagship products, premium and super-premium brands of this era rarely carried SRPs stamped directly on the packs or on the boxes of the product. This gave retailers the ability to adjust prices based on market conditions. As an example, 1991 *Stadium Club* carried an SRP of $1.25 per pack. However, the "Readers Write" of BBCM during 1991–1992 is littered with objections about having to pay $5 or more per pack. Similarly, although no SRP is cited, it is unlikely that Topps released 1993 *Finest* with a SRP of $25 per pack, but complaints (always by buyers) are rampant throughout hobby periodicals during 1993–1994 about the exorbitant cost of the product. This lack of a clearly provided SRP by the manufacturer carried over into later years when manufacturers began releasing the "same" product through hobby and retail channels, although the hobby product typically had better odds of pulling a rare card. The retail package typically contained an SRP while the hobby package did not.

Secondary Market

Baseball cards were one of the hottest investments in the 1980s, with the increase in the price of the 1952 *Topps* Mickey Mantle card being the usual example cited.[31] Baseball cards were also mentioned along with art as a means of diversifying one's investment portfolio.[32] The secondary market in the 1980s and early 1990s was defined by individuals stockpiling cards, particularly rookie cards, of players and swapping them like shares of stock, and by collectors attempting to discover variations and errors in their cards in the hopes of finding a rarity. Advertisements for lots of 50, 100, and even 1000 of the *same* card were prevalent.[33] In the early 1990s, demand for parallel and insert cards began to spike. Rookie cards, which provided the most speculative potential given that the player pictured on the card had little to no major-league experience, were in particularly high demand. Many magazines touted the fact that a three-cent Dwight Gooden rookie in 1985 had reached $2 by the end of the year, with little mention of those rookies who did not pan out. Prior to limited insert sets, finding an error or variation was the method of obtaining a card that was relatively scarcer than the others. The search for errors and variations became so popular that BBCM began a column called "Errors and Varieties" in its June 1988 issue. Finally, along with high secondary market prices came counterfeiters attempting to profit from uninformed collectors. These concepts are discussed in detail below.

Figure 12.2 shows complete set prices taken from BBCM from April 1988 until December 1994 for selected brands. The top-left panel shows the price path for complete sets of 1953, 1957, and 1958 *Topps*, the top-right panel the price path for the 1961, 1965, and 1969 *Topps* sets, the bottom-left panel the price path for the 1970, 1975, and 1979 *Topps* sets, and the bottom-right panel the price path for the 1988 *Fleer*, 1990 *Score*, and 1990 *Upper Deck* sets. These price paths are typical for sets of their era. Complete-set prices are used rather than individual-card prices because complete-set prices are typically less volatile. While complete-set prices tend to fluctuate as the key rookie cards in the set fluctuate, most of the sets from the 1950s and 1960s featured rookie cards of players who were inactive by 1988 and thus the values of those sets were not affected by on-field

FIGURE 12.2
Secondary Market Prices for Selected Sets from the 1950s–1990s

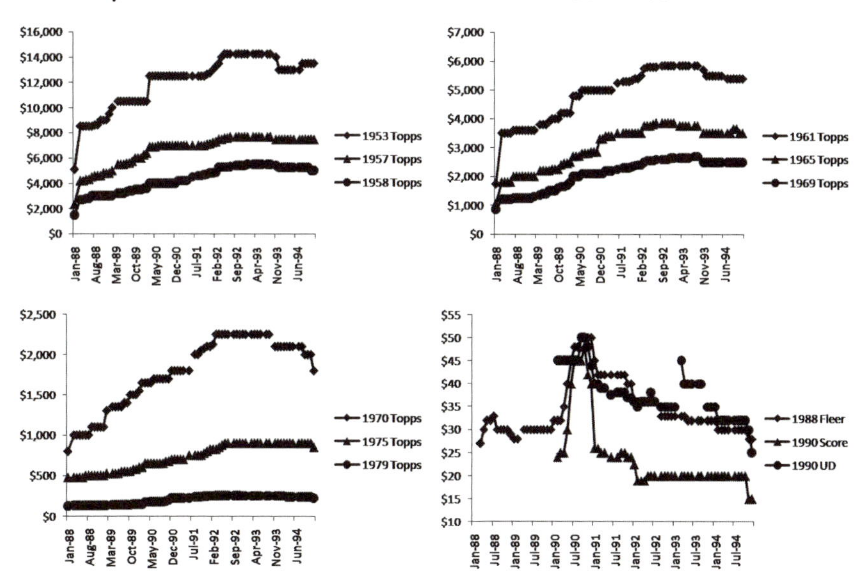

Source: Author's calculations, adapted from *Sports Collectors Digest* (various issues).

performance of the players.[34] As the panels for the 1950s, 1960s, and 1970s sets show, there were virtually no declines in the post–World War II material until late in 1993—over five years of growth![35] However, the more recent brands show sharper declines than the older brands and the decline occurs earlier than late 1993 in most cases. Part of the change is due to fluctuations in value of key rookie cards during this time period, but the general decline in set values for newer products reflects how the industry had changed in response to the introduction of insert cards. By opening packs to search for insert cards, collectors were able to build many sets and set values declined as the supply increased.

Rookie Cards

With the increase in visibility, speculators entered the market, and in the 1980s stockpiling of cards, particularly rookie cards, became a major craze. Although the definition of a *rookie card* has changed over time, it is generally defined by the hobby as the first nationally distributed card of a player in a brand of cards, as long as that player has not had a card in a brand of cards from the manufacturer of that brand or another manufacturer in an earlier year. Rookie cards are a staple in the hobby, and their appeal to collectors has driven some recent changes in when manufacturers release products.

The rookie-card concept is best explained by example. In 1983 *Topps*, *Donruss*, and *Fleer* all contained their first cards of Tony Gwynn, so all three cards are considered rookie cards. Both 1984 *Fleer* and *Donruss* contained a card of Kevin McReynolds, so they were considered his rookie cards. Topps, however, did not have McReynolds under license then, and did not release its first card of McReynolds until 1988. The 1988 card has never been considered a rookie card, although it is considered his First Topps Card, a label that had more importance in 1988 than it does today. Moving forward a few years to when manufacturers were releasing more than one brand of cards in a year, consider the case of Derek Jeter. In 1993 Jeter had cards in eight brands (*Bowman*, *Pinnacle*, *Score*, *Select*, *SP*, *Stadium Club Murphy*, *Topps*, and *Upper Deck*) from three manufacturers (Pinnacle, Topps, and Upper Deck). All eight cards are considered rookie cards. However, neither Fleer nor Donruss produced a card of Jeter in 1993, and when they first produced cards of Jeter in 1995 and 1996, neither card was considered a rookie card.

Historically, rookie cards have been the most valuable cards because they were the oldest and usually the scarcest cards of a player. There are exceptions to this—Mickey Mantle's true rookie card is his 1951 *Bowman* card, but his 1952 *Topps* card is his most valuable card due to the fact that it is his first Topps card and that the card was included in the scarce high series of 1952 *Topps*. Recently, given that rookie cards exist in multiple products and that certain insert cards are now rarer, the focus shifted to obtaining the player's best card, which likely contains a manufacturer certified autograph. However, rookie cards still generally carry a premium over most later released base-set issues.

Error Cards

In addition to rookie cards, error cards played a prominent role in the 1980s market. The term *error card* refers to any card that has any type of mistake: photo of an incorrect player, incorrect biographical data for the player, incorrect team, incorrect statistics, misspelled words in text on the card back, and printing defects are just some of the potential error cards. In the 1930s and 1940s, when baseball card collectors had no checklists and were still cataloging which cards existed, finding a variation was like finding a new card. Thus, the Sherry Magee error card from the 1909 T206 set, in which his last name was spelled Magie, was valued more than others, even in the 1940s, because it was rarer. In the 1970s the Magie error was selling for $100.[36] This behavior carried over into the hobby in the 1980s as collectors looked for anything that could make their particular card rarer and hence more valuable. It has been suggested that in an industry built on scarcity and quality of cards that error cards would become the norm in the industry.[37] For a certain period of time it looked like that might hold true as the hobby was obsessed with finding and cataloging errors in the 1980s. The "Readers' Write" in BBCM was littered with questions about finding potential error cards and their value.

Error cards only have value above typical market value if they are corrected, resulting in the error cards being relatively scarcer than other cards produced. In the 1960s most error cards consisted of misspelled names, photo changes, and printing variations, and relatively few were corrected. The most valuable error cards are the 1969 Topps "white letter" variations for some players where the letters of the players' last names are printed in white rather than yellow. In the 1970s there were also relatively few error cards—the most valuable are the 1974 Topps "Washington, Natl. Lg." cards. There was a rumor that the San Diego Padres would move to Washington, D.C., in 1974, and Topps printed cards of Padre players with "Washington" for the team location and "Nat'l. Lg." for the team name. The Padres did not move, and Topps corrected the cards in later print runs. However, from 1975 to 1981 Topps only corrected one error. In 1982 there were only three corrected errors, and from 1983 to 1986 there are no corrected errors in Topps' cards. In 1987 a few cards have printing defects. Of the three cards missing the trademark logos, two were of the hottest players in the market, Don Mattingly and Dwight Gooden. This led to rumors that Topps deliberately left the trademark logo off these two cards to create interest in the product. In 1988 and 1989 there were few corrected errors and most of those involved printing flaws and 1990 *Topps* had one major error that was corrected. 1991 *Topps* contained Topps' most errors ever, with many errors containing incorrect biographical information, which was subsequently corrected. From 1992 until the present Topps has produce some cards with uncorrected errors, but corrects few of them.

The other manufacturers had similar patterns for error cards. In 1981 Donruss and Fleer had multiple printings of their cards, using the latter printing to correct errors made in the initial print funs. These errors were likely not deliberate but due to time constraints in bringing their products to market after being granted licenses by the MLB and MLBPA. This claim appears to be substantiated by the fact that Fleer had few errors in its 1982 product, one printing error in its 1983 product, and then no corrected errors from 1984 to 1987. Donruss had minor issues with misspelled names and printing variations in 1982 and 1983, no corrected errors in its 1984 product, and relatively few corrected errors in its product from 1985 to 1989.[38] In 1990 Donruss had some cards with reverse negatives, and its entire All-Star subset had incorrect text above the statistics on the card backs. In 1991 Donruss corrected a few errors and from 1992 and beyond there were no corrected errors. In 1988 *Fleer* contained multiple cards with misspelled names and incorrect photos of players that were subsequently corrected. In 1989 *Fleer* produced the most infamous "error" card, known in the hobby as the "Rick Face" card due to its designation by BBCM. The "Rick Face" card features Billy Ripken with an easily discernible obscenity visible (i.e., no magnifying glass is needed) on the knob of the bat in the photo. Fleer used multiple methods to remove the obscenity in future printings, and the attention given to this card may have spurred other manufacturers to make errors. In addition to the Rick Face card there were other minor corrected errors in 1990 *Fleer*. From 1990 to 1992 Fleer had only a handful of corrected errors each year and after 1992 there were no corrected errors.

The two newest entrants, Optigraphics and Upper Deck, were not immune to errors. During 1988-1990 *Score* contained a handful of corrected errors, mostly misspelled names. In 1991 and 1992 *Score* still contained many errors but none were corrected, and by 1993 even the uncorrected errors had been reduced to a single one. In 1989 and 1990 *Upper Deck* contained various errors (such as incorrectly identified players or reversed negatives) but by 1991 Upper Deck reduced the number of corrected errors to two and from 1992 and beyond it was rare to see a corrected error. Some individuals believe that Upper Deck deliberately produced errors in 1989 in an attempt to create scarcity.[39] The only notable corrected error after 1992 was in 2002 *Upper Deck Vintage* and was a printing flaw where the names of the players on the home-run leader card were missing. Pacific, the last manufacturer to enter in this time period, had two corrected errors in its initial product in 1993 and none thereafter.

By 1993 there were relatively few corrected errors. The cause of this reduction can likely be linked to several factors. First, with improvements in printing technology the variations that existed due to printing flaws were reduced. Second, error cards were primarily valued on the secondary market for their scarcity, but manufacturers had begun to create numerous insert sets that were scarcer than the base set, reducing the need for errors to fill this scarcity void. Finally, since the manufacturers were now producing multiple products it is likely that creating a separate printing simply to correct a few mistakes was not as profitable as creating a new product. The error craze came to an end, but Upper Deck commemorated it by releasing a parallel set in 2002 *UD Authentics* called "reverse negative," in which the parallel cards were all printed with reverse negatives.

Insert Cards

Insert premiums had been around since the 1950s, but mainstream interest in them did not occur until the early 1990s. The Fleer All-Star set in 1986 is recognized as the first modern insert set, and for some time these insert cards were priced by BBCM. However, in May 1989 the cards were removed from BBCM's price guide. Donruss included Bonus MVPs as inserts in some of its later print runs from 1988 to 1990, but these cards are essentially as available as base cards from those brands. The 1990 *Upper Deck* Reggie Jackson autograph and 1991 *Donruss Elite* series sparked interest in inserts, and the initial parallel sets by Topps and Donruss also generated interest in insert sets. The *Elite* series, serial-numbered to 10,000, sparked such immense interest that stories circulate about individuals searching cases of 1991 *Donruss* with metal detectors in an attempt to detect the foil serial numbering. The insert set that sustained the most interest was Topps' 1993 *Finest Refractors* with a stated print run of just 241. *Finest Refractors* showed extraordinary growth at a time when the vintage market was leveling off and interest in newer product base sets waned. As late as 1996 *Finest Refractors* were still among the hottest cards on the market.

Counterfeits

With the increase in secondary-market values came counterfeiting attempts. Given the hobby's interest in rookie cards, most counterfeited cards were of the priciest rookie cards. Various issues of BBCM mention specific cards as potential targets for counterfeiters. Some innovations by the industry were designed to thwart counterfeiters. One was Upper Deck's inclusion of a hologram on the back of the card, making it difficult to reproduce. Another was the serial-numbering of cards—if a collector ever saw two cards with identical serial numbers he could be assured one of them was counterfeit. Also, the steady increase in quality of the cards in addition to the technological advances and inclusion of game-used memorabilia and autographs made it much more difficult for counterfeiters.

In the early 1990s card grading services emerged. While card grading services primarily focus on grading the card based upon its appearance, the more prominent services also check for counterfeits or cards that have been altered (retouched or trimmed) in an attempt to make the card appear higher quality. While there are numerous grading companies, three companies' products carry a premium on the secondary market—Professional Sports Authenticators (PSA), Sportscard Guaranty Corporation (SGC), and Beckett Grading Services (BGS).

PRODUCT PROLIFERATION AND INDUSTRY CONSOLIDATION (1995–PRESENT)

After the players' strike in 1994, the sale of baseball cards slowed considerably. New card sales for the sports-card industry peaked in 1991 at $1.2 billion and declined every year through 2001 when new card sales were at $350 million.[40] However, there has been a recent increase in sales as they climbed from $250 million in 2005 to $270 million in 2006.[41] This overall decline in the past fifteen years has led to a shifting industry landscape. Pinnacle acquired Donruss in April 1996, reducing the number of fully licensed manufacturers from five to four. In May 1998 Pacific was granted a full license to produce cards, returning the number of fully licensed manufacturers to five. The increase was short-lived as Pinnacle filed for bankruptcy in July 1998, returning the number of manufacturers to four. The brand names of Donruss and Leaf were acquired by a nonlicensed company, Playoff, Inc. (Playoff). Although Playoff was allowed to release one product that Pinnacle had already manufactured in 1998 (*Leaf Rookies & Stars*), it was not granted a license by MLB and the MLBPA until February 2001. However, the number of fully licensed manufacturers did not return to five in 2001 because Pacific decided not to renew its baseball-card license. In 2006 Playoff's application license was declined and Fleer filed for bankruptcy and was subsequently purchased by Upper Deck, leaving the baseball-card industry with less than three manufacturers for the first time since 1980.

The dominant trend throughout most of this period was the increased number of brands released each year by all manufacturers. In the late 1990s and early 2000s, manufacturers produced brands aimed at ever more narrow target audiences. For example, Topps produced three lines of Bowman cards (*Bowman*, *Bowman Chrome*, and *Bowman's Best*) all targeting rookie card collectors at three different quality levels. Some brands, such as Topps' *Topps Laser*, Pinnacle's *UC3*, and Pacific's *Crown Royale*, were produced to showcase a particular technology in a standard set as opposed to only using the technology in insert sets. Other brands focused on specific teams (Upper Deck's *Yankees Legends* and Fleer's *Red Sox 100th Anniversary*) or very specific themes (Upper Deck's *Challengers for 70*, which included those players likely to challenge the then-single-season record of seventy home runs). These brands were in addition to the manufacturers' already established flagship, premium, and super-premium brands.

Another trend was the dwindling production run of insert and parallel cards. Given the frenzy created by the 1993 *Finest Refractors* a further decrease in print run for some insert sets was a natural extension. Perhaps due to the MLBPA strike in 1994 and declining interest in baseball-related products in general, most insert sets in 1994 and 1995 remained at stated production levels around 1000 or 2000. There are some exceptions, but these were primarily parallel sets with unannounced print runs, such as Topps' *Stadium Club First Day Issue* (available 1:36 packs), Upper Deck's *Collector's Choice Gold Signature* (1:36 packs), and Pinnacle's *Pinnacle Artist's Proofs* (available 1:26 packs). In 1996 Pinnacle released *Select Certified*, which contained six different parallel sets. The most easily obtainable parallel cards in this set were the Certified Red, available at a rate of 1:5 packs. However, the Mirror Blue and Mirror Gold parallel cards had stated print runs of forty-five and thirty respectively, with insertion rates of 1:200 and 1:300 packs. In 1997 the boundary was pushed to its limit when Fleer and Pinnacle produced one-of-one inserts. Pinnacle's first one-of-one insert was a redemption card for a 24K solid gold coin of the specified player in *Pinnacle Mint*. These redemption cards were inserted approximately 1:47,200 packs. Pinnacle also cut up the printing press plates for 1997 *New Pinnacle* and inserted these plates in packs. The four-color printing process requires a total of eight plates, one of each color for both the front and the back of the card. Since the plates are different colors, each is essentially a one-of-one item. The first true one-of-one cards produced were by Fleer for *Flair Showcase*. These cards, called *Flair Showcase Legacy Masterpiece*, were viewed with mixed reactions.[42] The one-of-one parallels and other extremely low numbered cards would not become a product staple until Playoff began producing cards in 2001.

Interest in buyback cards increased during this time period. A *buyback card* is a card that was produced by the manufacturer at an earlier date, then bought on the secondary market by the manufacturer and randomly inserted into the manufacturer's current product. Topps had used buybacks in 1991 for its fortieth anniversary, inserting either actual cards or redemption cards for the original cards.[43] In 1996 Topps repurchased original Mickey Mantle cards and then packaged redemption cards for a lottery of the original Mantle cards. In 1997 Upper Deck repurchased cards from its 1993–1996 *SP* brands and had the pictured player autograph the repurchased cards. The autographed cards were then hand-serial-numbered and randomly inserted into packs of 1997 *SP Authentic*. Each card also came with a certification sticker on the back of the card and a certification card with a number that matched the sticker. The serial-numbered and autographed buyback card became a staple of future products, particularly those focused on retired players.

The use of redemption cards by manufacturers also became more prominent. Consumers can redeem redemption cards for the item specified on the card. Prior to the mid-1990s redemption cards were used primarily for items that could not fit into a pack of cards: an additional set of cards, a particular player's game-used bat, or a chance to win a trip to a World Series game. Currently, redemption cards are also being inserted for objects such as autographed cards and rookie or first-year cards, both of which fit in the card pack. The stated reason for issuing redemption cards for autographs is that the player autographing the card did not return the autographed cards to the manufacturer in time for the manufacturer to include them in the packs when the product was scheduled to ship. As for the rookie-card redemptions, these are typically for unknown rookies who may emerge during the upcoming season and tend to be inserted in brands released early in the baseball-card season. The reason for the inclusion of these redemption cards is to ensure that the brands released early in the season do not miss any of the key rookie players who may have an impact during the year. In either case, manufacturers could avoid inserting redemption cards by delaying the release of the brand, which occurs in rare cases.

In 1996 Donruss pushed the insert set to a new level with *Leaf Signature*. Packs of *Leaf Signature* carried a then-unheard-of SRP of $9.99 for four cards but each pack included at least one certified autograph card. The change with the largest impact occurred in 1997 when Upper Deck introduced the game-used memorabilia card to the baseball-card hobby.[44] A game-used memorabilia card is a standard-sized baseball card with a piece of the depicted player's memorabilia embedded into the card. The initial cards were inserted every 800 packs in 1997 *Upper Deck Series I*. Upper Deck used a similar process to create cut signature cards, which are embedded autographs of deceased players into cards. By acquiring canceled checks or authenticated autographs of deceased players Upper Deck was able to remove the autograph from the original object and create autograph cards of popular players such as Babe Ruth, Walter Johnson, and Honus Wagner.[45] Most of the other changes in the industry consisted of combinations of the above changes, such as serial-numbering game-used cards or having a player autograph a card that had game-used material in it.

Although innovations occur in the industry with some regularity, manufacturers generally do not gain a lasting advantage from innovating. This is due to the ability of other manufacturers to quickly incorporate the new innovations. The mid-1990s BBCMs contain numerous references to this imitation. Baseball-card dealer Candy Greenholtz states, "When card companies come up with new bells and whistles, others seem to follow."[46] In a question-and-answer session among hobby dealers Leer discussed the amount of imitation seen in the products.[47] In an attempt to stop imitation, Upper Deck filed suit to stop other manufacturers from producing cards with game-used materials embedded in them. Ultimately this lawsuit was settled out of court.[48]

Pricing Policies, 1995–2006

There has been a wide dispersion in pack prices since the early 1990s, given that different products are targeted for different consumers. As previously mentioned, 1996 *Leaf Signature* had an SRP of $9.99. While outrageous for its time, established collectors rarely balk at such prices today. Indeed, current products such as *Ultimate Collection*, *Epic*, *Topps Sterling*, and *Bowman Sterling* now carry SRPs upwards of $50 per pack of three to five cards and some carry SRPs into the hundreds of dollars. It becomes difficult to compare post-1992 pack prices for a few reasons. First, all the manufacturers were releasing multiple brands at this point in time. Second, the quality of the cards improved greatly, even for the basic brands, and as such comparisons with the pack prices in the 1980s become virtually meaningless. Price per card, unadjusted for quality, increased from thirteen cents in 1993 to approximately thirty cents in 1996, with the biggest increase between the 1994 and 1995 releases.[49] One reason for this increase was the MLBPA strike in 1994, which drove borderline collectors out of the hobby and left only diehard collectors. The demand shock also had different effects on products of differing quality. In the flagship brands the pack price rose sharply while the number of cards per pack remained constant. For example, Topps increased the price of *Topps* by fifty cents, from seventy-nine cents in 1994 to $1.29 in 1995, without changing the number of cards in a pack. However, in the premium brands slight price increases tended to be accompanied by fewer cards in the pack, driving up the price per card. Another exogenous demand shock occurred in 1998, this one positive, due to the pursuit of the single-season home-run record.[50] However, pack prices did not increase greatly. Instead, manufacturers continued to release more narrowly defined brands, perhaps signifying a shift in strategic behavior.

While the price per card of packs was increasing due to increasing amounts insert cards, the introduction of game-used cards corresponded to an even greater increase in price per pack. The process of embedding the memorabilia into the cards is much more complex than changing color schemes or adding serial numbers, and the players' jerseys also needed to be purchased. As an example of how game-used items affect price, consider 2001 *Pacific Private Stock*. Pacific released one version of this product as a hobby-only product and another as a retail-only product. Each pack of the hobby-only product contained a game-used card and carried an SRP of

$14.99 while the retail-only product did not include a game-used card and carried a $2.99 SRP.

Release Policy

Table 12.2 shows the number of brands by manufacturer from 1995 to 2006. A few comments are in order for Table 12.2. The years correspond to the year as designated by the manufacturer and not the actual calendar year of the release date. This is due to the fact that actual release dates for all products in this time period are not available and because some multiseries products were released across two different calendar years. For most of the years, Table 12.2 covers the process of counting brands by the calendar year designated by the manufacturer shifting the beginning of the calendar year from January to mid-November. Once one manufacturer released a brand for the upcoming year no other manufacturers would release a brand for the current year.[51] Also, all brands in 1996 that were previously Donruss created (*Donruss*, *Leaf*, and *Studio*) are listed as Donruss brands for 1996, and 1998 *Leaf Rookies & Stars*, which was produced by Pinnacle but released by Playoff, is counted as a Pinnacle product in Table 12.2.

A slight change in release strategy was triggered by Playoff's release of *Leaf Rookies & Stars*. Due to legal action by MLB and MLBPA, Playoff was prohibited from releasing *Leaf Rookies & Stars* until December 1998.

TABLE 12.2
Number of Brands by Manufacturer, 1995–2006

Year	Donruss	Fleer	Pacific	Pinnacle	Playoff	Topps	Upper Deck
1995	4	4	2	8		8	4
1996	6	6	2	10		9	4
1997		7	2	18		10	5
1998		10	8	16		14	7
1999		12	10			14	17
2000		12	11			14	16
2001		15	2		11	21	24
2002		19			15	23	19
2003		21			18	24	21
2004		18			21	22	20
2005		10			21	24	25
2006						20	19

Source: Author's calculations, adapted from James Beckett, Rich Klein, and Grant Sanground, eds., *Beckett Almanac of Baseball Cards and Collectibles,* no. 7 (Dallas: Beckett Publications 2002).

Because of its late release date, which was after the four current manufacturers had already released their flagship 1999 products, Playoff was able to include rookie cards of some players who had few other cards released during 1998. About the same time, Upper Deck released a product called *Upper Deck Black Diamond,* which contained the first Upper Deck issued J. D. Drew card. However, Upper Deck designated the product with a 1999 date, and even though the two products were released within days of one another in December, the hobby decided that the Playoff product contained a Drew rookie card and the Upper Deck product contained did not. Due to this designation by the hobby, the secondary market values of the cards differ greatly, and 1998 *Leaf Rookies & Stars* is heralded as one of the top products of the 1990s while 1999 *Upper Deck Black Diamond* is just another brand. Perhaps because of this, Upper Deck released 2000 *Black Diamond* in two series. The second series was released in December of 2000 and was called *Upper Deck Black Diamond Rookie Edition.* Thus, the practice of squeezing in releases at the end of a calendar year in order to produce a few additional rookie cards began.

Table 12.2 shows that the increase in brands each year by each manufacturer was fairly constant, with a few notable exceptions. The increase in Pinnacle brands from 1996 to 1997 is due to its acquisition of Donruss in 1996, while the increase in Pacific brands from 1997 to 1998 is due to its acquisition of a full license from MLB and the MLBPA in 1998. Topps' and Upper Deck's sharp increases in brands in 1997–1998 and 1999–2000 are most likely driven by the increased demand for baseball-related products ignited by Mark McGwire and Sammy Sosa's pursuit of Roger Maris's single-season home-run record in 1998.

The otherwise constant upward trend in brands can be attributed to a few factors. One is that due to investors stockpiling cards in 1984–1991 there was a glut of cards from this era still on the market once the speculators sold out. Most collectors had little use for 100 or 1000 of the same card, so in an effort to regain the sales lost by the exiting speculators, manufacturers turned to producing additional brands. The same collectors who purchased one brand could now be brought back into the market with subsequent brands, increasing sales. Thus, it is possible that collectors still wanted to purchase baseball cards but did not want to purchase the exact same brands repeatedly. In essence, collectors exhibited preferences for newness.[52] Purchasing the same baseball-card product is akin to a moviegoer repeatedly seeing the same movie, and while some individuals repeatedly view the same movie in the theater, most moviegoers typically view a different movie during each trip to the theater. Thus, an individual exhibits preferences for newness if that individual wishes to purchase from a general class of goods (say baseball cards or movies) but does not wish to purchase the exact same good repeatedly.

Another possible reason for the increase in brands was to solve the durable goods monopoly problem that exists in baseball cards. By producing another brand, manufacturers may have found a credible method of shortening the lifespan of a product. There is evidence that most new entrants to the baseball-card market experienced this type of problem. In 1981 both Donruss and Fleer produced cards based upon collector demand. As the year progressed, if their product sold out they would print more to meet demand. After realizing that they were alienating their customers due to the adverse effects on prices in the secondary market, both Donruss and Fleer discontinued this practice in 1984. The story of 1990 *Score* has already been discussed earlier. There are also rumors that Upper Deck followed a similar practice of overproducing specific cards in the early years of its existence.[53] While the precise reason for the shift to increasing the number of brands is unclear, it is certainly clear that the focus of manufacturers shifted from selling as much as they could of one brand to selling all they had produced of one brand as quickly as possible.

A Temporal Hotelling Game?

As shown in the preceding sections, competitive practices in the baseball card industry have evolved greatly. A final step is to look more closely at the specific release dates for products to determine if competitive practices have evolved to such an extent that manufacturers are not releasing products at the same time but are spacing them out over the course of the year, in essence playing a temporal Hotelling game.[54] The aforementioned discussion on the use of redemption cards also suggests that manufacturers desire to stay on schedule with their releases. The earliest reported release dates in BBCM occur at the end of 1997, but once Pinnacle went bankrupt all of the manufacturers began listing release dates for their products. Upper Deck appears to be the last of the manufacturers to follow this strategy, beginning in late 1998.

The data here consist of the release dates for the eighty-three releases that occurred during the 2002 calendar year, taken from issues of *Sports Collectors Digest*. Of the eighty-three releases, there were seventy distinct release dates. The most releases occurring on any day was three, once in June and once on December 31. Topps and Upper Deck are the only manufacturers to release multiple products on the same day. Most of these multiple release dates occurred between the end of the baseball season and Christmas Day, suggesting that there may be time periods when demand is high enough to disrupt any attempts at spacing releases.

Figures 12.3 and 12.4 show the actual date of each release by manufacturer. The vertical gridlines are placed every five days, which is approximately the average length of time between release dates. Brands with suggested retail prices greater than $10 are set slightly above the lower-priced brands for each manufacturer. While there are some periods of overlap and some periods without any releases, the general idea that the manufacturers in the baseball-card industry may be spacing their product releases is supported. In addition to the potential breakdown in product spacing during the holiday season, Figure 12.3 also shows that there was a fair amount of overlap in late April of 2002 and early May of 2002. The abundance of releases during this time period may be explained by the threat of a MLBPA strike that would have occurred in late August or early September of 2002. Manufacturers, knowing from firsthand experience that the player's strike of 1994 depressed card sales for nearly three years, may have felt pressured to release the brands earlier in the year than they had planned. Other years have similar release patterns to 2002, although the releases tend to be slightly more spaced since there were no threats of player strikes in those years. Thus, 2002 is the least likely candidate for the temporal Hotelling game, yet releases tend to be more or less spread throughout the calendar year.

FIGURE 12.3
Actual Release Dates by Manufacturer, January 1–June 31, 2002

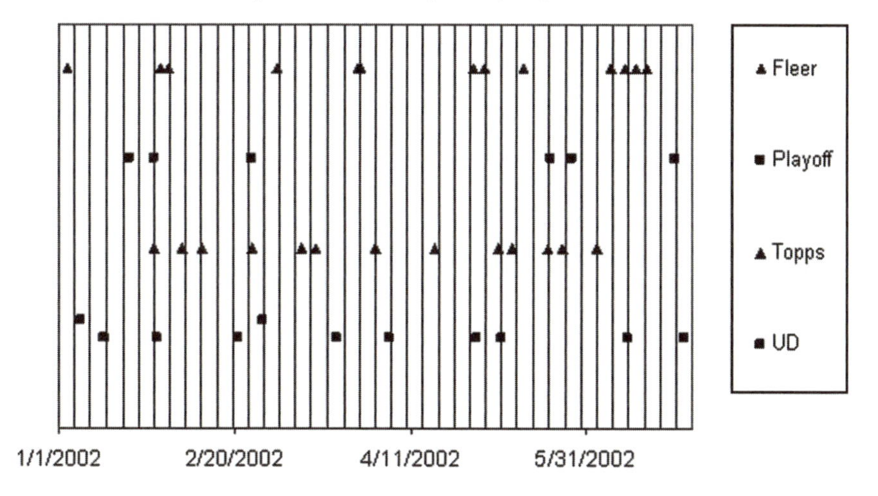

Source: Author's calculations.

FIGURE 12.4
Actual Release Dates by Manufacturer, July 1–December 31, 2002

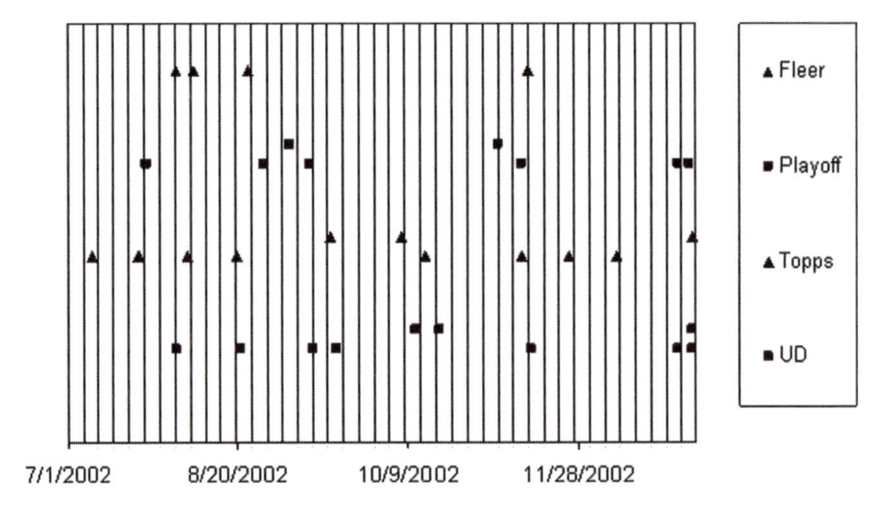

Source: Author's calculations.

Secondary Market

The secondary market from 1995 to 2006 is characterized by stable prices for most brands in which the key rookie cards feature players who are no longer active and a bubble-like pattern for newly released products. For older cards, the only changes in prices tend to occur at the high end of the graded card market as serious collectors seek to improve the overall quality of their vintage sets. The bubble-like pattern for new releases may be driven by preferences for newness on the part of collectors, which can be found by looking at the monthly surveys in BBCM during the early 2000s. Each month BBCM listed the top five items that were the hottest on the market according to surveys of dealers and consumers, and in eighteen consecutive monthly issues from August 2000 to January 2002 only two brands were able to sustain the highest ranking for more than one month, 2001 *Topps Heritage* (four months at number 1) and 2000 *Greats of the Game Autographs* (two months). In all there are fifty-six products listed in the possible ninety spots throughout the eighteen-month span, showing an incredible amount of turnover as consumer focus shifts from product to product. Also, there is an abundance of anecdotal stories describing the preferences for newness of consumers of baseball cards. The lead sentence in an article on *Finest Refractors* is, "The baseball card hobby has been marked by a fickle collector base that collectively jumps from one 'hottest issue of the week' to the next."[55] Those sentiments are echoed by veteran card dealer Kit Keifer:

> There is always going to be more demand for a current year's product, at least for a couple of weeks," Keifer says, half joking. "The window of opportunity for new sets seems to be getting smaller and smaller. With chase cards (inserts), dealers and collectors have preconceived notions of supply. More often than not, they are wrong.[56]

The quick peak and then sudden decline in value on the secondary market for products just released was not always the case, as insert sets from the mid-1990s, such as 1993 *Topps Finest Refractors* and 1994 *Flair Hot Gloves,* maintained strong secondary market prices well after their initial release. However, Figure 12.1 and Table 12.2 show that the number of brands increased so much in the late 1990s that Upper Deck alone produced as many brands in 2001 (twenty-four) as all four major manufacturers produced in 1994. Given the rapid rate at which products are currently introduced in the market, it is easy to see how high secondary-market values are not sustained for a long period of time. Also, the sheer number of products reduced the novelty of some of the inserts. In 1997 the owner of the one-of-one *Flair Showcase Legacy Masterpiece* Ken Griffey Jr. was offered $10,000 for it—and turned it down. The 1997 *Upper Deck Game Jersey* Ken Griffey Jr. card had a high book value of $600–$800, and now has a high book value around $200. Even the first Babe Ruth game-used bat card, which caused a great deal of controversy when Upper Deck obtained a Babe Ruth game-used bat and then cut it up to embed the bat pieces into the cards, has fallen dramatically in price. The decrease in the prices of these cards has come about simply because there are more of these types of cards available in the market today—Playoff littered the hobby with low-numbered parallel versions in most of its products, virtually every Upper Deck product today has a Ken Griffey Jr. game-used card, and while very few products have Babe Ruth game-used cards there are more today than there were in 1999. Collectors have added a new complaint to the old standards of too much product and too-high retail prices—declining secondary-market values. Perhaps in response to collector concerns, MLB and the MLBPA have recently begun to restrict the number of products produced in a given year. Table 12.2 shows only thirty-nine brands were produced in 2006, down from eighty in 2005. While part of this reduction is due to a decrease in the number of manufacturers, the twenty Topps brands and nineteen Upper Deck brands represent the fewest for both manufacturers since 2002.

SUMMARY

The baseball card industry has been continually evolving in both the production of picture cards and in the competitive practices among the manufacturers. Despite the decline in revenues from the peak in 1991, potential entrants can still be found. However, the decline brought forth innovations that could not possibly have been imagined in earlier years, and innovations are still to be found. In fact, Topps released the first-ever DNA cards in 2007, cards which featured a strand of hair from George Washington (the U.S. president, not the Chicago White Sox outfielder in 1935–1936) embedded in the card. Along the way, the nature of the industry allowed manufacturers to adjust their strategic behavior in response to changing market conditions, and the fact that entry was limited by MLB and the MLBPA allows one to clearly observe how this behavior changed. Despite these changes, as long as baseball cards continue to be produced and collected collectors will always have two beliefs: there is too much product on the market, and retail prices are too high (except when they go to sell, then they are not high enough).

NOTES

1. Greg Ambrosius, "Time for a Change," *Sports Collector's Digest* (June 28, 2002): 72–74.

2. Pankaj Ghemawat and Barry Nalebuff, "Exit," *RAND Journal of Economics* 16 (Summer 1985): 184–194; Drew Fudenberg and Jean Tirole, "A Theory of Exit in Duopoly," *Econometrica* 54 (July 1986): 943–960; Pankaj Ghemawat and Barry Nalebuff, "The Devolution of Declining Industries," *Quarterly Journal of Economics* 105 (February 1990): 167–186; John Londregan, "Exit and Entry over the Industry Life Cycle," *RAND Journal of Economics* 21 (Autumn 1990): 446–458; Pauli Murto, "Exit in Duopoly under Uncertainty," *RAND Journal of Economics* 35 (March 2004): 111–127.

3. Troy Kirk, *Collector's Guide to Baseball Cards* (Radnor, Pa.: Wallace-Homestead Book Company, 1990).

4. Tim O'Shei, "Stamp of Approval," *Beckett Baseball Card Monthly* (July 1997): 98–101.

5. To distinguish between brands and manufacturers any time a brand is referenced it will be italicized. Thus, Topps refers to the manufacturer while *Topps* refers to the flagship brand of Topps.

6. Nick Portantiere, "Factory Tour: Topps," *Beckett Baseball Card Monthly* (April 1996): 20–24.

7. Jim Geschke, "Factory Tour: Upper Deck," *Beckett Baseball Card Monthly* (February 1996): 20–24.

8. "85 Things You Always Wanted to Know about Baseball Cards But Were Afraid to Ask," *Beckett Baseball* (September 2007): 18–23.

9. Topps has changed its legal name multiple times in the past fifty years. Bowman was technically purchased by the Topps Chewing Gum Company.

10. *Bowman Gum, Inc. v. Topps Chewing Gum, Inc.*, March 31, 1952, and *Haelan Laboratories, Inc. v. Topps Chewing Gum Co.*, May 25, 1953.

11. Marvin Miller, *A Whole Different Ballgame: The Sport and Business of Baseball* (New York: Birch Lane Press, 1991).

12. John A. Vernon, "Baseball, Bubble Gum, and Business," in *Diamonds Are Forever: The Business of Baseball*, ed. Paul Sommers (Washington, D.C.: Brookings Institution Press, 1992), 91–108.

13. Miller, *Whole Different Ballgame.*

14. *Fleer Corp. v. Topps Chewing Gum*, 1980.

15. This list is by no means exhaustive.

16. Miller, *Whole Different Ballgame.*

17. George Solomon, "Nobody Flips over a Gogolewski or Dalrymple," *Washington Post/Times Herald*, April 15, 1973, D1.

18. Ibid.

19. Bob Addie, "Neither Wars nor Recessions Gum Up Baseball Card Business," *Washington Post*, April 24, 1975, E2.

20. Dwight Chapin, "This Man Is a Card-Carrying Member . . . ," *Los Angeles Times*, June 14, 1974, E1.

21. George Vrechek, "Collectors Searching for the Fountain of Completeness," http://www.oldbaseball.com/refs/1930s.htm (accessed November 26, 2007).

22. Chapin, "This Man Is a Card-Carrying Member."

23. *Topps Chewing Gum v. Fleer Corporation*, 1982.

24. Optigraphics changed its name to Pinnacle Brands, Inc. (Pinnacle), in 1992.

25. Optigraphics had attempted to solve this problem in 1988 by packaging *Score* in what was essentially a plastic bag that needed to be torn to be open. However, packs were still "searchable" given that the bag was see-through.

26. Portantiere, "Factory Tour: Topps."

27. Tol Broome, "Factory Tour: Pinnacle Brands," *Beckett Baseball Card Monthly* (March 1996): 20–24.

28. This process changed in 2006 as MLB and the MLBPA began limiting which minor-league players could appear in major-league sets.

29. Optigraphics had released *Score* and *Sportflics* in both 1988 and 1989, but as has already been mentioned, the inclusion of *Sportflics* as a competitor to the other brands is borderline at best.

30. It appears that this happened with 1995 *Topps DIII* as only the first series was produced.

31. Bill Sing, "Investment Outlook: How to Get Ahead Assessing 1988: '88 Ups, Downs and Might-have-beens: Soybeans and FCA Fizzled, but Baseball Cards Hit a Homer," *Los Angeles Times*, late ed., East Coast, December 4, 1988, A1.

32. Robert Hershey, "Consumer's World; Coping: with Financial Planning," *New York Times*, late ed., East Coast, January 14, 1989.

33. Robert Thomas, "Investors Hope a Rich Future Is in the Cards," *New York Times*, late ed., East Coast, April 10, 1988, A1, as well as many advertisements *in Sports Collectors Digest* during this time.

34. The notable exceptions are the 1968 and 1969 Topps sets that include the rookie card and second-year card of Nolan Ryan, who was the only superstar player still active in 1988 from these sets.

35. There are some changes in the listed card grades during this time. From January 1993 to February 1995 cards from 1968–1979 are listed in Near Mint–Mint condition. In February 1995 BBCM changed its listed grades to Near Mint for the 1968–1973 products and while leaving the 1974–1979 products at Near Mint–Mint.

36. Steve Cady, "Sports-Card Buffs Gathering for a Trip to Nostalgia," *New York Times*, May 26, 1973, 33.

37. Michael Stoller, "On the Economics of Antitrust and Competition in a Collectibles Market: The Strange Case of the Baseball Card Industry," *Business Economics* 19 (July 1984): 18–26.

38. In 1984 each of the first twenty-six cards in Donruss has a variation and there are two cards that have versions with and without card numbers. However, these variations are due to separate printing for its packs and factory sets.

39. Peter Williams, *Card Sharks: How Upper Deck Turned a Child's Hobby into a High-Stakes, Billion-Dollar Business* (New York: Macmillan, 1995).

40. Ambrosius, "Time for a Change."

41. Jennifer Davies, "A Huge Trade Looms in World of Sports Cards," http://www.signonsandiego.com/sports/baseball/20070708-9999-1n8cards.html (accessed November 26, 2007).

42. Tim O'Shei, "Party of One," *Beckett Baseball Card Monthly* (November 1997): 115–117.

43. Theo Chen, "Pure Premium," *Beckett Baseball Card Monthly* (January 1993): 14–16.

44. Upper Deck had previously issued game-used memorabilia cards in 1996 hockey and football products.

45. Reid Creager, "Cutting Edge Cards," *Beckett Baseball Card Monthly* (May 2002): 112–113.

46. Tol Broome, "The Attraction of Refraction," *Beckett Baseball Card Monthly* (September 1996): 114–118.

47. Tom Leer, "Pulse of the Hobby," *Beckett Baseball Card Monthly* (November 1996): 101.

48. U.S. District Court for the Eastern District of Pennsylvania, Civil Action No. 00-CV-4570.

49. Kit Keifer, "Dollars and Sense," *Beckett Baseball Card Monthly* (March 1997): 100–108.

50. Thomas Heath, "McGwire's Heroics Driving Up Profits: Griffey Jr., Sosa, Gonzalez Also Helping Boost Baseball's Popularity, Finance," *Washington Post,* final ed., July 8, 1998, C07; Alexander Peers and Ken Bensinger, "Art and Money," *Wall Street Journal*, Eastern ed., August 28, 1998, W10.

51. This practice changes around 1998. See the following paragraph about the release of 1998 *Leaf Rookies & Stars* for more detail.

52. Robert Krider and Charles Weinberg, "Competitive Dynamics and the Introduction of New Products: The Motion Picture Timing Game," *Journal of Marketing Research* 25 (February 1998): 1–15.

53. Williams, *Card Sharks.*

54. "85 Things You Always Wanted to Know about Baseball Cards."

55. Broome, "Factory Tour."

56. Ibid.

About the Editors and Contributors

Brad R. Humphreys is the Chair in the Economics of Gaming and an associate professor in the Department of Economics at the University of Alberta in Edmonton, Alberta, Canada. He holds a Ph.D. in economics from the Johns Hopkins University. He was previously an associate professor at the University of Illinois at Urbana-Champaign and the University of Maryland, Baltimore County. His research on the economic impact of professional sports, the economic determinants of participation in physical activity, and competitive balance in sports leagues has been published in scholarly journals, including the *Journal of Urban Economics,* the *Journal of Policy Analysis and Management*, the *Journal of Economic Behavior and Organization*, the *Journal of Sports Economics*, and *Contemporary Economic Policy*. His research has been featured in numerous media outlets, including *Sports Illustrated*, the *Wall Street Journal*, and *USA Today*. In 2007 he testified before the U.S. Congress on the financing and economic impact of professional sports facilities.

Dennis R. Howard is the Philip H. Knight Professor of Business at the Lundquist College of Business, University of Oregon. He joined the Lundquist College in 1997 after serving six years as the director of the Graduate Program in Sport Management at Ohio State University. He has published numerous articles on the marketing, financing, and management of sports in such journals as the *Journal of Sport Management*, *Marketing Management*, and *Sport Marketing Quarterly*, and is coauthor of the textbook *Financing Sport*. He is the founder and editor of the *International Journal of Sport Finance*.

Carlos Pestana Barros is an assistant professor of economics at Instituto Superior de Economia e Gestao (ISEG) in the Technical University of Lisbon, Portugal. He has a Ph.D. in economics from ISEG. His research on the economic efficiency of professional sport leagues, including those in Portugal, Germany, Greece, and the United Kingdom, has been published in scholarly journals including *Applied Economics, Applied Economic Letters, Journal of Sport Economics, European Sport Management Quarterly, Marketing Quarterly, Sport Management Review, International Journal of Sport Marketing Sponsorship,* and *International Journal of Sport Management and Marketing*. He served as guest editor for two special issues of *International Journal of Sport Management and Marketing*.

David J. Berri is an associate professor in the Department of Economics at California State University–Bakersfield. He holds a Ph.D. in economics from Colorado State University, and he was previously an assistant professor in economics at Coe College in Cedar Rapids, Iowa. His research on various topics in the economics of sports has been published in numerous refereed journals, including *American Economic Review*, *Economic Inquiry*, *Applied Economics*, and *Journal of Sports Economics*. He is lead author of *The Wages of Wins*, a book that was favorably reviewed in the *New Yorker*, *New York Times*, and SportsIllustrated.com. In addition to his academic research, he has also written columns on sports and economics for the *New York Times*, *Yale Economic Review*, and *VIBE Magazine*.

John Charles Bradbury is an associate professor of health, physical education, and sport science at Kennesaw State University in Kennesaw, Georgia. He has authored a book on the economics of baseball, *The Baseball Economist*, and has published articles in journals such as *Economic Inquiry*, *Journal of Public Economics, Journal of Sports Economics, Public Choice*, *Public Finance Review*, and *Southern Economic Journal.* He has also served on the faculties of the University of the South and North Georgia College and State University. He received his Ph.D. in economics from George Mason University in 2000.

Michael C. Davis is currently an assistant professor in the Department of Economics at the University of Missouri–Rolla. He received his Ph.D. in economics from the University of California–San Diego. His research has examined the importance of winning on local economies and the determinants of the locations of sports teams. Outside of sports economics, he has studied the dynamics of gasoline prices. His research has been published in scholarly journals, including *Atlantic Economic Journal, International Journal of Sports Finance, Journal of Money, Credit, and Banking* and *Managerial and Decision Economics.*

Gregory H. Duquette is a doctoral student in physical education and recreation at the University of Alberta. His research interests include sports teams as a strategic resource in place branding and the relationships between sport, status, and community identity.

Daniel S. Mason is an associate professor with the faculty of physical education and recreation and an adjunct professor with the School of Business at the University of Alberta in Edmonton, Canada. His research takes an interdisciplinary approach and focuses on the business of sport and the relationships between its stakeholders, including all levels of government, sports teams, leagues, the communities that host teams, agents, and players' associations. His research has been funded by the Social Sciences and Humanities Research Council of Canada and Alberta Gaming Research Institute, and he has published more than forty articles in refereed publications such as *Contemporary Economic Policy, Economic Development Quarterly, European Journal of Marketing, Journal of Sport and Social Issues, Journal of Sport History, Journal of Sport Management, Journal of Urban Affairs, Managing Leisure,* and *Urban History Review.* In 2004 he was named a research fellow by the North American Society of Sport Management.

Michael Mondello teaches finance in the graduate Sport Management Program at Florida State University. His graduate education includes a Ph.D. from the University of Florida. His research interests focus on financial and economic issues related to sports organizations, including completive balance, economic impact analysis, contingent valuation, ticket pricing, and the professional development of the academic field of sport management. He has published research in the *Journal of Sports Economics, Economic Development Quarterly, Journal of Sport Management,* and *Sport Marketing Quarterly.* He has presented papers and served as a keynote speaker at various international and national conferences. In 2007 he was recognized as a research fellow by the North American Society of Sport Management. In addition to his teaching and research responsibilities, he currently serves on the university's athletic board and finance committee, is a member of the faculty senate, and previously served on the board of directors of the Tallahassee YMCA.

Kevin G. Quinn is an associate professor of economics at St. Norbert College near Green Bay, Wisconsin. He earned his Ph.D. in energy economics and his MBA in economics and marketing from the University of Illinois–Chicago. He holds a B.S. in mathematics and physics from Loyola University of Chicago. He served as St. Norbert's faculty representative to the NCAA and chaired the institution's athletic committee for seven years. He also served as secretary of the ten-institution Midwest Conference and was elected president of the Illinois Economic Association in 2008–2009. Despite living in Packerland, he remains an unrepentant Bear fan.

Mark S. Rosentraub is dean and professor of urban affairs at the Maxine Goodman Levin College of Urban Affairs of Cleveland State University. His research interests focus on urban redevelopment, public finance, and the economic and intangible value of sports, the arts, and other amenities for urban centers. His most recent book, *The Economics of Sports: An International Perspective* (coauthored with Robert Sandy and Peter Sloane), was published in 2004. His *Major League Losers: The Real Costs of Sports and Who's Paying for It* was published in 1997, and a second, revised edition was released in 1999.

Mário Teixeira is a Ph.D. candidate in sport management at the University of Evora in Evora, Portugal.

Peter von Allmen is a professor of economics and a former chair of the Department of Economics and Business at Moravian College in Bethlehem, Pennsylvania. His primary research focus is in sports economics, including incentives and individual sport compensation, team sports compensation and monopsony power, and the influence of international players on competitive balance in the NHL. He has also published research on family labor supply models and postsecondary pedagogy in economics. He is the coauthor of two textbooks: *The Economics of Sports* (with Michael Leeds) and *Economics* (with Michael Leeds and Richard Schiming). In 2006–2007, he was a fellow of the American Council on Education, a yearlong leadership-development program. In addition to his responsibilities in the economics department, he serves as the chief of staff for strategic planning at Moravian, reporting to the president of the college. He earned his B.A. in economics at the College of Wooster and his Ph.D. in economics at Temple University.

Arthur Zillante is an assistant professor in the Department of Economics at the University of North Carolina–Charlotte. He received a Ph.D. in economics from the Florida State University in 2004. He previously worked as the IFREE visiting postdoctoral scholar at the Interdisciplinary Center for Economic Science at George Mason University in Arlington, Virginia. His research on auctions and experimental economics has been published in scholarly journals such as *Southern Economic Journal*, *International Journal of Game Theory*, and *Journal of Economic Behavior and Organization*. Although his current research focuses on profitably and efficiency in market mechanisms, his initial education about the forces of supply and demand came as a ten-year-old trading baseball cards on the school bus.

Dennis Zimmerman is an economist who writes on the economics of taxation and the economics of sports. He worked for many years at the Congressional Research Service and the Congressional Budget Office. He has written many articles and a book on the private use of tax-exempt bonds for the Urban Institute. He is currently the director of projects for the American Tax Policy Institute.

Index